THE PEOPLE'S HOUSE OF COMMONS:
THEORIES OF DEMOCRACY IN CONTENTION

Canada's House of Commons has come under considerable attack in recent years. Many critics have contended that the House has been unresponsive to public opinion, and that its party leaders have too much control, while leaving individual MPs essentially powerless. The House has also faced challenges by the courts since the introduction of the Charter, a powerful bureaucracy equipped with specialized knowledge, and new telecommunications systems that are redefining the transfer of information.

Through an examination of academic, judicial, political, and legal commentary, *The People's House of Commons* explores the role of the House as a public institution. While addressing much of the criticism that has been levelled at the House, political scientist David E. Smith considers the competing political models and inherent tensions and their effect on public understanding. Smith maintains that court decisions are transforming the political system from one dominated by parties to one that promotes individual participation. He argues that reforms such as fixed election dates or stronger parliamentary committees have constitutional significance since their implementation would alter the practice of responsible government, which for more than a century has been party government.

A definitive work by one of Canada's foremost experts in the field of political science, *The People's House of Commons* explores the ramifications of many of the changes currently being proposed to Canada's political system, with particular reference to their effect on prerogative power, parliamentary privilege, party discipline, bicameralism, and the role of the opposition.

DAVID E. SMITH is a professor emeritus in the Department of Political Studies at the University of Saskatchewan and Senior Policy Fellow, Saskatchewan Institute of Public Policy.

DAVID E. SMITH

The People's House of Commons

Theories of Democracy in Contention

UNIVERSITY OF TORONTO PRESS
Toronto Buffalo London

© University of Toronto Press Incorporated 2007
Toronto Buffalo London
Printed in Canada

Reprinted 2008, 2009

ISBN 978-0-8020-9255-7 (cloth)
ISBN 978-0-8020-9465-0 (paper)

Printed on acid-free paper

Library and Archives Canada Cataloguing in Publication

Smith, David E., 1936–
　　The people's House of Commons : theories of democracy in
　　contention / David E. Smith.

　　Includes bibliographical references and index.
　　ISBN 978-0-8020-9255-7 (bound)
　　ISBN 978-0-8020-9465-0 (pbk.)

　　1. Canada. Parliament. House of Commons.　2. Democracy – Canada.
　　3. Legislative bodies – Canada – Reform.　I. Title.

　　JL161.S65 2007　　328.71'072　　C2006-906098-3

This book has been published with the help of a grant from the Canadian
Federation for the Humanities and Social Sciences, through the Aid to
Scholarly Publications Programme, using funds provided by the Social
Sciences and Humanities Research Council of Canada.

University of Toronto Press acknowledges the financial assistance to its
publishing program of the Canada Council for the Arts and the Ontario
Arts Council.

University of Toronto Press acknowledges the financial support for its
publishing activities of the Government of Canada through the Book
Publishing Industry Development Program (BPIDP).

For my grandchildren, Emma, Deanna, and Ryder

Contents

Preface

There was a time when the Parliament at Westminster and its Dominion progeny were celebrated for the good effects their structures and practices produced. Whether stated or left to be inferred, the invidious comparison drawn was with the Congress of the United States, where private interests and money were said to rule. By contrast, party government, leadership, and discipline were believed to ensure that Parliament promoted the public interest. Today, parliamentary government, in Canada and Great Britain, is scorned for the same reason it once was esteemed: discipline is condemned for silencing individual members and the constituency opinion they seek to voice, while the interest that used to be promoted as public is revealed, say critics, to privilege some sections and classes while excluding others. Westminster used to stand as a parliamentary metropole to be imitated; today, political as well as cultural metropoles are out of fashion, difference not similarity now the object sought.

What has happened to undermine assumptions so long held, and why? More to the point, how to accommodate in existing constitutional structures attitudes that no longer presume Parliament's predominance? Canada has witnessed the movement of politics out of the confines of hierarchy and deference towards a broadening horizon of participation. The courts and the Canadian Charter of Rights and Freedoms are arrayed along that horizon; so, too, are the direct democratic values and rhetoric promoted by the Reform party and maintained by its conservative successors. Broadening out explains this book's title, *The People's House of Commons*, and is the basis for its thesis that parliamentary politics in Canada now embraces the competing claims of three rival models: parliamentary democracy, constitutional democracy, and

electoral democracy. The challenge for the popular chamber is to articulate core principles that integrate the competing claims. In fact, the
challenge is far greater than that because at its base what is at issue is the
largely unwritten, monarchical constitution that makes no provision for
the people and rests uneasy with the concept of a law higher than itself.

Rules changes notwithstanding, alterations to the conduct of lower
house business are far more difficult to achieve than critics of Parliament appreciate, for the very good reason that they frequently touch
on constitutional matters, especially in regard to the operation of
responsible government. The same can be said of electoral reform,
most proposals for which are based on the premise that the problem of
representative government today lies in the inadequacy of the representation the electoral system produces. The answer, according to British political scientist Kenneth Minogue, invariably takes some form of
'sociologizing of the process of representation,' which in turn requires
a reduction in party discipline if its influence is to be exercised.[1]

Another theme with unacknowledged constitutional implications is
concern to enforce accountability. Once again, fixing responsibility was
something parliamentary government was supposed to be particularly
good at achieving. The complaint now is that this is no longer the case;
the answer, to turn the concept on its head by detaching accountability
from the political process. Enforcement through codes and courts, commissions and officers of Parliament is a favoured alternative. Alterations of this kind would have fundamental implications for such
principles of the constitution as ministerial responsibility and parliamentary privilege, as well as the concept of the tripartite Parliament as
an organic entity.

The People's House of Commons is a study of the Commons in context.
Among other subjects, it discusses relationships between the lower
house and the crown, Senate, charter, courts and law, political parties
and social movements, federalism, the media and telecommunications,
and the electoral system. It begins with a chapter on 'The State of the
Commons' and ends with another on 'The People's House of Commons
and Its Study.' Despite sustained criticism of Parliament's lower house,
particularly for being 'unresponsive' to public opinion, that chamber
and Parliament generally remain remarkably understudied. The depth
of the examination that is required goes beyond what can be accomplished in a single volume. This explains the recommendation in the
conclusion that the people's house be one, albeit important, part of a
comprehensive study of constitutional processes in Canada. Chapters

2, 3, and 4 examine the models of parliamentary democracy, constitutional democracy, and electoral democracy that contend for attention in current political debate, while chapters 5 and 6 adopt a longer perspective and ask 'What Is the House?' and 'Who Are the People?' Answers to these deceptively simple questions require exploration of Canada's society and history as much as they do its politics.

The People's House of Commons is the last book in a trilogy devoted to Parliament, the first two volumes being *The Invisible Crown: The First Principle of Canadian Government* and *The Canadian Senate in Bicameral Perspective*. If *The Republican Option in Canada: Past and Present* is considered part of the examination of the parliamentary tradition in Canada – and there is compelling reason to support that view – then the series is a quartet. As with the previous works, I want to acknowledge the interest and help colleagues and friends have expressed and offered in the course of this book's writing. Specifically, I wish to thank Nathan Elliott, now working on his doctoral degree in Canadian history, for making accessible to me the cornucopia of political data available on the Internet. Like other current and former graduate students who have helped me on the project – David Brock, Megan Furi, Michael Jordan, Dan MacFarlane, and Will Robbins – Nathan Elliott showed an interest and enthusiasm for the study of Canadian politics that discomfits the media's easy claims of general political cynicism among the Canadian people and especially the young. It is for this reason and because of the undisputed significance of Canada's premier political institution that I dedicate this book to my grandchildren – Emma, Deanna, and Ryder.

I retired from the University of Saskatchewan in June 2004. Most of this book has been written since then, and I am indebted to the University of Saskatchewan and, particularly, the former dean of the College of Arts and Sciences, Ken Coates, for providing support that allowed me to complete the manuscript in a timely fashion. In the summer of 2005, I moved to Regina. There the Saskatchewan Institute of Public Policy, through its director, Ian Peach, offered me a new research home from whose windows I may marvel at the magnificent Beaux-Arts dome of the Saskatchewan Legislative Building. Architecture still speaks, and at Wascana, on Parliament Hill, and in the Palace of Westminster, the most recognizable and imposing structures of their respective societies affirm a civic commitment, past and present, to the ideal and practice of parliamentary government.

The manuscript was completed the week of the thirty-ninth federal general election in January 2006. With the largest number but still a minority of seats in the Commons, the Conservative party led by Stephen Harper formed a government. In the interval between the election and the publication of this book, the new government made statements and took action directly pertinent to some of the topics discussed in the following chapters. One instance was the creation of a parliamentary committee before which the prime minister's nominee for appointment as a justice of the Supreme Court of Canada appeared and was questioned. Another was a publicized dispute between the prime minister and the ethics commissioner, an independent officer of Parliament. Although the details of these (and other) events are anecdotal, they support rather than challenge the book's thesis that rival theories of democracy pervade debate in the people's House of Commons.

Finally, I wish to thank Lorrie Burlingham for her continued cheerful and speedy accommodation to my typing demands, Ursula Acton for her unfailing accuracy as an indexer, and Margaret Allen for her skilful copyediting.

Regina, Saskatchewan

THE PEOPLE'S HOUSE OF COMMONS:
THEORIES OF DEMOCRACY IN CONTENTION

1 The State of the Commons

The House of Commons is Canada's premier legislative institution, although legislation is produced only when the three parts of Parliament – crown, Senate, and Commons – work in concert. Of the three, however, the Commons chamber, despite the qualifier 'lower,' or the more antique 'nether,'[1] is pre-eminent, and for the reason opponents of Confederation early recognized: '[T]he people's house will be the all-important and all-powerful branch, for they will be able even to overturn the executive of the country.'[2] That was the opinion of Albert Smith, Liberal premier of New Brunswick and a founding father, speaking in 1866, but expressing a sentiment entrenched since at least the time of that archetypal non-liberal, the Duke of Wellington. It was Wellington who observed in one of his pungent epigrams – and this even before passage of the 1832 Reform Act with its crucial but modest extension to the franchise – that 'the House of Commons is everything in England, and the House of Lords nothing.'[3] The 'exclusiveness' of the Lords, said another critic, 'wounds democratic feeling.'[4] The point of these British references is to call attention to the singular pre-eminence in Canada of the House of Commons. There never was a time when the House was politically equal, let alone inferior, to the Senate. Parliamentary upper chambers were in eclipse even before the Fathers of Confederation created the Senate of Canada, a truth they acknowledged in their design for the new upper house.

The power of Canada's Commons has always rested in its inclusiveness. Through its members the House incorporates the people into the constitution: it is their voice that is heard, not that of the parties, the premiers, or the provinces. In the face of a federalized cabinet, with portfolios allocated to provide provincial representation, and a partisanized chamber, where independent members are a rare phenomenon, this is a contentious claim. Still, it is a necessary one. To concede otherwise would be to relinquish an essential democratic element of the constitution. The House is a representative body, the only one that can claim to speak on behalf of all Canadians. The voice of the people can be heard through the Senate, too, but the Senate was never intended to be a representative institution.[5] That is both its strength and its weakness: it is accountable neither to the people nor to any external body.

It is because of its election that the House becomes the repository of popular sovereignty. Such language, once favoured by late-nineteenth and early-twentieth-century writers like Alpheus Todd and Sir John Bourinot, is rarely heard although no less accurate today as a description of Canadian democracy.[6] Legal sovereignty rests in Parliament and popular sovereignty in the people. The vital connection between the two is the member of Parliament. No office holder is elected by all Canadians, but that does not mean that no one represents all – MPs do, 'because they speak for all.'[7] The constitutive power of the Canadian constitution rests, if not exclusively then predominantly, in the House of Commons. Here is the basis for defending the Clarity Act introduced by the Chrétien government and passed by Parliament in 2000. The act constituted the government's response to the opinion of the Supreme Court of Canada in the Quebec Secession Reference.[8] The court advised that where a province used a referendum to effect secession, the question asked and the result obtained be clear. Section 2:1 granted the House of Commons (but not the Senate) authority to determine the answer to both matters. The Senate resisted this provision of the act on the grounds that passage by one house of a bicameral Parliament did not meet the constitutional standard for royal assent. The particulars of that debate are not germane to this discussion except in so far as they highlight the privileged role accorded the lower house.

Nor is it necessary to support this provision of the act in order to accept the primacy of the House. The people are incorporated into the constitution through representation in the chamber. Periodically, general elections provide an opportunity 'to test [public] opinion ... and bring the legislature into accord with the public mind.'[9] This is Bourinot speaking again, and his interpretation is worth a moment's reflection. Unlike many modern interpreters who favour metaphors of balance, Bourinot speaks of harmony between the people, the legislature and the crown. His sense of the system – itself a malapropism since Parliament is not a composite but an organic unity and since the people possess no constitutive role except through Parliament – conforms more accurately to traditional governing practices than later critics are ready to admit.

Consider, for instance, the prerogative of dissolution: that is, the power the governor general has, exercisable on advice of the prime minister, to dissolve Parliament and to call for the issue of election writs. Prior to the federal general election of 2004, much criticism attended the indecision of the prime minister (Paul Martin) as to when to seek a dissolution of the thirty-seventh Parliament. The prime minister's discretion to name (in effect) the election date was deemed unfair since it could be used to the government's advantage. In its place a proposal for fixed election dates found favour. For the moment, dissolution needs to be seen as a power with the potential to effect harmony between the people and Parliament.

Another feature of the House of Commons that supports the claim to its primacy as an organ of public opinion is by-elections. Whether by-elections are held singly or conjointly, their results may be treated as a barometer of government policies. Until the 1930s, and extending back almost a century, by-elections in Canada were statutorily required when sitting members (in Ottawa, the provinces, or the colonies before that) were appointed to cabinet. It is seven decades since governments had to submit to that test of approval. On the subject of their cessation, it should be noted that, were Canada to adopt a system of proportional representation (be it a list or an alternative vote model variant) in place of single-member district, simple-plurality elections, by-elections might no longer be held. Constituency vacancies occurring between general elections would be filled by any one of a variety of procedures, including selection of the runner-up from the previous general election.

In a familiar passage from *The English Constitution*, Walter Bagehot described the cabinet as 'a buckle which fastens the legislative part of the state to the executive part of the state.' The same metaphor could as well describe the House in its job of binding the people to those who exercise power. Important as this function may be, the role of the House is about much more than a structure and its elements. The House gives institutional expression to the concept of a national community. The word *nation* evokes a long and contested history centring on the question whether Quebec is a distinct – that is, separate – *nation* (with the communal organic sense that the word signifies in the French language), one of at least two that make up the Canadian state. That debate, begun in the 1960s, remains unresolved despite momentary lulls. Indeed, the proposition that Canada contains more than one *nation* has found additional support from Aboriginal peoples, who until 1960 were themselves denied the right to vote in federal elections. The passion fuelling these powerful counter-visions of Canadian nationality cannot erase the reality that the House of Commons symbolizes the unity of the Canadian people achieved through the conversion of individual acts of voting.

For the House of Commons, its pre-eminence lies in being elected; for the voter, in casting the ballot. Voting is the sign of citizenship, no more so than when it is denied. Canada stood with other Western countries in withholding votes from women until after the First World War, but behind them when during that war it gave the vote to women relatives of men-at-arms while disenfranchising male immigrants who had come to Canada after 1902 from areas of the German and Austro-Hungarian empires. Denial of the franchise on racial grounds lasted for nearly a century, with (as already noted) treaty Indians and Eskimos (except veterans) being denied the vote. In this civic apartheid they were joined, until the late 1940s, by most Canadians of East Asian and East Indian descent.[10] This is not an exhaustive list of the excluded, because that uncomfortable project is not the purpose of this discussion. Rather, it makes the point that the suffrage is a sign of inclusion – a modern instance is that prisoners, once automatically deprived of the vote, now have it restored – and a denominator of democratic life.

By incorporating the people, the House creates the nation. And that act of incorporation is repeated at more or less regular intervals. In its 'discontinuous' life, the House is unlike the Senate, which never lapses. Fifty years ago Norman Ward, an authoritative interpreter of Parliament in Canada, could say that 'the modern electoral system ... lies dormant most of the time ... Between elections, only the staff of the Chief Electoral Officer at Ottawa, comprising less than a dozen civil servants, is steadily at work.'[11] Far from being 'the loose-limbed colossus' Ward once described, Elections Canada (as it is now known) is continuously active, overseeing the decennial drawing by independent commissions of federal electoral constituency boundaries, along with the compilation and maintenance of the permanent electoral register that replaces the former door-to-door enumeration prior to each election. To that should be added an expanded investigative, informative, and exhortative role, as witness the commissioning of studies of declining voter turnout, the organizing of conferences as part (in its own words) of its 'mandate' to promote 'youth voting,' and frequent addresses by the chief electoral officer to Canadian and international gatherings on a range of voting-related subjects.[12]

Like that clichéd pebble thrown into a pond whose ripples extend far in all directions, the actions of House members touch all Canadians. This is in contrast again to the Senate, whose attention tends to be directed towards sectional or regional concerns: for example, poverty, or soil degradation, or fisheries. Of course, the Senate deals with all legislation, whatever its subject, coming from the Commons, but its predisposition is to initiate more focused inquiries. Partly for this reason, partly because the Senate is only one-third the size of the Commons, but most of all because the senators are not elected, the public sees the upper house as a unity. The consequence, as a British scholar observed long ago of the House of Lords, is that its 'reputation ... depends on the character of the least reputable.'[13] On the other hand, MPs lead a double life; the public distinguishes between the member and the House and, as will be shown later, favours the individual over the institution. Why this is and the implications that flow as a consequence are important to this study. Nonetheless, the dichotomy helps to concentrate attention on the Commons.

There are of course other reasons why the Commons is the cynosure of Canadian legislative politics. The practice of drawing ministers almost solely from the lower house is one (in Canberra, as many as one-third of the ministers may sit in the Senate); the constitutional requirement that spending measures be introduced by ministers in the Commons is another; the focus on leadership and the electoral horizon in a situation where as yet (as of mid-2006) there is no fixed election date is a third. To these should be added the partisanship that pervades the whole picture. Membership in Canadian political parties may never have been large, and voter turnout may be in decline, but electoral support for other than party candidates is rare. It is a partisan world – and has always been: '[T]o be out of office was to be out of [that] world.'[14] That comment was made at the end of the First World War, at a exceptional moment when an attempt was underway in Ottawa to moderate the practice of partisanship, and nearly seventy years after another politician, this time in the Parliament of United Canada, had lamented that in the United Province 'partizanship rules everything.'[15] These are not isolated or selected comments. To say that partisanship is a prominent, apparently permanent, feature of Canadian politics may be dismissed as a trite observation. Still, it needs to be said, for partisanship, especially in the absence of 'general political principles,' as James (Viscount)

Bryce observed of Canada in his magisterial survey of Anglo-American democracies, is not the result of some unfortunate defect in national character or lapse of intelligence.[16] Partisanship is the modus operandi and lingua franca of Canadian politics. Its persistence warrants study particularly as support for new, less partisanized conceptions of governing increasingly gain favour.

Critics of partisan politics are as much a feature of the Canadian political landscape as partisanship itself. Advocates of procedural reform inside and electoral reform outside Parliament are of long lineage. So too are those who deride legislative debate as irrelevant to the 'real' needs of the people, to whom MPs of all stripes, they say, pay insufficient attention. This observation is not new, but it deserves notice in any discussion about the primacy of the House of Commons. Bagehot's *The English Constitution*, referred to above, offers the theoretical ground for Canada's parliamentary constitution. Certainly, Bagehot did more than anyone else in the nineteenth century to conceive of the parts of Parliament and their interaction as a 'constitution.' In other words, he brought people to believe that there was a unity to its operation. He went farther: not only was there a unity, there was a meaning behind its operation. As he explained it, there were efficient institutions (pre-eminently, the House of Commons), and there were dignified institutions (most obviously, the monarchy and the House of Lords). The English constitution worked, he said, because popular deference was given to the dignified parts, while the efficient part was allowed to do its mundane job of governing. The people loved a show, and the monarchy and the Lords provided just that diversion.

In Canada, two-thirds of Bagehot's constitutional materials were unavailable – no aristocracy and a surrogate sovereign. If deference were a necessary ingredient, then in response to what? Modern claims about the decline of deference in Canada need to be treated cautiously, not because it has not happened but because the cause of deference in the first place is qualitatively different from that in Bagehot's analysis.[17] In a vast transcontinental state where land was cheap, neither property nor class nor education provided a reliable or continuous basis for deference or, more to the point of the argument, for allegiance to government. Deference in Canada meant deference in electoral politics: the legitimation or obedience that Bagehot saw 'the constitution' in Britain as eliciting came in Canada through the forum of electoral politics. Here was another factor that worked to elevate Canada's Commons.

As an aside, it is worth recalling that the Fathers of Confederation could not have read Bagehot's celebrated essays, since they began to appear as journal articles only in 1865 and as a collection in 1867. By contrast, 'the most detailed accounts of British parliamentary institutions to appear in 1867 ... came not from Bagehot but ... from the librarian of the Legislative Assembly of United Canada, Alpheus Todd, who used Bagehot's articles.'[18] Todd's precedence in this matter reinforces the thesis of the pre-eminence of the Commons. His career in the service of the legislatures of Upper Canada, United Canada, and the Dominion of Canada was tied (in his words) to 'elucidat[ing] the working of "responsible" government.' In this undertaking he predated not only Bagehot but also Erskine May, the later recognized authority of parliamentary usage. Todd deserves to be acknowledged along with Robert Baldwin and Louis-Hippolyte LaFontaine for his contribution to parliamentary government – less, however, as an advocate than as a delineator.

With Wellington, one might say that Canada's House of Commons is 'everything.' Or, perhaps, *was* everything, since today as much is said about the House by those who would supplant it as would reform it. Of the latter, there is always a legion of improvers: those who would change legislative procedure to allow for greater committee consideration of bills, or reduce the power of party whips, or increase the authority of the speaker; those who would change the electoral system to make it a proportionally rather than a plurality-based entity, and thus, putatively, more representative; or those who would reform the Senate. The list goes on and on, because the House exerts both centrifugal and centripetal force, affecting through the electoral and party systems Canadians in all parts of the country, while influencing the conduct of government by cabinet, prime minister, and senior public servants. Notwithstanding the critics who say it is becoming impotent, the House through its members touches the activities of countless thousands.

And yet, the House of Commons has a problem, and it knows it – no one is happy with its performance. Neither the public nor the media nor the members themselves approve of what the House does. Letters to the editor and talk radio freely criticize members of Parliament, although hardly more severely than do the members. The members have lost their confidence, and maybe their way, in the crossfire of criticism. 'Everyone' thinks he or she can do a better job. The collective is used loosely here, since it includes not just opponents in the legislature, or even legislators personally. The Commons as an institution has competitors. The media and investigative journalists see themselves as the real opposition. That is, when they are not sharing the task with the Senate, which, C.E.S. Franks says, becomes aggressive when it sees an inexperienced House in the hands of partisan opponents.[19]

These are only a few of the competitors. There are the courts, to which citizens look for protection of entrenched rights following the adoption of the Charter of Rights and Freedoms, but which, far more sweepingly, can be viewed as creating a 'constitutional state [that] replaces a defective form of governance by depriving legislatures of their general supremacy over the essential features of liberal democracy.'[20] If, as the central institution of parliamentary democracy, the House of Commons is being challenged on one side by courts as upholders of constitutional democracy, then on the other it is under attack by advocates of electoral democracy, who view representative government as second best to control by the people. As electoral and parliamentary organizations, parties contributed to the prominence of the Commons. Conversely, new social movements and modes of protest politics divert attention from the familiar parliamentary-constituency network of activity and direct it towards extra-parliamentary strategies and concerns.[21]

More examples of competitors could be given, the bureaucracy being one, but the theme is clear. The Commons is under siege, figuratively, by trespassers. Its pre-eminence is in danger. Here is the political science equivalent of the 'tragedy of the commons,' the destruction by all of what is valuable to all. Nor are parliamentarians exempt from this indictment. Consider, for instance, willing support expressed for expanding the mandate (and number) of officers of Parliament. Whatever their virtues, these officials do work once expected of Parliament or limit what parliamentarians might do in the future. Increasingly in the public eye and often involved in controversy, they provide the Canadian counterpart to Bruce Ackerman's theory of a new, fourth, or 'integrity branch' of government in the making in Anglo-American democracies.[22]

Despite the creation by statute of the Office of the Auditor General in 1878 and that of the Chief Electoral Office in 1920, there are few published studies of officers of Parliament and none of a comparative nature.[23] Absence of attention to the part, so to speak, is indicative of lack of interest in the whole. This is to say that, despite Parliament's centrality, it is a subject of declining study. The last book-length institutional treatment was by C.E.S. Franks;[24] in the 1990s, the Canadian Journal of Political Science published nine articles that include in their title the word Parliament or the name of any one of its three parts; between 1991 and 2001, the program of the annual meeting of the Canadian Political Science Association listed on average fewer than one session (similarly defined) per year in its 'Canadian' section. The categorization is disputable since some papers in the same section deal, for example, with political parties and party discipline. Still, such professional incuriosity deserves notice, especially when placed alongside frequent presentations each year in the public policy and public law section of the program (on such subjects as the charter, the judiciary, the courts, and policy making). Disciplinary unconcern stands in contrast to heightened interest manifested by parliamentarians and the public. Representative of the first is the Canadian Study of Parliament Group (CSPG), founded in 1978, and open to anyone interested in Parliament. Professional political scientists constitute only one type of member, although the publications of CSPG are largely of their authorship.[25] For about the same length of time, the Canadian Region of the Commonwealth Parliamentary Association has published the *Canadian Parliamentary Review*. Here academics publish alongside but less frequently than members and officers of federal and provincial legislatures.

The study of Parliament, it would seem, has migrated from academic departments in two opposite directions. One is towards practitioners and researchers of politics, the other towards an engaged public. Two illustrations make the point. First, there is Democracy Watch, established in 1994, whose self-described 'mandate' is 'to ensure that Canadian citizens have a greater and more meaningful role in government and business decision-making in Canada.' Among 'the steps to empower Canadians' posted on the group's web page are reforming the electoral system, introducing mechanisms of direct democracy, developing a civics curriculum, and increasing accountability of the judiciary to the public. According to its own count, Democracy Watch in 2004 made 41 television appearances to discuss the issues of accountability, public access, and electoral reform.[26] For radio, the total was 98 appearances, and for newspapers and magazines, 185. In 1994 and using the same categories, the numbers were 14, 11, and 52. The second public organization is Fair Vote Canada, founded in 2000, which seeks 'a fair voting system – a fundamental requirement for healthy representative democracy and government accountability.'[27] The adjective *public* used to describe these organizations requires comment since they claim neither a mass membership nor intensive organization. Instead, their 'public' nature derives from the accessibility that comes with their Internet persona and from the traditional mass media's readiness to quote their rebuke of current practices.

The themes common to the critiques offered by Democracy Watch and Fair Vote Canada – greater accountability and accessibility on the part of politicians – are not theirs alone. Some of Canada's best-known journalists and academics have joined in the indictment: Jeffrey Simpson authored a book entitled *The Friendly Dictatorship*, Michael Bliss wrote articles for the *National Post* with titles such as 'Southern Republic and Northern Dictatorship' and 'Canada's House of Ill Repute,' while Donald Savoie advanced a thesis about the 'concentration of power in Canadian politics' in a book called *Governing from the Centre.*[28] Not in a century has there been such a constellation of critics and not in the country's history criticism that aimed so directly at the heart of the constitution. That heart is monarchy, and much of the complaint about the impotence of Parliament (which for the purpose of this discussion is really the Commons) and the impudence of the prime minister and his officials originates in the prime minister's use of prerogative powers (in regard to appointments and the conduct of foreign affairs, for example) that adhere to the Canadian crown but are exercisable on his (or her) advice. Too strict party discipline is part of the accusation, one that members of Parliament (particularly on the government side) increasingly echo. Often, but not always, the discipline question is linked to an exercise of power by government that originates in Canada's monarchical arrangement of power.

Questions of accessibility and accountability, discontent with discipline, the exercise of prerogative power, the expanding role of officers of Parliament – all of these matters and more combine to keep attention focused, despite competition from the courts and media, where it has traditionally been paid – on Parliament, and especially the House of Commons.

Not in a century has there been such a range of critics – perhaps thanks to the institutionalization of criticism outside of Parliament in the form of bodies like Democracy Watch and Fair Vote Canada – but criticism itself has a precedent. Consider, for instance, R. MacGregor Dawson's *Constitutional Issues in Canada, 1900–1931.*[29] Published seven decades ago, this collection of federal and some provincial government documents, plus newspaper and periodical articles, is striking in its contemporaneity. Forty-seven per cent of its pages are devoted to the three parts of Parliament and the cabinet; another 15 per cent to parties, and a further 13 per cent to constitutional amendment. The remaining pages deal with the civil service, the judiciary, and dominion-provincial relations. In the parliamentary section the issues are familiar ones, such as party discipline in the House, questions of confidence, and Senate reform. In retrospect, speakers may change but sentiments remain the same – almost. Missing is the vocabulary that talks of access and accountability. Its source, what one American writer has called the language of 'moral entrepreneurs,' will be discussed in a later chapter.[30] In the present context, the point to note is that, whatever new dimension arises in a discussion of public trust, the object of concern – the actions of elected persons – assures a central role for the House of Commons.

The habit of criticism of government, promoted in civics literature as a strength of democracies, has been broadened in Canada since the 1980s into an institutional critique. Consider, for example, 'A Conference on Parliamentary Reform' with the title 'Re-Inventing Parliament,' held at the University of Lethbridge in 1994 and co-sponsored by the Canada West Foundation, which describes itself as 'an independent, non-partisan, non-profit public policy research institution dedicated to introducing western perspectives ... through initiatives for active citizen education and engagement in the Canadian public policy process.' According to the 'Executive Summary' of the conference report, 'conference participants identified a number of deeply rooted problems currently plaguing Canada's system of parliamentary government,' the first of which was 'Canadians [sic] lack of confidence in, and respect for, their institutions of government.'[31] Lack of governmental accountability, prime ministerial dominance, and excessive party discipline appeared as other 'problems.' Recommendations for change included less party discipline, a greater role for parliamentary committees, reforms to the Senate and the electoral system (with some variant of proportional representation being introduced), and the introduction of such direct democratic instruments as citizens' initiatives, referendum, and recall.

This decade-old conference is recalled not because it was unique but because its conclusions articulated a viewpoint that has become more common. Again, it is less the substance of the specific recommendations than the breadth of their presumption that qualifies them for discussion here. In light of the subject of this book, two observations are in order. The first is to note the composure with which the summary communicates the finding that 'Canadians lack confidence in and respect for, their institutions of government.' In a later elaboration, the conference report notes that scepticism 'does not result from the *elected governments* themselves as much as it results from the shortcomings of the *system*' (emphasis in original). The second comment concerns that last word: what does 'system' mean in the context of this discussion? All of the recommendations, except for 'fundamental reform [that is, election] of the

Senate,' deal with procedures of the House of Commons, or electoral reform, or the inclusion of 'direct democracy mechanisms' whose effect would inhibit the present work of the Commons. The evergreen quality of the recommendations of 1994 are borne out by an article in *Policy Options* a decade later under the title 'Expanding the Federal Democratic Reform Agenda.'[32] Less discipline, stronger committees, and electoral reform reappear. What is new is concern for accountability.

From the perspective of these, and many other studies, Parliament means something more than the Gothic Revival structures on Parliament Hill in Ottawa, or the lawn, framed on three sides by monumental and distinctive architecture, the site for more than a century and a quarter of protests, festivities, and memorials. Before Confederation, governments emerged from within the House of Commons; loose party discipline made jostling for power possible just as it made it necessary. With Confederation, John A. Macdonald perfected the art of controlling the House and making governments from outside the chamber – indeed outside Ottawa. Patronage was now used to entice voters in the constituencies to support Macdonald's candidate rather than, as in the past, to bring members on side in the House. (Like William Gladstone, who became prime minister of Great Britain in 1867 and held power for most of the rest of the century, Macdonald had the completion of the railways to thank for making a national party organization possible. Church politics, the franchise, and political unity – Quebec rather than Ireland – were other similarities.)

The House of Commons incorporates the people as a nation, but this is possible only through political parties. For this reason, Parliament is about more than committees, debates, and life on the Hill. The people's house is about both house and people. The point needs to be stressed, because one of the difficulties in talking about the House of Commons is boundaries, not in the electoral sense but rather in terms of the reach of the House. Where does it end, or begin? This is a question that does not arise when discussing the Senate, since its constituency is all Canadians. The Senate was purpose-built: there are some similarities with the House of Lords, but in its vital features of appointment, size, and powers, it was quintessentially Canadian. By contrast, the House of Commons is a vestigial chamber, emulating, borrowing from, imitating, and mimicking the Commons at Westminster, one of whose features – the fundamental feature – is its view of itself as the sovereign voice of the sovereign people. Federalism with divided jurisdiction might limit the self-image of Canada's House. Nonetheless, from the beginning the Commons was about more than a building; it was about building and symbolizing a nation.

The divided jurisdiction of federalism limited the self-image of Canada's House. But by how much, and with what consistency over the years? For example, have four decades of province building narrowed the Canadian nationalist vision? (In the matter of jurisdictional consciousness, the House [and the Senate] looked out as well as in: until 1982, the Parliament at Ottawa had to acknowledge the ever-decreasing legal pre-eminence of Westminster.) Federalism disperses power; parliamentary government concentrates it. There is an inherent tension between the two governing arrangements, whose resolution has provided generations of students ample scope to theorize. How much greater is the tension where the relationships between the central and respective provincial governments become asymmetrical? Perhaps that question might more usefully be phrased as 'How much asymmetry can these relations absorb before parliamentary government can no longer function?' There has to be a perceived national community if majority rule in the House of Commons is to be the basis of decision making. After all, the House is the chamber that legitimates legislation.

At one time that role was shared with national political parties whose own structures replicated and reinforced the federal arrangement of power. If, as some critics say, Canadians lack confidence in their *system* of government, of which the House is a key part, then the regional decline of national parties must be a contributing factor, for it was the parties that incorporated different parts of the country into a national political community.[33] This explains why R. MacGregor Dawson gives more space to political parties than to federalism in his book *Constitutional Issues in Canada, 1900-1931*. It also explains why he saw political parties as a fit subject for inclusion in the constitutional category.

Seventy years later, the word *constitution* never refers to political parties. One of the most quoted books of the last decade to deal with Canadian federalism is Peter Russell's *Constitutional Odyssey: Can Canadians Become a Sovereign People?*[34] The odyssey it describes is the confederation journey – as it transpires, a journey without end. Nor is the constitution the property of federalist scholars alone. In 1982, following federal-provincial agreement on a domestic amending formula and adoption of the Canadian Charter of Rights and Freedoms, the British North America Act, appropriately amended, was renamed the Constitution Act. The point of these examples is that the word *constitution* has assumed a different meaning from what it once had. The charter and its guarantees have become in some quarters synonymous with the constitution. As a result a rival to parliamentary democracy has arisen in the form of constitutional democracy.

But that is not the only rival. Adoption of the charter, following parliamentary joint committee hearings that saw the government's original rights proposal broadened, encouraged a view of a people's constitution that did not conform to constitutional reality. Great expectations and, sometimes, disappointment have resulted. Entrenched rights might limit the jurisdiction of Parliament and the provincial legislatures, but the constitutive power of neither was altered by the charter. In fact, legislative authority grew as a result of the expanded categories of subjects requiring unanimous provincial assent for amendment under the renamed Constitution Act. The admission of new provinces, once the privilege of Parliament to determine, is an example. Another is the notwithstanding clause of the Constitution Act (33.1), which allows Parliament or a legislature to persist for five years with a statute or portion thereof notwithstanding conflict between it and most sections of the charter.

More than that, a new s.92A of the Constitution Act confirmed exclusive provincial legislative authority over exploration, development, and conservation of non-renewable resources. The coincidence of the Constitution Act's affirmation of entrenched rights and freedoms for Canadians on one hand and authority over natural resources for the provinces on the other deserves mention. Concern about protecting natural resources was largely a preoccupation of Alberta and Saskatchewan and originated in their governments' strong opposition to the federal government's National Energy Policy. Section 92A was viewed as insurance that federal trespass on the affected provinces would not happen again. The reason for mentioning the resource conflict in the context of the Commons is to underline a related development. Opposition from Alberta to the National Energy Policy and the federal government that introduced it also re-energized long-standing Alberta opposition to national political parties that were viewed as unsympathetic to western Canada's needs. Notwithstanding a new government and a new party in power in Ottawa between 1984 and 1993, disaffection on the prairies produced the Reform party, whose founder and leader was Preston Manning. The significant features of Reform lay in what it rejected: a federated structure of provincial organizations – Reform was a national party only, and a party held together by discipline; autonomy and independence were its distinctive principles.

Thus, the Constitution Act fed two developments whose core principles ran counter to each other and to Canada's tradition of parliamentary democracy. First, there was constitutional democracy, which emphasized the supremacy of the charter and what the Supreme Court of Canada in the *Quebec Secession Reference* called 'foundational constitutional principles': '[W]ith the adoption of the *Charter*, the Canadian system of government was transformed to a significant extent from a system of Parliamentary supremacy to one of constitutional supremacy.'[35] Second, in seeking to assuage a western sense of grievance by inserting a regionally specific jurisdictional amendment, the first ministers affirmed the legitimacy of the complaint and, by extension, the indictment of political parties that carry policies against strong opposition.

This was the atmosphere that produced the 'Triple-E Senate' proposal – to make the upper house equal, elected, and effective. As well, that decade saw the promotion of a party that rejected party discipline – in the constituencies, in the caucus, and in the Commons – and thus parliamentary democracy as it traditionally operated in Canada. In its place, Reform promoted electoral democracy. In the eyes of Reform's proponents, Parliament was at best a debating society whose deliberations were irrelevant to the citizen. In place of debate, Reformers advocated consultative mechanisms in the form of plebiscites, referenda, and the use of recall. How to operationalize these proposals in federal politics was another matter. It is important to note that, like constitutional democracy, electoral democracy helped personalize politics. As rivals to parliamentary democracy they can be seen as attempts to create space where a different kind of politics can occur.

What kind of politics and how effective a substitute or even alternative to parliamentary democracy remain matters for discussion. Is there any counterpart, for instance, for the symbolic or integrative role the Commons regularly plays as a result of the ritual of election? It can be argued that the refinement of representation – what MPs do – produces a 'condensation of values.'[36] The phrase comes from anthropology, but it seems particularly apt as a description of the royal assent ceremony before it was altered in 2003: the representative of the crown personifies the nation; the Senate embodies the federal principle; and the Commons represents the people through their representatives. The work of the Commons (and the Senate), where debate and orderly procedure in the form of readings and committee examination build consent leading to the creation of law, offers another, but less constitutionally whole, analogy.

Law is not found but created by Parliament. The cumulative sense, reflected in the consecutive numbering of parliamentary sessions, and the theme of progressive development – from colony to nation, the achievement of responsible government, the rounding-out of Confederation – are familiar features of Canada's institutional heritage. Canadians, as William Kilbourn described them, are 'a people of the law rather than the prophets.'[37] Continuity and tradition are virtues, but they are also qualities that disguise the distinction between present and past. The past restrains the present – Tom Paine's 'sepulcher of precedents' – but it also informs it; consider the resurrection in 2004 of all former minority governments to guide the actions of those in power after the general election.[38] Again, is parliamentary reform an attempt to recapture the past or achieve a hitherto unrealized ideal? The temporal dimension of legislation is but one of the layers of significance of parliamentary democracy that distinguish it from constitutional and electoral democracy. Representation – the skein of representation in the context of legislatures – is another.

2 Parliamentary Democracy

Parliament is composed of two chambers of the people, but only the Commons can be said to represent the people. However imperfectly the House embodies the principle of representation by population – and it is imperfect, as can be seen, for instance, when Saskatchewan with one-third of Alberta's population in 2001 has one-half its number of seats in the Commons – the lower and not the upper chamber of Parliament springs directly from the choice of the people. Inadequately so, say a legion of critics, who blame the machinations of the disciplined parties that nominate most candidates and contest most elections, the unsophisticated method by which votes are cast and counted, the self-seeking individuals who win constituents' trust and then abandon it once in office, and a cloud of interests that at all times wield disproportionate influence over the political system.

Criticism of the Commons, which, unfairly as regards the Senate, is identified in the public mind with Parliament, is long-standing. Still, that heritage of complaint should not be treated as static in its particular grievances. The milquetoast MP in the grip of a corpulent plutocrat, a favourite subject of agrarian cartoonists early in the last century, has disappeared. Now it is the tentacles of party and not capital that critics say limit the freedom of the member. This bill of indictment is familiar enough. At issue here is less the individual charges than the parliamentary democratic ideal that informs the arraignment.

As this and the next two chapters will demonstrate, Parliament but, more accurately, the Commons – the 'people's house' – confronts a conflict of alternatives and choice over the role it should play. There is the traditional attribution of the Commons as the embodiment of parliamentary democracy. Only in this form can 'a nation ... interrogate itself.'[1] This is a description offered by a former speaker of the National Assembly of France, but it applies to Canada and for the same reason as in France: the elected chamber incorporates the nation. It does this in diverse and sometimes contradictory ways.

First, there is territorial incorporation. Along with monetary arrangements, the terms of union for all provinces have included representation in the Commons and membership in the Senate. It is a distinctive Canadian tradition that skilful political negotiations and not dispassionate mathematical formulae determined parliamentary numbers. That is why, when British Columbia – with a smaller population than Manitoba – entered Confederation, it secured more seats in the Commons. Unlike the United States, where representation in Congress is limited to states, representation in the Canadian Parliament is not limited to provinces. In 1887 the North-West Territories was granted two senators and four seats in the Commons, a precedent that continues in the twenty-first century with each northern territory sending to Ottawa one senator and one member of Parliament.

In a country as vast as Canada, territorial incorporation, as well as the mechanisms to contest and conduct an election, constitute an underacknowledged dimension of the people's house. More customary, however, is discussion of the franchise. Voting is the hallmark of citizenship, both symbolically and practically. Exclusion of First Nations from the federal franchise until 1960 has not been deemed, retrospectively, a prohibition of major practical import, although alternative legal remedies – perhaps in part as a consequence of electoral exclusion – have had a determinative influence on Canadian politics. By contrast, denial of the franchise until almost half a century ago remains symbolically a permanent reminder of discrimination and exclusion. First Nations were not the only residents of Canada so treated. Until women cast their the vote nationally for the first time in the federal election of 1921, half the country's population was disfranchised. Again, in his book *Redress*, Roy Miki says that Japanese Canadians 'who wanted to participate in the democratic process, fixated on the lack of the franchise ... Without the right to vote, they were not permitted to enter professions such as medicine, pharmacy and law, to hold public office or to work in certain occupations.' More than that, exclusion fed passivity to the point of failing to 'mount a challenge to the racist policies.'[2] (The first Canadian of Japanese origin was elected to the House of Commons in 2004.)

The reason for this selective excursion into the history of the franchise is to underline the singular importance of the people's house as an agent of legitimation. Or, delegitimation even, in the case of those who were citizens. Lorraine Weinrib describes rejection by the Commons of a 1906 petition from representatives of Canada's Jewish community in which they requested exemption from application of the Lord's Day Act: 'The answer they received was not merely negative. It was exclusionary and condescending.'[3]

Thus, at different times, the House of Commons admitted and the House of Commons excluded, but in each instance, the House of Commons defined Canada. Here is a reason to study the Commons, one as important to understanding Canadian politics as concern about the impact of different electoral systems upon its composition or the passage of laws. But racially discriminatory voting practices and exclusionary sabbatarian legislation are in the past. The Charter of Rights and Freedoms is twenty-five years old, and the Supreme Court of Canada has interpreted its provisions to, among other things, extend the franchise even further (to prisoners), invalidate on the grounds of unequal treatment the invidious distinction between citizen and non-citizen status in the matter of employment, and broaden the interpretation of freedom of religion in the context of Sunday observance.[4]

Does Supreme Court interpretation of the charter deprive the people's house of its 'interrogative' function? The unqualified answer to that inquiry must be no. What has happened is that the Commons no longer monopolizes the discussion, and for that reason it cannot afford to allow itself to be viewed as condescending to public opinion, no matter how minor or marginal or unpopular that opinion may appear to be. The soliloquy has become a dialogue. In the context of court and parliamentary relations in Canada, the term *dialogue* has assumed a rarefied meaning – judges and legislators working together to improve the law. Critics of the courts have treated dialogue as a euphemism to disguise the judiciary's intrusion into legislative matters. That is not the sense of the term here. Rather, it is about the courts interpreting rights, entrenched beyond legislative influence, and through interpretation expanding the sense of who the people are.

Broadening out by the courts probably reinforces, may even accelerate, the incorporating function of the legislature. Still, it does not rival or supplant it. The court complements the Commons because neither institution equates people with citizens. The 'people' of the people's house includes more than the electorate. In respect to children that is self-evident. Their interests, as far as may be met by political means, are assumed to be the interests of members of Parliament, be they, for example, protection from exploitation or the provision of day care. Non-citizens, either as refugees or landed immigrants, are people, too. Congregated in Canada's largest metropolitan centres, this diverse sub-population has a presence and profile in a limited number of constituencies that influence in an identifiable way the politics of the Commons and the role members of Parliament adopt as representatives of the people.

In the parliamentary democratic ideal, the House of Commons is the stationary centre of a Ptolemaic-like political universe. The reasons for this are easy to state. Outside of Lower Canada (later Quebec) with its Roman Catholic church and the seigneurial system, nothing preceded electoral politics. Absent a hereditary aristocracy and an established church, the appointed legislature councils, that is, the upper chambers of the colonies, were seen for what they were – institutions to limit electoral democracy. Institutions, it should not be forgotten, imposed by imperial authority. Partisan organization or, better still, tendencies following upon unsuccessful rebellions in Upper and Lower Canada, led to the achievement of responsible government and the displacement of imperial power. First the assemblies and then the Commons became the centre of attention.

The electoral root of the Commons as well as the legislative fruit of its labour help explain its pre-eminence. These features, along with the function of territorial incorporation, are grounds enough for placing parliamentary democracy first among the triptych of models for discussion. Necessary but not sufficient, however. Parliamentary democracy is privileged in all senses of the term. It is ancient, established, politically dominant, and, unlike its doctrinal rivals – constitutional and electoral democracy – it lays claim to 'possess ... inherent constitutional privileges necessary for the efficient operation of the legislative body.' That claim the Supreme Court of Canada has recognized in *New Brunswick Broadcasting Co. v. Nova Scotia (Speaker of the House of Assembly)*.[5] At issue was whether the exercise of parliamentary privilege to prohibit the use of television cameras in the Nova Scotia House of Assembly was subject to charter scrutiny. The court determined that parliamentary privilege fell within the group of principles constitutionalized by virtue of the preamble and was therefore not subject to charter scrutiny. Legal immunity as part of privilege was not absolute, however, but only for actions done within 'the necessary sphere of matters without which the dignity and efficiency of the House cannot be upheld.' Charter limitations on the scope of parliamentary privilege, in respect, say, to the exercise of managerial powers, invalidate neither privilege nor the unique authority Parliament may claim as a result of privilege.[6]

In a 1957 article, 'Called to the Bar of the House of Commons,' Norman Ward discussed eighteen cases between Confederation and 1913 (the last instance) of individuals 'summoned or ordered to appear at the bar,' one of whom was committed to prison.[7] In his conclusion, Ward quoted, approvingly, Beauchesne's authoritative opinion that 'the power of commitment ... becomes the keystone of parliamentary privilege.'[8] It is fifty years since Ward's article appeared and more than ninety since the last 'summoning.' Has a power so little used atrophied? Apparently not. In 2003, the Government Operations and Estimates Committee, dissatisfied with former Information Commissioner George Radwanski's administration of his office, was reported ready to call that officer of Parliament before the House to answer contempt charges.[9] In the event, Mr Radwanski resigned his position before committee action proved necessary.

There is a statutory basis for the privileges of the Canadian Parliament – s.18 of the Constitution Acts, 1867–1982, originally Parliament of Canada Act, 1875, 38-39 Vict., c. 38 (U.K.) – but they originate in ancient usage and form part of the common law. In an early opinion (1841), the Judicial Committee of the Privy Council observed that 'the reason why the House of Commons has this power [of committing a person for contempt] is *not because* it is a representative body with legislative functions.'[10] Here is one source of the exceptionalism of Parliament, one that is underappreciated by scholars, the media, the people, and even parliamentarians.

Of course, Parliament and, more particularly, the Commons is a legislative body and a representative body. Of course, that is the work everyone with an interest in the matter pays attention to. Nonetheless, parliamentary privilege and the common law inheritance of which it is a part deserve examination, and not out of excessive respect for historicism. On the contrary, the presumptions that sustain parliamentary privilege and the distinctiveness of Parliament as an institution are increasingly under scrutiny and subject to criticism. This is happening not so much as a result of a coordinated campaign with a coherent purpose – to replace the parliamentary order – but as a loss of conviction on all sides in its superiority. Hence the power of slogans such as 'the democratic deficit,' multi-partisan in appeal within the Commons and popular with press, public, and academics outside, even though 'the origin of the phrase lies within the European Community; specifically, in debates about the relationship between economic and political integration in general and the legitimacy of non-majoritarian institutions in particular.'[11]

By what route the phrase migrated to Canada is unknown, but its transmutation in meaning – from a concern about 'ill-fitting' power to an attack on concentrated power – is clear enough. Emotive descriptions of Canadian government as a dictatorship or autocracy are exaggerated variants on 'the-decline-of-legislatures' thesis popular in the literature of comparative politics four decades ago.[12] As with the 'decline' thesis then, so today's lamentations echo in other parliamentary systems. The Constitution Unit, University College London, has published timely and cogent monographs since its founding in the mid-1990s to coincide with a program of constitutional reform in Great Britain unprecedented in the past century: proportional representation in European elections, adherence to the European Convention on Human Rights, freedom of information legislation, House of Lords reform, new legislatures in Edinburgh and Cardiff. Yet, voter turnout in the 2001 election was the lowest since 1918. (In 2005, there was a 2 per cent increase, to 61.3 per cent.) 'Is Britain Facing a Crisis of Democracy?' a 2004 publication asked in its title, and concluded that 'talk of a "crisis" is premature,' although British democracy was 'certainly fac[ing] a challenge.'[13]

The same cause, low voter turnout – 60.5 per cent in Canada's 2004 federal general election – has prompted the same label – crisis, only in Canada as an assertion of fact by, for example, the Civics Channel, a non-profit, non-partisan organization.[14] According to this source, 'apathy' and 'cynicism' are the culprits. If this is true, they are not new phenomena: consider the title of an article written in 1993 by Stéphane Dion and published in *Canadian Parliamentary Review* – 'Rising Cynicism: Who Is to Blame?' – or a burgeoning literature since then with titles such as 'Failing Legitimacy: The Challenge Facing Parliamentarians,' 'Toward a More Responsive Parliament,' 'Can Parliamentarians Become Real Players?,' 'Is the Decline of Parliament Irreversible?,' 'The Roots of our Democratic Malaise,' and *'Just Trust Us': The Erosion of Accountability in Canada.*[15]

Concern about the state of Parliament today, which more often is expressed as concern about the Commons, to whom government is accountable, is widespread and overwhelmingly negative but politically and constitutionally unfocused. There is a kaleidoscope of complaints: about committees and their operation, about chairs and their selection, about party discipline and government exploitation of discipline to control the House, and about the impotence of backbenchers on both sides of the chamber. The work of the House, say some critics, has become the business of others – the courts, the media, premiers, regulatory agencies, and bureaucrats. In *Parliament under Blair*, Peter Riddell, political columnist of *The Times*, recounts many of the same grievances heard in Great Britain but cautions, too, that 'the belief that Parliament is no longer supreme or central to political life has almost been too glibly accepted.'[16]

Canada's federal Parliament was never so supreme as the Parliament at Westminster, just as today it (and every provincial legislature) confronts a limitation on its powers in the form of the Charter of Rights and Freedoms without comparison in Britain or other Commonwealth countries. Still, within the jurisdiction assigned it by the Constitution Acts 1867 to 1982, and recognizing the constraints a charter of entrenched rights imposes on parliamentary power, the Canadian Parliament remains, as it has since 1867, the country's pre-eminent political institution. The reason why is not hard to find. The Commons has a distinctive role to play in unifying the country (the Senate plays its part, too, but the role of the Commons is both more purposeful and more obvious). Canada's is a double federation – of provinces and of English and French-speaking cultures. It is true that bilingualism, multiculturalism, and Aboriginal rights are recognized in sections 16, 27, and 35 of the Constitution Act, but the dichotomy of language and culture that pressed for constitutional recognition late in the eighteenth century was acknowledged in and through the House of Commons at Confederation. Redistribution, which until the 1940s saw Quebec the basis for calculating the allocation of seats to other provinces, now sees Quebec guaranteed seventy-five seats irrespective of the province's population decline relative to the national total (except for Ontario, Alberta, and British Columbia, grandfathering benefits all provinces to some extent). Through its Standing Orders and by convention, the House offered a model of bilingualism long before enactment of the Official Languages Act in 1969. Alternation in the speaker's chair of persons fluent in one or other of the two languages, along with appointment of a deputy speaker possessing a full knowledge of the language *not* that of the speaker, testified to the integrative capacity of the lower chamber. In its operation and in its composition, the Commons was tailored less to fit Canadian federalism than it was to promote that polity at the centre.[17]

It needs to be said that the House was not alone in performing this function – the dual legal system of common and civil law offered a further bond of unity. Nonetheless, the House and the political parties that populated it were given unique responsibility to make the federation sound – one they still have. The decline in voter turnout in recent federal elections (reversed, slightly, in 2006) is more than a sombre lesson in civics. Canadian parties and Canadian voters believe (because they have been so taught) that national political parties are essential to Canadian unity.[18] Third parties, ideologically oriented (for instance, the New Democratic Party) or regionally based (the Bloc Québécois), complicate the goal of national unification. That this is a goal of parties that seek to govern is evident even in a cursory reading of the history of the Reform party, the Canadian Alliance, or the Conservative party formed in 2003 through amalgamation of the Canadian Alliance and the Progressive Conservative party. How low can voter turnout fall before the legitimacy of a government is in doubt? As with other questions that arise in the context of parliamentary elections – such as what result constitutes a defeat for a government where no party wins a majority – considerations of who voted (and did not vote), and where, would be relevant. In short, in this particular instance, how is low turnout to be read?[19]

In the present context, where the focus is on parliamentary democracy, the proposition to pay attention to is the following: voter turnout is important because the House of Commons is important. And so are its members. Pierre Trudeau's description of members of Parliament as 'nobodies' is much quoted, but for contrasting reasons: to illustrate the arrogance of prime ministers and to document the impotence of MPs. The first claim may or may not be accurate, but the second is false, or so imprecise as to defy refutation. Members of Parliament by definition are not the prime minister or leaders of political parties. The respective influence of the one, the few, and the many is different. Discipline is a levelling device and is recognized as such in Canada, where complaints about its use focus as much on what it demonstrates – hierarchy and inequality – as they do on its consequence – stifling the individual member as the voice of constituency opinion.

Hierarchy is fundamental to parliamentary democracy in a constitutional monarchy, just as it is central to recent criticism of that form of government in Canada. By definition, hierarchical power is vertical and concentrated in appearance, but its consequences (and the consequences of the reforms its critics propose) are horizontal and diffuse in effect. From one perspective this is the familiar question of how to reconcile monarchy and federalism, a constitutional form pioneered by Canada in 1867. The answer was to create a federation of compound monarchies, each province of which within its jurisdiction might claim the statutory and prerogative power necessary to realize its constitutional objectives.[20] However, the question to be discussed here does not concern federalism but rather the people's house and parliamentary democracy. Until late in the twentieth century, there is little evidence of opposition to the conventions of parliamentary democracy. Little but still some, since the Progressive party once challenged party discipline.[21] James G. Gardiner, a former Liberal premier of Saskatchewan and twenty-one-year minister of agriculture in the Mackenzie King and Louis St Laurent governments as well as inveterate foe of all sympathies non-Liberal, labelled that challenge 'the Old Manitoba form of democracy.'[22] By this he meant an unhealthy reverence for constituency opinion to the detriment of the party as a whole. After six decades in hibernation, the competing claims of party discipline and constituency or member autonomy reappeared in the 1980s, largely in the Progressive rhetorical guise of demands for free votes and opposition to the confidence convention.

The subject for the present is not this familiar complaint of parliamentary democracy but rather a new critique, the source of which is prerogative power inherent in the crown (that is, the sovereign through her representative, the governor general) exercisable on the advice of its first minister.[23] The essence of the prerogative is its imprecision, which for this reason confers on the crown's advisers discretionary power of great breadth. The point about the prerogative needs to be made because it is so seldom acknowledged in the criticism directed today at parliamentary – but often called prime ministerial – government. In the words of Michael Bliss

What has been accepted as normal and amoral is going to be condemned as immoral and corrupt, and eventually legislated out of existence.

Consider these examples. Since 1867, the Prime Minister of Canada has had the constitutional responsibility for appointing Senators and for advising the Governor-General when to call elections. It has been normal to appoint Senators as a reward for party service and to call elections for a date that will maximize party advantage. I believe that many Canadians now consider it morally corrupt to appoint people to the Senate solely for party service. Many Canadians now consider it morally corrupt to time elections for partisan reasons – which is why a number of provinces are moving toward fixed election dates.

Many Canadians now consider all patronage appointments to positions in Crown corporations to be morally corrupt. Letting contracts and giving grants and subsidies without open, advertised competition is coming to be seen to be corrupt. Interventions by Members of Parliament to obtain jobs and contracts for their political supporters – even summer jobs for favoured students – is coming to be seen to be corrupt. All other forms of partisan favouritism are coming to be seen to be corrupt in a society that believes in equal opportunities and non-discrimination. In other words the whole traditional culture of Canadian partisan politics is starting to be seen to be corrupt. Thus the notion of a culture of corruption.[24]

Discretionary power as corrupt power. Here is a proposition that explains much about modern political attitudes in Canada: the demand for parliamentary participation in, or surveillance or veto of, governor-in-council appointments; proposals for an elected Senate (which first appear only in the late 1980s); pressure to legalize the political realm – that is, to promote statutory over non-statutory processes (a central issue in the debate over ethics regulation); support for fixed election dates, thereby creating 'a level playing field' in place of prime-ministerial privilege. The list could be lengthened and the implication of its contents explored – for instance, parliamentary involvement in the nomination and appointment of justices of the Supreme Court of Canada. In short, monarchical parliamentary (federal) government in Canada has evolved into a highly complex arrangement of understandings and influences that are neither easily articulated nor altered without compensatory adjustment. This was the same reason that Australians, who by a wide margin favoured making their country a republic, rejected that proposal in a constitutional referendum in 1999. They could not agree on an alternative republican arrangement of power in place of the existing monarchical arrangement. More to the point of this discussion, they could not agree on how to disperse (or limit) the crown's prerogative and statutory powers exercisable on advice.[25]

As surrogate monarchies whose sovereign is the sovereign of the United Kingdom, Canada, Australia, and New Zealand are among a handful of countries who share an unusual constitutional status in the modern world. Still, monarchy is only part of what makes parliamentary government inherited from the United Kingdom distinct. Another aspect is that it is *inherited*. Few passages are more familiar in Canadian

politics textbooks than the phrase from the first paragraph of the preamble of the Constitutional Act, 1867, which expresses the colonial
'Desire to be federally united into One Dominion ... with a Constitution
similar in Principle to that of the United Kingdom.' The phrase has had
wide implications, among them support for an unwritten bill of rights
before the Bill of Rights introduced by the Diefenbaker government in
1960 was enacted.[26] Latitude for interpretation of the phrase is not a
matter for discussion now, but the presence of the phrase is, because it
demonstrates that Canada's parliamentary democracy is not a work of
construction but an inheritance. Here is a distinction often ignored.

In the 1990s, gridlock was a popular metaphor used to describe congressional government in the United States. Congress, critics said, did
not 'work,' either because of widening separation of powers or because
of declining bipartisanship. Interestingly, neither of these putative
causes could be cited for stasis in Canada. Nor, more importantly, does
this diagnosis of Washington's political malady apply to Ottawa. Parliamentary systems do not 'work,' or, for that matter, 'not work,' in the
sense in which U.S. critics use that term. Therefore, it is more than misleading – it is a misperception – to suggest that 'given the challenges of
modern society,' Parliament can no longer play its scrutinizing role – or,
that 'Parliament was designed for an era when things were simple and
manageable. That's when Parliament and government worked well
together.'[27] Parliament was never *designed*. To the degree that its 'parts'
are worthy of separate comment, they are more noticeable for their
overlap – for example, government in the people's house, crown subject to ministerial advice, and senators appointed by the crown on ministerial advice – than for their independence. The point is worth
emphasizing.

Parliament comprises both executive and legislature, with a telescop-
ing of responsibilities that produces a concentrated perspective. In his
biography of Gladstone, Roy Jenkins speaks of 'the futility of politics
without office.'[28] Notwithstanding that high politics touching the charter, federalism, and national unity have moved outside the parliamentary orbit, the people's house remains Canada's principal political
forum. The reason why is that the government is here, and it is drawn
overwhelmingly from the members of the House of Commons. So obvious is this statement that to say it requires justification. Parliamentary
government is just that – government in and of Parliament. In the colonies that joined to form federal Canada in 1867, first there was representative government (the Constitutional Act, 1791, as far as the colonies of

Upper and Lower Canada were concerned) and then there was responsible government, in 1848. From that date, politics in Canada was always more about government than it was about representation. Imperialism (internally, as regards acquiring and controlling the colonies of the North-West and British Columbia and externally as regards the march to dominion autonomy) helped explain the centripetal forces acting originally on national government. That was the North American variation on the monarchical theme. More enduring was Parliament's structure itself: control of the House required command of a majority of the constituencies. The vehicle was the national political party; the fuel, patronage.

Much has changed since the time of Sir John A. Macdonald and Sir Wilfrid Laurier, but the strength and structuring influence of partisan feeling remain. This is an essential feature of parliamentary politics, one whose importance reformers depreciate and even ignore.[29] Inverting the traditional hierarchy of government and representation, writers in the 1990s and early 2000s concentrate attention on matters of representation. The Canadian Democratic Audit, a nine-volume inquest into the health of Canadian democracy, sets as its 'benchmarks: public participation, inclusiveness, and responsiveness.'[30] Declining voter turnout along with decreasing membership in traditional civic and party organizations are both cause and consequence of a discouraging audit.[31] On all sides, words like *disaffected*, *disengaged*, and *dysfunctional* are employed to describe what is seen as a civic malaise.

There is nothing atypical about the volumes in this series. Indeed, they are representative of their type, which is to say, of commentary on Canadian legislative politics. The images employed are of reflection, of sameness, of wholeness, or, more accurately, a miniature whole. The argument is powerful because the reflection inevitably is found to be flawed, the part imperfect. Middle-aged, well-educated, highly paid white males have the advantage (and take it) everywhere. How to counter their privilege? The audit advances some unusual recommendations, but in light of the preceding discussion one might be noted. In the volume *Advocacy Groups*, the authors advocate 'an arms-length government agency to provide ... funding to groups representing marginalized segments of society.' Such a body would 'depoliticiz[e] the process of funding these groups.'[32]

From where does this reflective view of representation arise? And when does it come to dominate academic thinking? It is not found in Norman Ward's study *The Canadian House of Commons: Representation*, published in 1950, with a second edition in 1963. Divided into five parts, including Introduction and Conclusion, it has three substantive sections devoted to describing redistribution, the qualifications and condition of membership in the House, and, finally, the mechanisms of election (for instance, voters' lists and the franchise). Nor is it found in the study Norman Ward and David Hoffman did for the Royal Commission on Bilingualism and Biculturalism, *Bilingualism and Biculturalism in the Canadian House of Commons* (1970), although among the concepts of representation discussed there is the delegate theory, which awards primacy to constituency opinion as an influence on a legislator. But it is a long way from the delegate perspective to a position that talks about dysfunction and disengagement, says 'government outcomes should respond to the views of Canadians,' and advocates 'return[ing] the House of Commons to the people of Canada because they [outcomes] do not [respond] ... It is up to the members of parliament ... to take parliament back.'[33] This populist language has received the imprimatur of the political establishment, too: Paul Martin spoke, for instance, of 'giving Parliament back to the people.'[34]

Similarly, there is a chasm between mandating responsiveness, on the one hand, and pronouncing Parliament 'the crucible of national debate ... and the framework for national reconciliation,' on the other.'[35] Are these collective and selective versions of parliamentary democracy themselves reconcilable? They are, but only when representation is seen as a process of refining diverse opinion, not all of which comes from the people. On the contrary, government carries proposals to the people through Parliament. Representative government is superior to responsive government because its product – compromise – draws strength from a broadened base of support.

Representative government in a parliamentary system such as Canada's requires political parties. It was parties that made constitutional monarchy and responsible government possible in the colonies of British North America. Their and the legislature's historic function was to discipline power. Parties linked the people to power and in so doing made Parliament 'the pre-eminent legitimating institution.'[36] The contrast between that tradition and the current depiction, which attributes 'the public's disenchantment with the political community ... [to] the impoverished role of the parliamentarian and ... the contempt in which elected officials themselves hold democratic institutions,' is striking.[37] Exaggerated language, perhaps, but the uncertainty and inconsistency about much of what is said and written concerning Canadian parliamentary democracy in the twenty-first century requires explanation. Where once it was common to hear candidates and voters say they participated in electoral politics to make a difference, now that same reason is given for abandoning electoral politics. Even among those who show no disposition to leave, a growing number advocate detaching Parliament from the people and subjecting it to statutory and judicial control (discussed in chapter 3) or detaching the people from Parliament as a constituent entity in their own right (discussed in chapter 4).

3 Constitutional Democracy

There were rights and freedoms in Canada, just as there was constitutional government, before the advent of the charter. What was absent was supremacy of a higher, constitutional law. A discerning assessment of the implications for parliamentary government of the Constitution Act, 1982 (of which the Canadian Charter of Rights and Freedoms is a part) is to be found in the *Report* of the Royal Commission on the Economic Union and Development Prospects for Canada.[1] Published in 1985, the *Report* precedes later, enduring controversies that take as their focus the respective roles of Parliament and the courts in the era of the charter. Present at the creation, so to speak (the royal commission was appointed in 1982), its perspective – uncomplicated by practical experience – cannot be recaptured; still it is a viewpoint with a lesson to teach.

It is unremarkable to say that the charter transformed the Canadian constitution. The real point at issue is to understand the nature of the transformation and, for the purpose of this discussion, to determine its effect upon the people's house. If in the words of the royal commission *Report*, 'The Charter is a new pillar of the Canadian constitutional order,' how (to maintain the metaphor) does this new element alter the architecture of the existing constitution? What implications flow from the declaration in the Constitution Act, 1982, that 'the Constitution of Canada is the supreme law of Canada, and any law that is inconsistent with the provisions of the Constitution is, to the extent of the inconsistency, of no force or effect' (s. 52:1).

If some critics are to be believed, the Supreme Court of Canada, which as the highest judicial body is the principal object of censure, 'has become a law unto itself' and, in consequence, is '"hijacking" democracy.'[2] Whether or not that language is judged emotive, the import of the charge it makes for parliamentary democracy is clear enough: Parliament has been superseded, which is to say – and it is said – that the people and their interests have been displaced by judges who act on behalf of a new class. Most famously known as the 'Court Party,' half of the title of a much-quoted book on this subject, *The Charter Revolution and the Court Party*, the class is said to embrace those whose concerns run to such matters as national unity, social equality, civil liberties, and post-materialist interests such as the environment.[3] Synonyms for the 'Court Party' are the 'knowledge class,' the 'intelligentsia,' and, inevitably, the 'elites.' The invidious distinction between constitutionalism, the courts, and elites, on the one hand, and parliamentary democracy and the people, on the other, is easily drawn or, better still, imagined, since the discussion of electoral democracy in chapter 4 suggests that more than one set of tensions is at play in the realization of democratic values.

The court-Parliament dichotomy provides the basis for one of the most persistent critiques in academic circles, as perusal of the program of the annual meeting of the Canadian Political Science Association bears witness. Because the topic is a perennial favourite invigorated by an array of controversies over judgments, appointments, litigation, and the legal mobilization of interest groups, there is no need to elaborate the argument (there is literature enough on this already).[4] Except in one respect: the proposition that the eclipse of Parliament is due to an activist judiciary is overly simplistic. Indeed, the court-Parliament dichotomy itself is too stark, too hermetic in the contrast it posits. The relationship between the judiciary and Parliament is more entwined and less compensatory – one gaining at the expense of the other – than the watertight compartments of the dichotomy imply.[5] This chapter argues that together they offer not a dual but a double perspective on the constitution. Constitutional democracy revalues rather than devalues parliamentary democracy.

In his study of the Declaration of Independence, Garry Wills writes that 'the Declaration is not only part of our history; we are part of its history.'[6] Substitute *charter* for *Declaration*, and that insight applies equally to Canadians. The charter may have transformed the constitution; there may have been a charter revolution, but the charter is not a device or force external to Canada. On the contrary, Canada is part of the charter. Mobility rights (s.6), official languages (s.16), proceedings of Parliament (and its statutes and records) (ss. 17 and 18), proceedings in courts established by Parliament (s.19), communication by the public with federal institutions (s.20), minority language educational rights (s.23), multicultural heritage (s.27), rights respecting certain schools (s.29), recognition of existing Aboriginal and treaty rights (s.35), and equalization and regional disparities (s.36) – none of these rights makes sense absent the context provided by Canadian history and politics. All speak to continuing, often historic, concerns.

If Canada informs the charter, then judicial interpretation of the charter re-informs Canada. How to reconcile the charter guarantees of freedom of conscience and religion (s.2a) with public funding of denominational schools (s.93:1 of the Constitution Act, 1867)? In an advisory opinion in 1987, the Supreme Court of Canada, through Justice Wilson (unanimously supported by her colleagues), wrote: '[S]pecial treatment guaranteed by the constitution to denominational, separate or dissident schools ... sits uncomfortably with the concept of equality embodied in the Charter because [it is] not available to other schools.' Yet, 'it was never intended that the Charter could be used to invalidate ... a provision such as s.93 which represented a fundamental part of the Confederation compromise.'[7] Or, again, take s.23 guarantees regarding minority language educational rights and observe how the Supreme Court in 1990, and again in 1993, 'breath[ed] life into the express purpose of s.23' by requiring first the Alberta and then the Manitoba government to design and implement a system of school governance incorporating s.23 rights.[8]

Much could be said about these two examples of the court and the charter, beginning with the fact that they are only two and, therefore, unrepresentative. The difficulty is to know what is representative. The reason for discussing the two cases is to emphasize that in each the court revived in the case of Ontario or expanded in the cases of Alberta and Manitoba guarantees arising out of the charter and with roots in the Confederation or parliamentary settlements of 1867 and 1982, respectively. Equally important, according to Michael Behiels, in his study *Francophone Minority Communities*, successes in court signified the renaissance of these communities, which earlier had secured inclusion of s.23 in the charter. In their achievements, the Francophone minority communities had become part of what Behiels describes as 'the remarkable ongoing democratization of Canada's constitutional development.'[9]

No group, save Aboriginal peoples (s.35), has depended more than those representing minority language interests upon the charter and the courts to secure their rights. Yet to recognize that activity, even its primacy, and nothing else distorts understanding of the achievements of those s.23 benefits. The same might be said of Aboriginal groups, whose pace is different from those of minority language groups but whose priority – the recognition of rights – is the same. It is customary to depict Aboriginal groups as judicially focused. Their lack of interest in legislatures arises from their having been denied the franchise (until 1960, federally) and having been dependent upon bureaucracy to meet their needs. One consequence of this bias was the development of a 'concept of "being Indian" that differed from mere enfranchisement.'[10] Still, electoral interest and activity are emerging alongside recourse to the courts to secure interests.[11] Two issues need to be distinguished in this discussion – the legalization of politics and the politicization of law.[12]

The interposition of law and politics begins with Parliament's debate on the charter in 1980. This is another familiar story, although no more authoritatively told than by one of its central participants, Roy Romanow. In his first-hand account of the Special Joint Parliamentary Committee, to which the constitutional package with a domestic amending formula as well as the proposed charter was submitted, Romanow notes that the committee held '106 meetings on 56 hearing days. It sat for 270 hours and heard presentations from six governments, ninety-three groups and five individuals.'[13] Nationally televised, the testimony, which was overwhelmingly in favour of the charter, also had the effect of legitimating the charter. Another close observer at the time of the joint committee hearings was Barry Strayer, later a judge of the Federal Court of Appeal but then in the Privy Council Office. His recollection was that 'we were engaged in ... a process to establish political legitimacy for constitutional change.'[14] Here is the source for the proposition that Parliament is the base for public legitimation of the charter and thus the courts, a claim justices of the Supreme Court have felt called to reiterate. An early but representative example is by then Justice Lamer in 1985: 'It ought not to be forgotten that the historic decision to entrench the Charter in our Constitution was taken not by the courts but by the elected representatives of the people of Canada. It was those representatives who extended the scope of constitutional adjudication and entrusted the courts with this new and onerous responsibility. Adjudication under the Charter must be approached free of any lingering doubts as to its legitimacy.'[15]

The 'peoples' package,' as the Trudeau government in its struggle with the provinces invidiously labelled the charter and the other elements of patriation, injected an element of populism into the political transformation of the 1980s, but with this difference – there was no popular sovereignty. There could have been, for the federal government proposed using a referendum to resolve disagreement over an amending formula. As it happened, the provincial leaders (minus René Lévesque) agreed on a formula that kept amendment in the hands of politicians. Doubtless the charter enjoys great support from the people, but that popularity does not signify a constitution whose source rests in the people. Popular opinion runs (less than before, perhaps, but still principally) through Parliament. How then do the charter and Parliament 'fit'? The answer to that question is of more than factual importance, for together the charter and Parliament complement not contradict one another.

An early appreciation of what is described as 'congruence' between charter and Parliament can be found in the Supplementary Statement to the *Report* of the Royal Commission on the Economic Union and Development Prospects for Canada by Commissioner Clarence L. Barber. By this means, he says, the charter brings 'the courts ... more effectively into the competition that characterizes the political system.' The effect 'over the longer term [will be to] tighten the democratic link between governments and citizens.'[16] Where the stress is on complementarity between courts and legislatures, then, use of language that speaks of the first 'overruling' the second sounds more than harsh – it is misleading and feeds a view of the relationship between courts and legislatures as antipathetical.[17]

Constitutional democracy and the higher law it embraces intensifies rather than depreciates parliamentary democratic government. The argument that 'the judicialized politics of rights' undermines representative democracy because rights are absolute and absolutes are antipolitical omits what is most important to note – that rights reinforce democracy.[18] Consider *Figueroa v. Canada (Attorney General)*, where sections of the Canada Elections Act providing that political parties must nominate candidates in at least fifty electoral districts in order to obtain registered party status and thus qualify for certain benefits were found unconstitutional because they were inconsistent with s.3 of the charter: 'Every citizen of Canada has the right to vote in an election of members of the House of Commons or of a legislative assembly and to be qualified for membership therein.' Figueroa, leader of the Communist Party of Canada, argued that being a registered party under the impugned sections 'cost our party money.' More relevant for the present discussion, he observed that, 'The Canadian people consider it to be important, that you're not really legitimate if you're not registered, if you're not official.'[19]

Here is a revealing comment on the institutionalization of politics, with implications for parties and elections, at a time when both are reputed to be in disrepute. In its judgment the court allowed Parliament a year in which to determine alternative requirements for registration that would meet the court's unanimous view as typified in the following passages:

> Full political debate ensures an open society benefiting from diverse opinions and a social policy sensitive to the needs and interests of a broad range of citizens. Participation in the electoral process has an intrinsic value independent of the outcome of elections. The right to run for office provides an opportunity to present ideas and opinions to the electorate and the right to vote provides an opportunity for citizens to express support for ideas and opinions. In a democracy, sovereign power resides in the people as a whole and each citizen must have a genuine opportunity to take part in the governance of the country through participation in the selection of elected representatives ...
>
> [T]he ability of a political party to make a valuable contribution to the electoral process is not dependent upon its capacity to offer the electorate a genuine 'government option' ...
>
> In each election, a significant number of citizens vote for candidates nominated by registered parties in full awareness that the candidate has no realistic chance of winning a seat in Parliament – or that the party of which she or he is a member has no realistic chance of winning a majority of seats in the House of Commons. Just as these votes are not 'wasted votes,' votes for a political party that has not satisfied the 50-candidate threshold are not wasted votes either. As a public expression of individual support for certain perspectives and opinions, such votes are an integral component of a vital and dynamic democracy.[20]

The government's response was to introduce a bill to amend the Canada Elections Act (and the Income Tax Act). Bill C-3 reduced to one the number of candidates a party must endorse in order to register; among other provisions, it also defined a political party for the first time.[21] Strong arguments may be offered as to the beneficial and adverse effects of a ruling that transforms the traditional view of a political party. Jeffrey Simpson, one of Canada's most widely read political columnists, speaking specifically to the *Figueroa* decision, said, 'the political system should adapt to new circumstances. It should bring the Supreme Court and other high courts fully into the political process, where the courts are anyway, by letting them decide much earlier what should or should not be done in public policy. Then legislatures could rubber-stamp or fine-tune what the courts decide, and all Canadians would understand who's making the important decisions.'[22] Simpson's thesis – that in the 'Age of the Charter,' Parliament is 'an institution of secondary importance' – emanated from the dichotomous or compensatory school (so to speak) of court-legislature relations – one rises or falls at the expense of the other.

A different interpretation leading to a less pessimistic conclusion sees the court expressing popular opinion, specifically 'more openness in the political process than politicians have seen fit to afford.'[23] *Figueroa* is a telling example of this approach. The fifty-candidate threshold arose out of a conception of political parties as spatial entities – intended to transcend geography and, ideally, to unite Canada itself. The one-candidate minimum speaks to a very different conception – parties as the voice of opinion. Here constitutional democracy with its higher law opens the door to the possibility of a new party system. More is necessary for that to happen than one judgment by the Supreme Court of Canada. In the first decade of the twenty-first century there is growing discussion about reform to Canada's plurality electoral system. In the winter of 2005, the Standing Committee on Procedure and House Affairs began to consider processes by which to approach the study of electoral reform.[24] Of course, the future is unknown. Thus observers are free to speculate that, because of *Figueroa*, were some form of proportional electoral reform to be introduced, then 'a more representative and influential House of Commons' could result, and as a consequence, strengthen Canadian democracy by reinvigorating political debate and reducing the dominance of the governing party.'[25]

Bill C-3 reconstitutes Canada's electoral process by setting minimum numbers of candidates and by statutorily defining a political party for the first time. Predictably, dissent at perceived judicial trespass on legislative preserve followed *Figueroa*, even though the principal effect of the decision was to broaden representation of popular opinion in the people's house. It is important to note that the presumption of the decision is to enhance participation, and it is that charter value with which the former section of the Canada Elections Act conflicted. Participation is a reflection of 'one of the core values underlying both the purpose of the Charter and a number of its specific rights and freedoms.'[26] It is reasonable to infer from *Figueroa* that the court's concern with the fifty-candidate threshold lay in the difficulty it saw the public having when trying to participate fully in electoral politics. Elections are not the preserve of parties, especially not those that sit in the House of Commons and pass the electoral laws.

How then to explain the Supreme Court's decision in *Harper v. Canada (Attorney General)* in 2004 to uphold sections of the Canada Elections Act that limited the amount third-party, that is lobby, groups might spend during election campaigns? Critics of these provisions, the most prominent being the National Citizens' Coalition, who challenged the spending limits, called the offending sections a 'gag law' because they constituted a restraint on freedom of expression. In a 6–3 decision, the judges acknowledged that the law abridged freedom of expression, but they also found the limitation reasonable in the name of 'the overarching objective ... [of]electoral fairness.' The object here, and consistent with *Figueroa* (to which the judgment makes frequent reference), was to counter the depressing effect of inequality – be it number of candidates or unequal funds – on participation in an election. As the court said in *Harper*: 'Equality in political discourse is thus necessary for meaningful participation in the electoral process.'[27]

From the perspective of this discussion, the issue is not the appropriateness of the court's judgment but what it says about constitutional democracy in Canada under the charter. It is the role of the court to reinforce values already alive that are central to parliamentary democratic government. Reinforcement is not a synonym for confinement. On the contrary, as in these two cases, it stands for enhancement. This is the substance of the charter's transformation of Canadian politics. Because legislative institutions are made up of elected representatives who have to secure re-election, they must, said Beverley McLachlin, the chief justice, in 2004, 'be supplemented by other non-elected bodies, like courts and ombudsmen.'[28] Supplemented not supplanted: this is the rationale of the dialogue that reputedly occurs between the courts, legislatures, and the executive:

> [T]he decisions of the Court almost always leave room for a legislative response, and they usually get a legislative response. In the end, if the democratic will is there, the legislative objective will still be able to be accomplished, albeit with some new safeguards to protect individual rights and liberty. Judicial review is not 'a veto over the politics of the

nation,' but rather the beginning of a dialogue as to how best to reconcile the individualistic values of the *Charter* with the accomplishment of social and economic policies for the benefit of the community as a whole.[29]

The result is a reciprocating relationship with an emphasis on motion – act-react – as opposed to one based on objects – thesis-antithesis. And even from that perspective there are contrasting interpretations of what is happening. According to Christopher Manfredi, 'adjudication is focused, piecemeal, passive and retrospective, all of which makes it very good at deciding particular cases, but not so good at formulating general policies.'[30] Compare that view to another that promotes the legal system as a way of empowering individuals, that is, 'legal mobilization,' where the legal process 'makes the individual a participant in governance rather than an object of government.'[31] Here is the gate in the wall that divides courts and legislatures and through which citizens increasingly pass, partly but not solely as a result of the charter. As well, since the 1970s Canada has developed public 'standing rules ... [that] are now among the most liberal in the western world,' and now, two decades after that, half the provinces have provided for class action litigation whereby 'a small group [may] bring a lawsuit on behalf of a larger group of people who stand to benefit from the litigation.'[32] The pattern is of a David-and-Goliath confrontation between (for the sake of argument) a minority of small farmers opposed to genetically modified grains speaking for the larger group in a suit against a firm (again, for the sake of illustration) such as Monsanto.

Class action lawsuits are one illustration of the modern political narrative whose theme is 'the people want to be heard.' In this particular instance, the issue is less about enforcing charter rights than about acknowledging the right to participate in the resolution of issues that arise out of extremely complex situations, of which genetic science is a prime example. At least two considerations propel matters touching on this subject into a judicial forum and away from legislatures. First, 'the legislature seems content to leave it up to the courts to regulate ownership of genetically modified higher life-forms, despite calls from a number of parties – including the courts themselves – to legislate on the matter.'[33] The complexity associated with genetic-science and reproduction lies at the heart of the issue, and of others (more central to the thesis of this book), such as confidence in elected officials to resolve the complexity: 'The things we [the House of Commons Standing Committee on Health] understood the least [said its chair, Bonnie Brown] was when someone talked about chimeras ... about exons; they were into all this scientific ... language nobody got. That's why the committee homed in on this human family stuff. The science was way beyond us.'[34]

The knowledge gap, or information deficit, or however that inadequacy is phrased, seldom arises in discussions of Parliament except in the context of demands for more resources for members of Parliament. How additional resources would remedy the particular problem the Health Committee faced is unclear. The quality of resources available to members of Parliament is relevant here only as an indicator of the attractiveness of the judiciary. In their study of politics in the United States, John Hibbing and Elizabeth Theiss-Morse discovered an apparent contradiction between 'people's desire to increase the influence of ordinary people yet also increase the influence of business people and unelected experts.'[35] Among the latter experts were judges. On the basis of Canadian research done to date, it is evident that Canadians share this sentiment and, for this reason, view with distrust governments whom they see 'as influenced by corporate funding.'[36]

Another response to complexity is to claim rights – that is, to reframe the discussion, reduce its scale, and move from the technical to the personal. The courts are the logical forum for arguments couched in this vocabulary. It is widely accepted that it is their job to interpret the constitution in a manner that will create a society that is more 'fair.'[37] Activists use the vocabulary of rights as both a shield and a sword, in contrast to the language of the legislature. In turn, media coverage of genetic science (for instance, the long-running legal battle between Saskatchewan farmer Percy Schmeiser and chemical giant Monsanto over patent infringement of Roundup Ready Canola) reinforces a view of constitutional democracy as preferable both in process and outcome to parliamentary democracy.[38]

The criticism of parliamentary democracy as party dominated and thus closed to the people, or as manipulated by the prime minister because of his monopoly of advice on appointments and use of the prerogative, owes much to the charter and 'the ethical principles' derived from it. According to the Report of the Royal Commission on Electoral Reform and Party Financing (1991), Canadians use these principles, for instance, 'to evaluate many election-related practices and they have found these practices wanting.' Political parties failed to affirm political values, key among which, the commission stressed, were access, equality, and fairness. While acknowledging that fairness is 'not an entirely contemporary concern, fairness as a fundamental value of electoral

democracy has become more prominent over time.'[39] There is every reason to believe this statement to be true, beginning with the poverty of
examples of fairness as a criterion before the 1980s. The *Report* of the
Royal Commission on the Economic Union and Development Prospects
for Canada says as much: '[T]he understanding of equality has changed
substantially at the popular level over the past few decades.'[40] Evidence
in support of that claim can be found in the *Report of the Committee on
Election Expenses* (1966). The committee, established by and reporting to
the secretary of state, recommended the electoral expense regime of
subsidies and support for political parties that continues in broad out-
line today. Among those of its recommendations that were adopted was
the introduction of tax credits for political donations in order 'to
broaden the base of political giving.' Nowhere in the *Report* do values of
fairness or equality enter into the discussion, although they might be
inferred from comments such as the following: '[T]he greater the number of people involved in a party's financing, the less the dependence on
a few big interests, and the greater a party's freedom of action in pursuit
of what its members conceive to be the public interest.'[41] Still, it would
be an inference.

Nonetheless, the intervening transition in public attitudes towards
government and politics is crucial to understanding the attraction of
constitutional democracy today and the criticism directed at parliamentary democracy. It is generally agreed that a primary cause for the
change lies in the defeat of the Meech Lake and Charlottetown Accords
and, more particularly, 'the role democratic processes' played in these
events. Meech Lake is customarily cited as an agreement that failed for
lack of democratic consultation, although several governments did
respond to public critiques in an ultimately futile attempt to salvage it.
By contrast, the Charlottetown Accord was preceded by 'a series of
miniature constituent assemblies' to promote public participation and
was submitted for approval to the people in a referendum. The first
attempt was largely conducted behind closed doors, the second largely
in full view of the media and the public. Yet the result was the same –
failure to achieve constitutional change. It is the common lesson of
these disparate enterprises that critics say has undermined public support for traditional (parliamentary) processes and a 'willingness to
defer to elected leaders.'[42] Oversimplified, perhaps, but this explanation accounts for the prevalence in the recent study of Canadian politics
of such alliterative phrases as 'the decline of deference' and 'the democratic deficit.'

Reference to values arises in the 1990s. The *Report* of the Royal Commission on Electoral Reform and Party Financing has already been mentioned. Another, contemporaneous, inquiry was the Citizens' Forum on Canada's Future, chaired by Keith Spicer. After 'an eight-month consultation ... of over 700,000 Canadians,' the Citizens' Forum confirmed seven universal beliefs as intrinsic to 'Canadianness': 'equality and fairness, consultation and dialogue, accommodation and tolerance, a commitment to diversity, compassion and generosity, respect for Canada's natural beauty, and projection of Canada's image of being committed to freedom, peace, and nonviolent change.' In the interests of balance, it should be noted that one of the commissioners of the Citizens' Forum, Richard Cashin, appended a separate comment to the forum's *Report*. In this he raised 'three basic concerns,' the first of which was that 'we have [no] way of knowing how representative the opinions we hear may be of the opinions of all Canadians. This is because the process of participation was self-selective.'[43]

A decade later that assessment had not changed: '[T]he charter mentality has most assuredly reinforced the decline of deference in Canadian society and the rise of individualism.'[44] Canadians 'skeptical of traditional authority,' said another best-selling author, contrasted sharply with Americans who were 'inclined to latch on to traditional institutional practices, beliefs and norms as anchors.'[45] Change in values, along with sensitivity to their influence, entered public discourse: 'Canadians view medicare,' said Roy Romanow, commissioner on the Future of Health Care in Canada, 'as a moral enterprise'; the Civil Marriage Act (same-sex legislation) was hailed by then Minister of Justice Irwin Cotler as a vindication of the charter rights of 'tolerance, respect and equality'; Auditor General Sheila Fraser, in her *Report on Matters of Special Importance* (in November 2003), called on the government 'to provide ... a foundation of sound values and ethics,' which, she said, should include 'fairness' and 'honesty.' In 1995, in a study of Canada's foreign policy the Department of Foreign Affairs and International Trade elevated three values – democracy, the rule of law, and human rights – as 'guiding principles,' while a study of Canada's military culture comments on 'the high value the [Canadian Forces] places on integrating military values with the values of Canadian society, leading to the CF itself becoming, like its parent society, more "democraticized, liberalized and civilianized."'[46]

The list goes on, and on. But to what purpose? Canadian politics have become values oriented, even values driven. The fundamental question here is what this transformation implies for the people's house and parliamentary democracy. Distilled to its essence, the answer is harsh: 'Half of Canadians believe "MPs are not responsive to the needs of constituents"' and 'three out of four Canadians agree with the statement, "I don't think that the government cares much what people like me think."'[47] Contrary to the view that making the House of Commons more responsive to voters is a 'perennial' concern, it is in fact a recent one, as a reading of the biographies of past cabinet ministers or studies of political parties will show.[48] Government traditionally was about rewards and support; political parties were about organizing to distribute the first and attract the second. Affirming values had no place in the lexicon associated with these activities.

The higher law of constitutional democracy embraces values, although it would be misleading to suppose the values discussed above approximate let alone exhaust the substance of that law. On the contrary, the principles of the constitution the Supreme Court has elaborated and that provide a frame for constitutional democracy speak only tangentially to such matters as fairness and tolerance. In the Quebec Secession reference, the court perceived 'an internal architecture' to the 'Constitution' comprising 'four foundational constitutional principles': constitutionalism and the rule of law, federalism, democracy, and protection of minorities. Significantly for this discussion, the court spoke of the first principle as 'implicit' (para. 50), the second as an 'underlying' practice (para. 55), the third as 'a sort of baseline against which the framers of our Constitution, and subsequently our elected representatives under it, have always operated' (para. 62), and the last, a principle that 'continues to exercise influence in the operation and interpretation of our Constitution' (para. 81).[49] Significantly, because the principles the court cites are abstract and require definition. The principle of democracy was 'not explicitly identified in the text of the Constitution Act, 1867 itself. To have done so might have appeared redundant, even silly, to the framers. As explained in the *Provincial Judges Reference* ... it is evident that our Constitution contemplates that Canada shall be a constitutional democracy' (para. 62).

In the *Provincial Judges Reference* (1997), the issue was the remuneration of judges and the independence and impartiality of judges.[50] In obiter dicta accompanying a six to one opinion, the court discussed protection for judicial independence in the context of the Constitution Act's preamble, which speaks of a 'Constitution similar in Principle to that of the United Kingdom.' In a lengthy dissent, Justice La Forest took

issue with what he described as 'a dubious theory of an implicit constitutional structure' that elaborates upon 'underlying, unwritten, and
organizing principles found in the preamble' (para. 319). In a subsequent case, this time before the Federal Court of Appeal, judicial independence was attributed to separation of powers, a doctrine again cited
as emanating from the preamble. In his judgment, Justice Strayer specifically rejected that argument, stating instead that the phrase '"a constitution similar in Principle to that of the United Kingdom" was
understood in 1867 to be a reference to an entrenchment of responsible
government, i.e. where the Executive is responsible to the legislature.
The very concept was the antithesis of separation of powers.'[51] More
important for a book on the people's house, he took care to clarify the
respective positions of Parliament and the constitution in Canada following adoption of the charter:

> Both before and after 1982 our system was, and is, one of parliamentary
> sovereignty exercisable within the limits of a written constitution, as evi-
> denced by courts striking down laws for inconsistency with the division of
> powers set out in *British North America Act, 1867*, sections 91 and 92. These
> were solely quantitative limits on the exercise of legislative power prior to
> 1982. The adoption of the Charter in 1982 added a multitude of qualitative
> limitations on the exercise of power, but the Constitution of Canada was
> and is supreme over ordinary laws.[52]

In response to the statement by the Supreme Court in the *Quebec
Secession Reference*, that 'with the adoption of the Charter, the Canadian
system of government was transformed to a significant extent from a
system of Parliamentary supremacy to one of constitutional supremacy,' Justice Strayer observed that 'it is uncertain what significance
should be given this statement, since the supremacy of the Constitution
was established well before 1982 and even before Confederation in
1867.'[53]

There was no clarification of the matter since the Supreme Court
refused leave to appeal from the decision of the Federal Court of
Appeal. Silence offered support to what some scholars argue is a
signal feature of Canadian politics – institutional ambivalence. In this
instance, there are the guarantees of the Charter of Rights and Freedoms on one hand and section 33 (the notwithstanding clause), which,
when exercised by a legislature, may abrogate those rights, on the
other.[54] Ambivalence may pass under other names. In federal-provin-

cial relations *asymmetry* is a favoured synonym, but in either guise it feeds uncertainty and confusion. Witness political and legislative debate in 2004 and 2005 over the interpretation of marriage: misunderstanding was apparent on the part of some participants who thought s.33 might be invoked to counter court decisions upholding same-sex marriages under the equality provisions of the charter. Arguably, in a parliamentary system with a higher law, ambivalence is inevitable. Indeed, one could go further and say that lack of specificity occasions, even demands, overlapping consent of judiciary and legislature. While it is true that legislatures and their laws must conform to the charter, politics in Canada is better seen as 'working out' a constitutional order that embraces Parliament and the charter rather than 'working within' one or the other.[55]

It is better because, absent popular constitutionalism, there is no theoretical ground for a hierarchical interpretation that places judiciary over Parliament. The people's charter emanated from Parliament. The justices have no claim, even indirectly, to popular consent. After he retired from the Supreme Court, Justice Willard Estey, in a characteristically blunt speech, noted that 'the closed circuit system [of judicial appointments] we use in Canada doesn't allow much input by the democratic basement of our community, the electorate.'[56]

Working out a constitutional order is a complex undertaking of multiple and diverse endeavours. Aboriginal rights may serve as an example. The range of initiatives encompasses the following: the guarantees of s.35 of the charter (to recognize and affirm 'existing aboriginal and treaty rights'); constitutional talks with first ministers in the 1980s on the subject of Aboriginal self-government; debate in journals and at conferences among scholars who, in their engagement with the subject, qualified in Alan Cairns's phrase as 'an intellectual vanguard in the service of a social movement';[57] judicial decisions on matters of Aboriginal title and rights that in turn feed public debate, as witness Preston Manning's call, when leader of the Official Opposition, for 'a judicial review committee of the House of Commons to ensure the supremacy of the elected representatives of the people of Canada and the accountability of the judiciary ... This committee should review decisions of the Supreme Court and advise the House when any decision appears to violate the purpose for which Parliament passed the legislation ... and whether legislative action is necessary ... to restore the legislation,'[58] and, finally, legislation to ratify, for instance, the Nisga'a treaty, which in 1999 and 2000 was before the two houses of Parliament for a matter of several months.

The constitutional order that is emerging embraces more than the justices of the Supreme Court says it does. As noted, parliamentary sovereignty was not acknowledged as one of the 'principles' of the constitution in the Quebec Secession reference, yet there can be no doubt as to its significance in the conduct of Canadian politics. Arguably, the constitutional order is taking form despite the court's pronouncements. Consider that in its principal opinion on the 'one person, one vote standard' – that is, Saskatchewan's constituency boundaries, enacted in 1989 and providing for categories of urban, rural, and northern seats with generous provisions for population disparity – the court found that the purpose of the right to vote enshrined in Section 3 of the charter is not equality of voting per se but the right to 'effective representation.'[59] By contrast, the Saskatchewan Court of Appeal, from which the case had come, had pronounced 'the idea of equality [as] inherent in the right to vote.' Notwithstanding these judicial opinions and notwithstanding an attempt by the Royal Commission on Electoral Reform and Party Financing to reconcile the irreconcilable – equality and effectiveness – the values invoked after the early 1990s to assess the performance of the plurality electoral system or of prime-ministerial government invariably included nouns and adjectives like *fairness, equality, representative, open, effective, accountable, inclusive,* and *choice.*

The foregoing eight 'democratic values' are listed in the *Final Report* of the New Brunswick Commission on Legislative Democracy and are described as 'principles [that] brin[g] a more humanistic and collective focus to the role of our democratic institutions and practices. They reflect our expanded notion of democracy today. For many voters, these have become the new measures of democratic expectation and legitimacy.'[60] The accuracy of this assertion is not at issue here. In the language of the subject matter itself, what requires emphasis is the 'representativeness' of the claim that is being made. The values the New Brunswick *Report* employs are anything but provincial – they are the accepted tests of performance for Canadian democracy in the first decade of the twenty-first century. During 2004 and 2005 the British Columbia Citizens' Assembly on Electoral Reform travelled the province holding public hearings. According to its *Final Report,* 'What we most wanted to learn was what values, hopes and desires should underlie our electoral system.'[61] Again, from the perspective of a study of the people's house, what calls for notice is that these criteria are less a matter of judicial intent, ideology, or effect than they are the product of political technique. Of the eight democratic values cited in the New

Brunswick *Report*, the Supreme Court has pronounced on only two of them – equality and effectiveness – and then in quite different terms than are found in the *Report*. The *Report* defines equality as meaning 'all votes should count equally'; the court had said that the right to vote guaranteed by the charter was 'not equality of voting power per se, but the right to "effective representation."' The *Report* discusses *effective* in governmental and legislative terms, that is, whether these institutions are able 'to take decisions, consider diverse viewpoints and respond to changing economic and social circumstances.' It has nothing to do with representation.

If these norms are part of constitutional democracy in Canada – and this book maintains that they are – it is essential to be clear that they are not judicially inspired. This is not to say that at some future date courts might decline to pronounce on the operation of Canada's electoral system, for example, from the perspective of how open the system is to participation by candidates or eligible voters. The origin of this extra-judicial, constitutional, and democratic-sounding language is of some importance to a study of the people's house. Clearly, multiple influences are at work, among them changes in educational curricula, transformation of modern communications, and global dispersion of liberal values – what one author has titled 'Liberal Democracy and the Empire of Speed.'[62] But there is more than these influences. What is striking about Canadian politics, and unstudied from a political science perspective, is the structuring influence on debate of royal commissions and commissions of inquiry.

Enough has been said already about the Baird, Lortie, and Romanow commissions and the Royal Commission on Aboriginal People (RCAP) to indicate the importance this study attributes to them in the context of political and public debate. The Somalia Commission with its critical comments that 'a shift toward "civilianization"' was undermining military professionalism could be included as well.[63] To these might be added also the provincial inquiries into matters of democratic reform that had reported as of January 2005.[64] All are creatures of government, all study 'problems' framed by government. In addition to, and as important as, their final reports, the commissions create ambitious research agendas. The Lortie Commission produced a four-volume report, but it also commissioned twenty-three volumes of research studies comprising 110 individual papers. RCAP was larger still. Too often, when talking about royal commissions, the emphasis is placed on the disposition of their recommendations. Equally important is the diffusion of ideas and values symbolized, first, in a commission's terms of reference, then in its research project, and, ultimately, in analysis of its report. Add to that the aggregation of scholars associated with the project – 120 authors produced the 110 papers published by the Lortie Commission. Academics, the media, the public, and legislators also take their political cues from such a force of concentrated scholarly energy, especially when the subjects under study are intensely personal – privacy, illness, racial prejudice, reproductive technologies, individual rights.

The Charter of Rights and Freedoms may be the tap root of constitutional democracy in Canada, but the consciousness of values it inspires is far broader than the sections of the charter imply and of longer descent. In speaking to Bill C-38, the Civil Marriage Act (2005), then Prime Minister Paul Martin referred not only to 'liberties,' 'rights,' and equal treatment 'under the law,' but also observed that 'the attention of our nation is focused on this chamber in which John Diefenbaker introduced the Bill of Rights.' In 1995, when moving second reading to Bill C-68, 'an act respecting firearms and other weapons,' Allan Rock, then minister of justice and attorney general, spoke of the 'objectives, ideals and values that motivated the government.' By third reading of this bill, he had distilled the political essence of those values: 'Canadians everywhere ... want the government to preserve the civil character of our society and strengthen the values that have always set us apart as a nation.'[65] Where once the country's distinction – in North America at least – had rested in its commitment to pioneering a federal parliamentary democracy, now its defining character was pronounced to rest in values rather than institutions, a transformation of uncommon importance for the future of the people's house in Parliament.

4 Electoral Democracy

Electoral democracy is the third way of conceiving the arrangement of political power. The phraseology is awkward but telling, for it reflects the central weakness of electoral democracy – it has no core. Rather, it is a utilitarian term intended to encompass instruments of direct democracy, such as initiative, referendum, and recall, as well as a philosophy of popular rule. By contrast, parliamentary democracy has the support of convention and tradition. It invokes great moments in British constitutional history – the Glorious Revolution, 1688, the Act of Settlement, 1701 – as well as Canadian – the Constitutional Act, 1791, the British North America Act, 1867, the Statute of Westminster, 1931 – and sententious pronouncements: 'The law of the realm cannot be changed but by Parliament.' A cloud of witnesses – Dicey, Dawson, Forsey, Jennings, and Marshall – testify to its vividness.[1] Parliament unifies – crown, Senate, and Commons – and is one in spirit if no longer act and word with the Mother of Parliaments. Constitutional democracy possesses a lineage and hagiography, too – Magna Carta and the Charter of Rights and Freedoms – a written constitution with a division of powers subject to judicial review, first by the Judicial Committee of the Privy Council and then by the Supreme Court of Canada. And like parliamentary democracy, it, too, is personalized, through famous judges on both sides of the Atlantic – Coke and Denning, Rand and Laskin – and their judgments.[2]

Electoral democracy can claim no comparable ancestry, nor does it afford a corporate presence in the form of House or bench. More than that, it is excluded from the symbiosis that sees parliamentary joined to constitutional democracy, where, for example, the chief justice of the Supreme Court of Canada acts as deputy governor general, the court passes upon the constitutionality of acts of the legislature, and the crown appoints on advice of its first minister members of the superior judiciary.

It may be true that, whatever their theory, all constitutions today are attributed to the people. Still, it is a questionable attribution in a constitutional monarchy such as Canada's, where there is no base for popular constituent power. In the United States, the people preceded government; in Canada, government preceded the people – and it still does. In 1852, during the interminable debate over what to do with the upper house of Canada's legislature now that the principle of responsible government had been granted – that is, make it elected or leave it appointed – George Brown, an opponent of election, explained the source of his objection: 'The elective principle is not a system of Government; it is merely a means of working out our institutions.'[3]

Proponents of an elected Senate – the Triple-E proposal for an elected, equal, and effective upper chamber – should pay attention to Brown's dictum, and for the reason he gives. Election of the Senate is at best a technique to achieve what its advocates seek – a provincial veto over government policies deemed to be prejudicial to the interests of the provinces. Alberta's opposition to the Trudeau government's National Energy Policy in the early 1980s would serve as an example. Triple E may embrace no organizing principle of government, yet its effect would be to challenge the conduct of responsible government, the principle that informs the existing arrangement of parliamentary power and one recognized by the courts.[4] An elected Senate would diffuse power – which is its purpose – from an arrangement characterized now by its concentration. That may or may not be judged a desirable object. What is beyond doubt is that it constitutes a calculated response to a particular, perceived problem, and nothing more. In this respect, Triple E is representative of the tradition of electoral democracy in Canada: it has no momentum of theory to sustain it.

The elective principle may not be, in Brown's words, 'a system of Government,' but it manifests enduring if not continuous attraction. Pre-rebellion vigour in the 1830s, post-rebellion slumber in the 1850s – that sequence of responses to the call for electoral democracy in the first half of the nineteenth century has been repeated in succeeding decades. Indeed, the episodic nature of its appeal is an important dimension to its study. This is not to say that at the beginning of a new century the reappearance of a call for electoral democracy, under the auspices of Preston Manning and the Reform party (and its successors), is merely a reprise of attitudes and phenomena that once espoused similar goals. Patently, this is untrue – and it would be odd if it were otherwise – since the context of the present resurrection is so different from the past. To begin with, no longer is electoral democracy summoned to the aid of a specific interest, such as western farmers, in opposition to other identifiable interests – in that instance, the railways, the grain companies, and the banks. Today the stakes are higher, the effect more pervasive: 'It may be that the era of pure representative democracy is slowly coming to an end ... Representative government is being complemented by more direct forms of involvement, from the internet to referenda.'[5] Some of the reasons for that 'end' have been discussed in the preceding chapters – entrenched rights and empowered courts, on the one hand, and strains on Parliament as a result of a decline in voter turnout and traditional forms of political activity, on the other.

This chapter supports this end-of-an-era view to the extent that it sees current pressures for electoral democracy in Canada as qualitatively different from past experience and debate. Some of the goals sought today – curtailment of government's use of confidence votes or reduction in party discipline – are familiar enough to students of Canadian politics in the decade before or after the First World War. Yet familiarity should not disguise what is original in the current democratic mission. To the unprecedented campaign for a Triple-E Senate should be added a reconstituted view of Parliament as a legislature whose duty is to oppose an executive. That separation-of-power perspective helps explain the commitment to renovated bicameralism and a hostility to Parliament that goes beyond mere anti-partisanship. The rationale behind both objectives lies in Preston Manning's conviction

> that one of the principal ways of getting things done politically in the first part of the 21st century will be through the building of principled coalitions or strategic alliances.
>
> Canadian politicians, particularly at the federal level, are singularly ill-equipped for and inexperienced in building coalitions. Our current system tends to keep partisans in water-tight compartments, and party discipline is used excessively to discourage any building of coalitions across partisan lines.[6]

Half a century ago, T.D. Weldon wrote a book about the ambiguity of political language. Political terms might be viewed as no more than exclamations like 'Hurrah,' or its opposite, 'Boo.'[7] There is nothing 'boo' in phrases like 'principled coalitions' or 'strategic alliances,' but then there is not much that is parliamentary about them either. The assumptions underlying this admonition by a former leader of the Official Opposition, an office itself destined to become anachronistic in a world of coalitions and alliances, require careful analysis on two counts. First, they transform the purpose of electoral democracy. No longer is it about injecting the popular will – through the initiative, for example – or submitting official policy for approval by the people, that is, the referendum. Nor is it about achieving specific policy objectives – roll back the tariff or entrench low freight rates (as an example, the farmers' Magna Carta, the Crow Rates). The vision is grander, or at least more sweeping, in its implications. Thus, the second reason to pay attention to Mr Manning's political prescription is the effect it will have on the conduct of politics. It will reduce Parliament to the status of a legislature whose job is to oppose or check the executive, as Congress does the president in the United States. Here – and not in fewer confidence votes or less party discipline – lies the importance of modern electoral democracy for the operation of the people's house. In the United States, coalitions and alliances must be formed – and reformed – to secure passage of every piece of legislation. That is why there is so much activity, so much pressure to get bills through the two houses. There is no government and certainly no focus of responsibility as in the Canadian system. Whether this is a preferable arrangement of power is for others to decide, although it may be relevant to note evidence of scepticism about the inclusiveness purported to follow upon the negotiations leading to coalitions. Many Americans resent what they call 'deal-making' and 'compromises,' and for very specific reasons: 'Th[e] belief that Congress members were inattentive, unresponsive, and out of touch,' and needed to be 'coerced into doing something.'[8]

It would be a misrepresentation to suggest that Preston Manning's views are necessarily those of the Conservative party founded in 2003. Still, support for the norms of electoral democracy, and particularly the attack on Parliament, is stronger here than in other parties. More to the point, however, is that the electoral democracy debate today in Canada is conducted almost exclusively using terms and assumptions that originate with Reform's first leader. As Aberhart (or later Ernest Manning) was to Social Credit, so Preston Manning was to Reform – leader and party were one. The same could not be said of early proponents of electoral democracy in the Progressive party, which had no long-term authoritative leader, or of the Co-operative Commonwealth Federation, which in T.C. Douglas possessed a mesmeric leader but which also depended upon an array of ministerial talent to propel controversial socialist programs through a combative legislature. Furthermore, Preston Manning and Reform stand apart from earlier advocates of electoral democracy in another crucial respect – they use the vocabulary of democracy as a weapon against parliamentary and constitutional democracy in their campaign to elevate electoral democracy.

And that is their objective – to transform the distribution of power in Canadian politics by redefining the institutions of government. Their progenitors – the Progressive party, Social Credit, and to a lesser extent the Co-operative Commonwealth Federation – never conceived so ambitious a strategy. Their objectives were regional in scope and (generally) economic in objective. This was the backdrop to debates in the House in the early 1920s over discipline and questions of confidence.

The modern vision of electoral democracy is a story whose conclusion has yet to be written. Will its critique of parliamentary democracy and constitutional democracy triumph and bring with it a new politics? The incompleteness of electoral democracy is part of its attraction and part of its distinctiveness. It has nothing concrete to offer when compared to Parliament and responsible government or to the judiciary, the charter, and the common and civil law. More than that, these last are national narratives whose origins predate but contribute to the unity of the country. Both are linear, both provide integrative frames of reference for a federal system of divided jurisdiction. Electoral democracy is better described as a nested narrative whose traditional theme of frustration and impotence touches individuals and regions more than nations. Preston Manning's variation on this theme constitutes a sharp break with Canada's history of electoral democracy. First, it is national in its perspective: the Reform party was not a federated party; the politics it sought to reconstitute was a national politics. Federalism enters the discussion through what might be called the principle of reduction – equality for all, special status for none. This was the basis for the Reform party's opposition to the Meech Lake and Charlottetown agreements, with their complicated provisions to reconcile and accommodate conflicting regional and collective interests. Decentralization was Reform's favoured solution to the problems of Canadian government.

Interpretation of those problems provides a second contrast that sets the present apart from the past. 'Indigenous prairie democratic thought,' says one scholar who has studied the Progressives, Social Credit, and the Co-operative Commonwealth Federation, was united in

its belief that corporate interests – banks, railways, and grain companies – were the cause of the west's problems.[9] Hence the battles to
secure lower freight rates, marketing boards, and cooperatives. The
establishment of the Canadian Wheat Board in the 1930s and its even-
tual monopoly over the sale of grain removed a long-standing source of
conflict and contributed in a major way to the disappearance of electoral democracy as a challenge to existing political practices.

It did so for some decades, in any case, since by the 1990s Reform had
taken up the cause of those grain farmers who challenged the board
and its monopoly and who were willing to go to jail rather than pay
fines incurred after they sold wheat in the United States outside the
marketing scheme established by the board.[10] From the point of view of
a study in Canadian politics, the significant aspect of this cause was not
the farmers' complaints but the board's monopoly. Reform's prince of
darkness no longer resided on Bay Street or St James Street but in the
towers housing bureaucrats and special interests that crowded central
Ottawa (or Winnipeg, in the case of the Canadian Wheat Board).
According to David Laycock, in his book *The New Right and Democracy
in Canada*, 'the "special interests" are groups that support the welfare
state, oppose tax cuts, and propose that social resources should be allocated on the basis of non-market principles.'[11] They have the inside
track to bureaucrats and policy makers, partly, maybe largely, because
government supports their activities. That support, often in the form of
money that comes from taxpayers' dollars, privileges some Canadians
over others. In this interpretation, Canada becomes a country of elites
and not one committed to equality.

This depiction is familiar. What has not received the attention it warrants is the political implications that result. The common people are
not heard because their representatives are subjected to the yoke of
party discipline. Only one voice is distinct in the governing caucus – the
party's – and that is determined by the special interests whose support
the governing party seeks. In this world, Reform presented itself as 'the
representative of the unrepresented,' the enforcer of accountability.[12]
Here is the rationale for the referendum: a popular alternative to a system otherwise elite driven. From this perspective, submission of the
Charlottetown agreement to the Canadian people in 1992 constituted a
victory for Reform, although it is acknowledged (and not only in Canada) that 'all major parties now accept that major constitutional change
should be accompanied by a referendum.'[13] That dictum comes from a
British political commentator and is a reminder once again that Reform

and its successors are the Canadian exemplars of an international critique of parliamentary democracy.

'Critique' is an apt description, for a characteristic of accounts of Reform is that they each tell a story. Laycock, for instance, speaks of the party 'constructing a new story about the people's enemies' and, later, of 'weav[ing themes] into a story about the crisis of democratic politics in Canada.'[14] Characters may change, but the moral remains constant. And there is always a moral. For in the tale of the little farmer and the big grain company, just as in the contrast between the common man and the special interests, there is, on the one side, dishonesty and betrayal and, on the other, virtue and fair dealing. Politics as parable. Electoral democracy is fed by both a new kind of criticism and new opportunities to advance it. The farmers' newspapers early in the last century – for instance, *The Western Producer*, within whose covers was published the 'Mainly for Women' page edited by farmer, writer, and feminist Violet McNaughton – took on the corporate interests of the time, just as the *National Post* has sternly drawn attention to the privileged treatment special interests receive today. Campaigns for electoral democracy are fuelled by perceived injustice. Now, as opposed to in the past, the focus is less on economic inequity – although issues such as the GST and Reform's highly publicized opposition to it remain important – than on ethical issues that are intensely personal – same-sex marriage, abortion, capital punishment, gun control. Party discipline is depicted as a poor guide in matters of personal morality. The ingredients exist for antagonistic confrontation: the focus is personal, individual, and, necessarily because of these factors, local or immediate. In short, electoral democracy presents issues in a different light from that of parliamentary democracy, or even constitutional democracy, where the judiciary is presented with facts of a specific case involving identifiable persons.

The role of media was critical to the success of Reform and the extra-parliamentary organizations that supported it, such as the National Citizens' Coalition (NCC). The NCC must be one of the most successful extra-parliamentary organizations in Canadian history. Aggregating and articulating public opinion against Parliament, with regard first to MPs' pensions and then the election finance law, the GST, and more, it created a constituency whose voice was heard in Parliament. Significantly, the NCC campaigns used the newspapers to communicate their message to the Canadian reading public and to provide a channel, via prepared statements to be sent to MPs postage free, to relay that message to Ottawa. Thus the NCC helped reduce the sense of difference between governors and governed that has been a feature of parliamentary government for hundreds of years.

Reform employed what might be called Canada's second political vocabulary, one the media were quick to disseminate. In addition, they too introduced what one British commentator has described as 'an increasingly critical edge' to their reports.[15] 'The "reality" which the media construct for the public' affects not only how citizens view politics – the launching of the *National Post* in the late 1990s (at a time when the opposition was disunited in the House of Commons) and the confrontational tone it adopted in its editorials and coverage of the Chrétien government helped feed the cynicism citizens increasingly expressed – but also how parliamentarians view citizens.[16] Abandon fixed ideas of rank and order and replace them with mechanisms by which ordinary Canadians might overcome everything that politically hampers them. And yet that interpretation is flawed, for much of what people dislike about Parliament is endemic to what is central to a modern parliament – party discipline and executive pre-eminence.

Regional protest parties occupy a special place in Canadian political literature. These parties, in particular the phenomenon of Social Credit, gave impetus to the study of political parties. A ten-volume study of Social Credit in Alberta written between 1950 and 1959 was the first and is still the most ambitious research project on Canadian political parties.[17] That this series should have had a protest party as its subject (one which within three years of completion of the project was to experience fission and, in another decade, exhaustion in its home province) was the result of a perspective on Canadian politics shared by national politicians and academics alike. The Progressives, Social Credit, and the rest were viewed as aberrations from the Canadian norm, to be accommodated if Mackenzie King had his way, destroyed if western Liberals like James G. Gardiner or W.R. Motherwell, ministers in the King cabinet, had theirs. Because Canadian parties are low in ideological content, any dissent or faction is subject to misinterpretation by politicians; they are seen as the plots of spoilers or the misguided.

For academics, the interpretations have been more sophisticated, but they too share what might be called the 'eccentric' view of third-party proliferation. Protest parties were understood as the product of frontier-metropolitan tension, or the response to a 'quasi-colonial' relationship, or another variant of North American agrarian radicalism. Each saw the protest as a reaction to forces generated elsewhere; each was centralist in its interpretation. In their view, the tide should ever flow from Ottawa, and never ebb. (None of the scholars in the Social Credit series was provincialist in his research interest; only one of the ten in this series on Alberta actually resided there, and he wrote about the Liberal party.) Politicians and academics still embraced what Frank Underhill called a 'literary theory of the constitution.'[18] Canada had inherited a British-style constitution, and deviations from what happened in Britain were just that – deviations, to be curbed by the governors and studied by the scholars. Both saw the political system as sound but subject to idiosyncratic attack.

In its pronouncements on the source of political legitimacy, the Reform party was exceptional, at least by the standards of parliamentary democracy and constitutional democracy. In its view of itself as a descendant of 'the reform tradition in Canadian politics,' it was quixotic.[19] The quintessence of the reform tradition is responsible government, whose practice, principle, and efficacy Preston Manning continues to dismiss. Yet, notwithstanding – even today – the distinctiveness of Reform's prescription for electoral democracy, its messengers cannot be dismissed as eccentrics or misbegotten. Canadian politics has changed, for reasons supporters of electoral democracy correctly identify: the gap between people and constituted authority has widened with the arrival of the charter and the 'phenomenon of "constitutional minoritarianism" [which] reflects the new constitutional status and identities that the Charter has conferred on racial minorities, women, official language minorities and other minority groups.'[20]

In its modern form, electoral democracy presents a complex challenge to existing understandings of government. If a theme were required to explain the source of the complexity, it is this: electoral democracy, as advanced initially by the Reform party and maintained still by its most publicized advocate, Preston Manning, telescopes issues – individual morality in a secular age, personal values under a Charter of Rights and Freedoms, region in nation, autonomy of members of Parliament in an institution defined by its corporate personality. The challenge to parliamentary democracy and constitutional democracy arises out of this interposition of attitudes and objectives. It has been said that 'what counts as "politics" ... receives much of its definition from the institutions of state (Parliament, parties, elections) through which it is organized.'[21] Early in the last century, attempts to import American procedures of direct democracy, such as the initiative and referendum, failed for exactly this reason: the courts ruled that they trespassed on the prerogative of the crown – that is, that the lieutenant-governor's discretion in the matter of approving a bill could not be abrogated.[22] Similarly, political parties of that era thwarted attempts to introduce the primary as a means of selecting candidates, and thereby protected the power of the leader.[23]

Politics is no longer accepted as being confined to what is approved by Parliament or the political parties. The expanded role of the courts in consequence of the adoption of the charter offers one alternative to the traditional restrictive view. Electoral democracy offers another, and not because the instruments of direct democracy are easier to invoke or used more frequently now than in the past, although in the 1990s Saskatchewan, Alberta, and British Columbia each introduced new legislation touching on initiative, referendum, and recall.[24] If the measure of electoral democracy today depended upon the exercise of direct democracy, it would represent no challenge to traditional political practice. On the contrary, the challenge of electoral democracy lies not in its achievements but in its promise. It is important to be clear about the content of that promise, which is, in short, to democratize politics, to hand it back to the people. Referring to Parliament and moral issues, although the rationale advanced could as well apply to a broad range of subjects, Preston Manning maintained that 'values (even when not shared by our media and political elites) are nevertheless an integral part of how many Canadians live their daily lives and make important decisions.'[25]

The dichotomy of democrats and elites is a fundamental proposition of modern electoral democracy, although not confined to supporters of one political persuasion: 'Liberal Party Run Like an Oligarchy: Grits,' an article about the Liberal party's 'glaring democratic deficit,' carries the same message.[26] The power of the proposition lies in its dismissal of difference and, thus, deference. The proposal has original appeal in a political system defined by hierarchy, prerogative, and the exercise of discretionary power. More than that, prime-ministerial government (or, in the provinces, government by first ministers) concentrates power, isolates decisions, and insulates those who make them both from the opinion of the people and from their elected representatives. This is the source of the complaint about extra-parliamentary agreements – Meech Lake, Charlottetown, fiscal arrangements, health care, and more. This is not news, but the premise from which it derives is new – at least in the unfolding of the concept of electoral democracy. The issue is not that the people should initiate such comprehensive undertakings, nor that they should always and in all circumstances be required to pass approval on them (although in the realm of constitutional accords it is probably now accepted). More central still, and of direct import for the subject of this book, is the belief – as in the United States – that the legislature is the sole remedy, the single legitimate, practical, and practicable forum for public policy.

Only from this vantage can the attraction of slogans like 'the West wants in', 'the people want to be heard,' and 'the common sense of the common people' be appreciated, although the last of these is ambiguous in that *common* can mean either ordinary or communal, a significant difference in political terms.

The primacy of the legislature explains Preston Manning's proposal that the House of Commons should establish 'a judicial review committee to ensure the supremacy of the elected representatives of the people of Canada.'[27] It provides context, too, for his equation of the House with a political marketplace in which popular support is mobilized 'to force [ideas] higher and higher on the political agenda,' and where it is 'necessary to build and maintain coalitions across regional and party lines.'[28] It may to some extent offer a rationale for the Triple-E Senate, although that proposal pays little attention to the complex operation of a bicameral Parliament where both chambers adhere to the elective principle. What legislative primacy does not make clear is the relationship between the member and the constituency. What is the nature of that constituency power? Take recall, for example. In *The New Canada*, Preston Manning advocated the introduction of a special initiative to recall members of the house, but with a 'quite high' threshold 'so as not to result in recall being used simply as a partisan device for unseating political opponents.'[29] As one commentator noted, 'Since that is precisely what a recall is designed and intended to do and since there are already ample means of expelling "corrupt" members of the house, one wonders why Reformers bother with recall at all, since they do not also advocate changing the regime.'[30]

Reform advocated recall in order to perfect representation, and that for two reasons. First, as with the referendum, recall contributes to making the legislature and the people one. Second, to the extent that unity is, or can be claimed to be, achieved, legislative supremacy follows. That at least is the theory to which Reform and its successors appealed when they described 'judicial rulings as undermining democracy in this country.'[31] Paradoxically, in this interpretation, instruments of direct democracy arm the legislature in its battle with government. The martial language is not extreme, for advocates of electoral democracy in the Reform mode reject the multiple and intersecting dimensions of government set down, for example, in *New Brunswick Broadcasting Co. v. Nova Scotia (Speaker of the House of Assembly)*:' Our democratic government consists of several branches: the Crown, as represented by the Governor General and the provincial counterparts of that office; the legislative body; the executive; and the courts. It is fundamental to the working of government as a whole that all these parts play their proper role. It is equally fundamental that no one of them overstep its bounds, that each show proper deference for the legitimate sphere of activity of the other.'[32]

As noted in an earlier chapter, the *New Brunswick Broadcasting* case was concerned with parliamentary privilege, whose function the court saw as a unifying factor. For those adopting the Reform perspective of the role of the legislature, there is nothing to unify. The principle of responsible government appears not to exist; the theory of ministerial responsibility is thrown in doubt; and a politically neutral civil service is placed in jeopardy. Only when the executive is seen as separate from the legislature is the following request by Preston Manning to the Commons committee on procedure explicable: that the committee 'recommend a procedure whereby Parliament may petition the Governor-General for the removal of a prime minister who fails to uphold the Constitution of Canada.'[33] The depiction of a legislative fastness is reinforced by a view of the Senate of Canada as 'a chamber of elites,' the senior judiciary as the personal choice of the prime minister, and the media as easily manipulable.[34] Traditional mechanisms of parliamentary democracy, however impaired their effectiveness, find faint support in this dichotomous vision of government versus legislature.

With one exception – officers of Parliament, whose impartiality and independence are powerful attractions to anti-politics politicians ready to indict parliamentary party government. Arguably, a discussion of officers of Parliament at this point in a study of the people's house may seem out of place. More obvious locations would be in the context of examining parliamentary democracy or the work of the House – but only if the officers are viewed as having an organic link to Parliament. From this latter perspective the officers expand Parliament's investigative capacity by increasing its expertise in evaluating legislation and government programs; by following up on a daily basis issues that MPs (and senators) cannot focus on because of their other responsibilities; by keeping Parliament informed, through annual reports of the progress of their respective recommendations; and in the case specifically of the commissioner of official languages, by ensuring that language equality remains a defining principle of the constitutional architecture of Canada, its Parliament, and its government.

According to this interpretation, the officers do more than just complement the work of Parliament: they actually afford parliamentarians the opportunity to play their role as parliamentarians. And it is a rapidly changing role. The large number of parties now registered with the chief electoral officer has provoked a new dimension to the office that relates not only to his role but also to the Canada Elections Act itself. The CEO's obligation of accountability encompasses a much larger number of parties than those represented in the Commons, and he must notify them and involve them in the same way as he does the traditional parties represented in the House. It is his legal obligation. Since all of the registered parties can raise money, they must all report to the CEO. They must also report on their financial administration if they receive the election subsidies under the political financing law that came into force in 2004.[35]

But there is another – extra-parliamentary – way of looking at officers of Parliament, and one that accounts for the discussion that follows in this chapter. According to this interpretation, the officers are assuming a coherent purpose and emerging as an identifiable but acknowledged branch of the constitution. Rather than being organically linked to Parliament, they are perceived to be – or are in process of becoming – detached from Parliament itself. Each officer becomes tantamount to an external body that relies more on the capacity of public opinion to draw attention and mount pressure on the executive to act, instead of relying on Parliament itself to make an effective and continuous effort to implement the recommendations made in the officer's annual report.

The rivalry between parliamentary- and electoral-democratic models is revealed in the contrasting roles each assigns to officers of Parliament.

It is important to make plain which officials and their establishments fall under the designation *officers of Parliament*. For this discussion, the genus consists of the auditor general, the chief electoral officer, the information commissioner, the privacy commissioner, the commissioner of official languages, the ethics commissioner of the House, and the ethics officer of the Senate. (Because they do not meet the criteria that follow, this designation does not include the speaker of the Commons, the librarian of Parliament, or table officers of the House. Nor in the past have the public service commissioner and the Canadian human rights commissioner qualified for inclusion. In 2006, the Harper government announced that it would merge the two existing ethics positions into one, whose future status as an officer of Parliament, as defined above, appeared in doubt.)

Selection criteria for this particular list are appointment and removal provisions, tenure, budget, and reporting procedures. In the instance of the seven officers just named, six are appointed following passage of a resolution by one or both houses of Parliament (the outlier is the auditor general, who is appointed by governor-in-council alone); all are removable by governor-in-council on address by the two houses; their terms vary: ten years for the auditor general, seven for the commissioners (except the House ethics commissioner, which is five), and mandatory retirement at age sixty-five for the chief electoral officer; except for the chief electoral officer, who draws from the Consolidated Revenue Fund, the budget of the other officers is determined by a governmental department; finally, each officer reports regularly to Parliament.

The two broad features officers of Parliament share are, first, independence from the executive, and second, accountability – this last itself manifested in contrasting ways: officers are accountable through their reports to Parliament, and government's accountability to Parliament is heightened as a result of the officers' activities. The interposition of officers of Parliament in the operation of responsible government raises the question whether their activities strengthen or undermine that foundational principle of the constitution. To take a specific example: does the work of the auditor general assist the Public Accounts Committee, or does it supplant the committee? Independence and accountability are contradictory principles, whose realization is further impeded by the triangular set of interrelationships that exist between officers, government, and the legislature.

Officers of Parliament either singly or as a collective are largely unexplored phenomena. This is so because each office is rooted in its own past – comparatively distant for the auditor general (1878) and the chief electoral officer (1920), less so for the commissioners (since 1968) – a past characterized by controversy – financial (the Pacific Scandal) in the case of the auditor general, electoral (manipulation of the franchise in the wartime election of 1917) in the case of the chief electoral officer – or concern at abuse of power by government – the information, privacy, and ethics commissioners. The commissioner of official languages is the exception, representing government's commitment to honour a constitutional principle. It should be noted that contributing causes since the 1970s have not been Canadian alone. Ever since the U.S. government and media were convulsed by the Watergate break-in and subsequent investigations, demands for oversight of government have grown.[36] Literature on the officers reflects the individual origins of their offices. Only the auditor general has received book-length treatment; at the same time, that office has received more attention than its counterparts in other forms of scholarly writing.[37] In the context of this discussion it is worth commenting that the topic – officers of Parliament in the plural – is rarely disussed. A retrospective assessment of the extant literature finds the commentary selective, hermetic, and untheoretical, qualities that mirror the offices themselves. Paradoxically, for an institution respectful of precedent, Parliament appears to have created officers of Parliament with no clear model in mind, either as to when such a response is appropriate or what that response will look like, beyond providing support for Parliament. This is an omission that requires attention, for pressure will grow from within Parliament (as well as from outside) to create new officers. Consider, for instance, the call by MP Carolyn Bennett, at the time of the Romanow Inquiry into Health Care, for appointment of a health care commissioner.[38]

While there may be no model officer of Parliament, there is a popular sense of one, and that is the auditor general. The reasons for the hold of this office on the public and political mind are obvious: it is by far the oldest of its type and, because of its annual (now more frequent) reports to the Public Accounts Committee and long-standing media interest in the content of those reports, the one with which people are most familiar. It is because of the auditor general's prominence that officers of Parliament are regularly described as watchdogs, usually 'governmental' watchdogs. This is a misnomer when applied to officers as a group. To be a watchdog implies exacting accountability, and such, for instance, has not been a function of the chief electoral officer until the recent legislation limiting financial contributions. Instead, the duty of that officer was to guarantee impartiality in the administration of elections. Accountability does not enter into the conduct of elections or the drawing of electoral boundaries for federal constituencies.

Similarly, are the commissioners (of privacy, information, or official languages) watchdogs? Are they even impartial? They, and those who study them, favour the word *ombudsman* to describe what they do. But can an officer of Parliament be an ombudsman and be neutral at the same time? Where does the commissioner of official languages fit in these descriptions? With a capacity to launch legal actions independently of complaints, or to intervene in proceedings by a complainant, or, in the words of the Official Languages Act, 'to seek leave to intervene in any adjudicative proceedings relating to the status or use of English or French' (s.78: (3)), the language commissioner is a singular agent for the advancement of a specific public policy. In the fulfilment of that task as it relates to the drawing of federal electoral boundaries, the language commissioner as an officer of Parliament may find himself or herself in conflict with another officer of Parliament, the chief electoral officer.[39]

Here is a range of activity performed by an array of actors. Clearly, their designation notwithstanding, the officers are not identical septuplets. How, then, to categorize them? They do not report to a minister, and therefore they sidestep the whole responsible government structure. Are they agents of their principal – Parliament? Their appointment and reporting provisions lend support to that proposition, except that, aside from the auditor general, Parliament (and the public) pay little attention to them. This is a complaint of long standing by the commissioners, and to the extent that it is true it signifies flawed accountability. Nor is Parliament alone in this astigmatism. Democracy Watch, Canada's self-described 'leading citizen group,' which makes empowerment of citizens one of its objectives, says virtually nothing on its web page about the work of the information, privacy, or language commissioners. Its concerns speak solely to matters of ethics, spending, and auditing.[40]

Political scientist Jennifer Smith has written that officers of Parliament contribute to the notion of the executive and legislature standing in opposition to one another.[41] This is the perception promoted by Preston Manning when he was leader of the Reform party and of the Official Opposition, and one he continues to advance in his commentaries on Canadian politics.[42] As Smith observes, 'lurking behind such a sentiment [the executive-legislature face-off] is the idea of an independent minded legislature, which means a legislature of independents, or nonpartisan elected officials.' More than that, there is a further implication in this sentiment that calls for notice: independent and non-partisan elected officials are not the same thing, and neither of them is the equivalent of an independent-minded legislature, if that means one free from executive control. Clarity on this point is essential. Tom Axworthy has said that 'if members of Parliament are to do their job, they need policy and research capacity equivalent to the executive ... We need a Canadian equivalent to the General Accounting Organization [sic] and the

Congressional Budget Office, two institutions central to the work of the U.S. Congress, the most independent legislature in the world.'[43] Independent from the executive, perhaps, but Congress is far from being non-partisan.

It is a Canadian view and an index to prevailing political assumptions here that *independent* and *non-partisan* are treated as synonyms. More than a curiosity is at issue in this observation. On the contrary, it goes to the heart of Canadian politics. Partisanship pervades Parliament (as it has since before Confederation). Officers of Parliament constitute a deviation from the norm, which is to say that they act so as to remove decisions from politicians. This is the signal characteristic the seven share. What does it signify?

No single thesis applies without qualification to officers, whose appearance spans more than a century and a quarter. Nonetheless, the bare-bones thesis advanced here is as follows: officers of Parliament originate in and reflect the anti-party sentiment that historically skirts the core of Canadian politics. How to reconcile this paragraph with the preceding one that talks of the strength of partisan sentiment? More study is required, but it is striking that the circumstances giving rise to officers of Parliament involve either a revulsion at party or a strong sense of the inappropriateness of party's linkage to the matter at hand. In this interpretation, officers of Parliament were created when Parliament failed to provide a forum in which to bridge partisan disagreement.

As happened after the wartime elections of 1917 and the Pacific Scandal four decades earlier, so today on all sides parties and Parliament are described as failures. Members of Parliament are 'voting machines,' the plurality electoral system itself 'unfair,' the will of the people 'ignored.' Politics has become dysfunctional, incomprehensible, and, according to Tom Axworthy (again), a 'poisonous atmosphere of distrust and cynicism ... currently exists between parties and citizens.'[44] The indictment is now so familiar that there is no need to elaborate it.

From the point of view of this discussion, the main weight of the critique is to disparage party and to look for an alternative. Officers of Parliament play that role – they become allies of Parliament and the people. In the words of the deputy auditor general, Parliament becomes 'our primary client,' and the media 'an important secondary audience.'[45] When Parliament fails as an ally, then officers of Parliament such as the information and privacy commissioners must elicit public attention by other means – hard-hitting criticism of government or organized media and public relations to promote their activities.

It is a staple complaint of a succession of information commissioners that no one – but most especially Parliament – appears interested in their work: '[Their reports] have never ... even prompted a question to the government in either the Commons or the Senate.' In such an uninquisitive atmosphere it becomes understandable why the former privacy commissioner, George Radwanski, 'frequently issued press releases and [gave] interviews to publicize his positions ... [even] before addressing MPs.'[46] The privacy and information commissioners need the alertness of advocacy groups like Democracy Watch, just as Democracy Watch would benefit from broadening its interpretation of what constitutes a subject of accountability.

As it currently stands, more than half of the officers of Parliament operate in a half-light, with the auditor general the centre of attention. This is unfortunate on two counts. First, the auditor general adopts a patronizing tone towards members of Parliament. MPs on the Public Accounts Committee are alternately complimented for doing their work and reminded that they 'do not have the time, the staff and the access to records that we do.'[47] One result of such candour, according to pollster Allan Gregg, is to 'undermine' public trust in government, a consequence that, if true, is both serious and paradoxical.[48] Or perhaps not paradoxical. Ipsos-Reid has discovered that the current auditor general is 'immensely trusted by Canadians because "she has no vested interest and is viewed by Canadians as being above politics."'[49] This is exactly what John Hibbing and Elizabeth Theiss-Morse found in their study *Stealth Democracy: Americans' Beliefs about How Government Should Operate*: 'Peopl[e] [they say] desire to increase the influence of ordinary people' and are willing to achieve this end by increasing 'the influence of ... unelected experts.'[50] Here is the populism that critics of the auditor general write about; here the explanation for that officer's elevation, in Jeffrey Simpson's phrase, to 'a kind of taxpayer folk hero.'[51]

The second reason for regretting that the Office of Auditor General has become the representative of its type is the anti-party sentiment its reports and comments elicit. The danger lies in the potential of which Aneurin Bevan warned Britain's Labour party long ago: 'Political parties [can] become the enemies of parliamentary democracy.'[52] The depreciation of Parliament's competency by any one of its officers ought to be a matter of concern or at the very least one to which all observers are sensitive, for the reason a recent study of officers of Parliament in Great Britain gives: '[E]xcessive involvement of unelected officials in supervising elected politicians can damage democracy, if independence alone is the dominant characteristic.'[53]

At stake here is not some form of intra-institutional rivalry. The auditor general and the other officers of Parliament represent much more than their narrow label implies. A reading of their reports to Parliament bears out that claim. Here they speak to Parliament; but they also speak for, if not on behalf of, public opinion. Depending upon the officer in question, the subject may range, for instance, over taxes, security, and the Internet; it may involve the private as well as the public sector; and it may extend beyond the federal into the provincial order of jurisdiction.[54] In their commentaries and in the attention their commentaries elicit, officers of Parliament assume some of the features of representation, not in the traditional, 'promissory' sense, as Jane Mansbridge describes it, but rather in what she calls 'gyroscopic' representation. Conscience, principle, and character describe this type of 'unaccountable' representative, since there is no direct linkage between elector and elected. In this situation, 'X' speaks for minority sentiment, regardless of geography and regardless of incentive.[55] There is some distance between Mansbridge's account of elected representatives – a black member of Congress speaking for blacks who do not live in his or her district – and officers of Parliament, who are unelected. Still, officers of Parliament inhabit a world of representation and articulate concerns some of the represented believe to be inadequately expressed by elected members. The thread that joins officers of Parliament is their common concern for integrity. In his call for a new separation of powers in the United States, Bruce Ackerman has proposed an 'integrity branch,' whose job would be to 'check and balance' tendencies towards abuse of power.[56] The characteristics he lists of members of this proposed branch echo those of Canada's officers of Parliament.

The gap between actual and ideal characteristics is a subject for another discussion. What matters here is that Canada has the ingredients of an emerging integrity branch of government – accountable to Parliament but also responsive to the public and sensitive to the constitution. If parliamentary democracy in Canada is under pressure from alternative conceptions of governing, to be precise, constitutional democracy and electoral democracy, then officers of Parliament stand at the frontier of these competing claims to authoritative rule.

The critique advanced by the Reform party, and its successors, claims allies in the officers of Parliament, but to what end – as reinforcements for its line of legislative resistance to government? This is true for some officers, such as the auditor general, who devote their attention to finding fault with government. Others, like the commissioner of official languages, generally go unremarked, but when there is comment it is negative. This happened in 2004, when the commissioner, in an unprecedented act, intervened in judicial proceedings arising out of Acadian discontent with boundaries proposed by the Electoral Boundaries Redistribution Commission for New Brunswick following the 2001 Census.[57] There is another attraction to officers of Parliament for those who think this way: officers of Parliament help restore trust in government. It was a tenet of Reform belief, maintained in the national media by its founder long after he had moved from public office, that the elected could not be trusted to police their own actions. The non-elected, in the person of officers of Parliament or chairs of public inquiries, such as Mr Justice Gomery appointed to investigate the sponsorship charges, were the better repository of public trust in a system marked by a dominant prime minister, disciplined parties, and suppliant media.[58] Stephen Harper, leader of the Conservative party during the campaign leading to the January 2006 federal election, reiterated this theme: '[T]he first piece of legislation I will introduce as prime minister will be the federal accountability act ... It will give more power to the Auditor General, the Ethics Commissioner, the Information Commissioner, and the Lobbyists Registrar [t]o make sure that *these* independent Officers of Parliament can *hold* the government accountable.'[59]

Trust and accountability – the rise of what has been called the 'audit society' – these are big topics and fit more properly in a later discussion, of the question 'Who are the people?'[60] For the present, and to draw the themes of this chapter to a close, it is important to note that the theory of electoral democracy as it exists in Canada is the source of two paradoxes. First, and contrary to its reputed and putative claims, electoral democracy is not a matter of simplifying politics. Initiative, referendum, and recall, as well as officers of Parliament and commissions of inquiry, add layers of uncertainty, for none can be called an undisputed instrument of accountability. More than that, they contradict emphasis placed on the primacy of the legislature as the voice of the people. A second, unexpected result of electoral democracy as advanced by Reform and its successors lies in this – the depreciation of the House of Commons in Canada's system of bicameralism.

The ambition of the Reform party, launched nearly two decades ago and, now, heard in the ranks of the Conservative party, is to decentralize, devolve, and disperse. A House that reflected these objectives would be less powerful than the present lower chamber and more susceptible to multiple influences. There is another way such a blueprint would enervate the people's house. The idea of representation that it embraces is representation only in the sense of reflection, as in a mirror. It is passive. By contrast, in the language of parliamentary democracy, representation is active. Parliament interprets and refines interests. The difference between the two finds a parallel in the distinction Susan Sontag once drew between photography, which discloses, and painting, which through its layers of application constructs[61] – Parliament not as image but 'the thing indeed.'[62]

5 What Is the House?

When in the Confederation Debates Macdonald explained how representation by population was to be implemented for the new House of Commons, he jauntily stated that 'the whole thing is worked by a simple rule of three.'[1] By that he meant the ratio of Quebec's population per member determined the number of members each province would have in the new lower chamber. A consequence of this practice was a chamber with no fixed ceiling on its numbers (until a new redistribution formula, introduced in 1946, did just that, only to be abandoned three decades later for a series of agreements that saw some provinces increase their number of seats but no province lose) and, more fundamental still, an attitude towards representation that might be described as malleable. It is the absence of a rigid adherence to numbers that helps to explain the greater absorptive capacity of Parliament, compared to the United States Congress, as seen in the presence of representatives of the three northern territories in the first and the absence of Puerto Rico in the second.

For present purposes, another rule of three – that is to say, the parliamentary, constitutional, and electoral theories of democracy as applied to the work of the people's house – is no more simple than Macdonald's, although equally necessary to a modern appreciation of Canada's political system. The need to fit theory with fact is designed not to exclude but rather to integrate in a coherent way competing ideas of political rule and thereby strengthen public understanding of this central institution of government. That this is a worthy object there can be little doubt: the competing theories feed the discontent with Parliament that is so widely reported: 'A recent poll revealed that of 12 professions, MPs stood second to bottom in terms of public trust' (1998); 'at present, according to surveys, only 4 percent of the population have confidence in their representatives' (1996).[2] Here is a contributing source for Donald Savoie's claim that 'national political institutions are in a state of disrepair,' or another depiction of Parliament as 'calcified.'[3]

That last adjective refers to function and not to architecture. The great stone edifices that symbolize the national government to the public mind may appear impervious (although structural maintenance is a continuing job), but the impregnable facade disguises two broad areas of change that have pronounced ramifications for the people's house, whether viewed from the perspective of constituents or that of members of Parliament. The first deals with the provision of constituency services. At one level this seems straightforward enough: MPs receive public money to establish local offices with staff in order to maintain closer contact with constituents. When questioned about their job, MPs invariably talk about the opportunities and demands such service presents: 'The riding appeals to me more than the House ... [T]his is where I get the nourishment. [Neglect of the constituency] is what causes the demise of governments.'[4]

Whether in the constituencies or in the House, MPs today, when compared to their predecessors, are models of purposeful endeavour. Gone are the benign days of Louis St Laurent, for example, when members had few resources, travelled little, and corresponded infrequently with their constituents. In Ottawa, says one close observer, 'members of Parliament have come to devote major portions of their time to providing assistance to individual constituents.'[5] David Docherty, whose book *Mr Smith Goes to Ottawa* is subtitled *Life in the House of Commons*, goes even farther: 'MPs,' he says, 'have come to see constituency service as a primary role.' Patrick Boyer, former MP and author of works on Canadian politics, casts that sentiment in a different light: 'Constituency demands,' he says, 'mak[e] MPs administrators of government programs, which takes them away from their primary role of holding government to account.'[6]

The time and resources devoted to the home front and away from the parliamentary arena might be seen as a cost. The late Alan Clark, a former Thatcher minister in Great Britain, so viewed it and gave it a name – 'democratic overhead.'[7] The cost is particularly steep in Canada, where constituents appear to have a different view of the significance of constituency work: 'While it is valued by those who receive it, it has only limited influence in getting a Member re-elected.'[8] To this paradox might be added the irony that nothing the MP does by way of constituency service has anything particular to do with Parliament, and it could be done, in a less personal manner perhaps, by a bureaucrat.

Still, it is the personal manner that counts. 'Before constituency offices,' according to Ed Broadbent, 'MPs were more seen originally as people you send to Ottawa simply to legislate, not provide service. And I think in my own case, I'm sort of part of this generation of participatory democracy ... I was 31 when I was elected and so I was very strong on the theory of democracy other than simply representative institutions.' Flora MacDonald, a former Progressive Conservative MP and cabinet minister, agrees: 'Communication by phone and fax and e-mail is good, but seeing someone in person is so much better.'[9]

The emphasis on the person – member or constituent – signifies the nature of the transformation that has occurred. Constituents could never be ignored, but where once the member voiced party concerns back home, now he or she voices – as much or more – the people's concerns in the House. According to political scientist Louis Balthazar, 'politicians ... have never tried harder to please than in our time. That may even be part of the problem. They are trying too hard.'[10] There are a number of reasons for the frustrations MPs experience today, some of which will be examined below, but that they are frustrated and that their unhappiness is the subject of continuous discussion by themselves and others cannot be denied. Witness the stream of publications of the Canadian Study of Parliament Group and the Parliamentary Centre, the latter a self-described 'Canadian not-for-profit organization devoted to improving the effectiveness of representative assemblies and governance mechanisms in Canada and around the world.' Of nine occasional papers listed on the centre's website, the majority deal with problems MPs encounter: 'Stress and the MP,' 'Managing Staff,' 'MPs Views on Committee Organization,' 'The Question Period: What Former Members Think,' 'Building Better Relations,' and 'E-Governance: Some Implications for Parliamentarians.'[11]

There is nothing original in the revelation that MPs experience cross-pressure in carrying out their duties – should they be guided by party discipline, their personal views, or constituency opinion? Norman Ward and David Hoffman wrote a study for the Royal Commission on Bilingualism and Biculturalism in 1970 on just this topic. They discovered that 'the majority of Canadian M.P.s are inclined to follow their own judgement against the wishes of their constituents, [but] are considerably less inclined to display the same independence when their personal views are in conflict with those of their party.'[12] In this trio of pressures there are echoes – muted, perhaps – of elements discussed already in the chapters on parliamentary, constitutional, and electoral democracy. What is new and demands explanation is the emphasis on the individual member rather than on the institution of Parliament, which is where Ward and Hoffman located it. Nor is this placement extraordinary, as David Docherty's book, and even more its title, testify. The allegorical Mr Smith, MP, recalls the junior senator played by Jimmy Stewart in the Frank Capra film *Mr Smith Goes to Washington*. Docherty claims only a verisimilitude between Canadian fact (his data were gathered using a survey of the thirty-fourth and thirty-fifth Parliaments as well as of candidates who ran unsuccessfully in 1993) and American fiction: '[T]he Canadian Parliament in the twilight of the twentieth century shares none of the fictional corruption of the American Senate in *Mr Smith Goes to Washington*.'[13] True, perhaps, but the shift of attention from chamber to individual introduces a less familiar language to parliamentary discussion. The rhetoric – like the film's eponymous character – comes from outside. Consider some of Docherty's chapter titles: 'Arriving in Ottawa,' 'Turning Expectations into Actions,' 'Coming to Terms with Parliament,' 'Home Style: Members and Their Constituents,' 'Life Cycle of a Political Career,' and 'Leaving Parliament.' Impermanence, illustrated in Canada by high turnover rates of MPs – as much as 40 per cent on occasion – produces amateurism in Parliament and personal uncertainty, since there is not much a member can do to change the party's position on issues once the leader has spoken (the plight of an MP in this position gained mythic stature after a medical doctor and member of the Liberal caucus wept while voting to support the Chrétien government's limited compensation for persons who had contracted hepatitis-C through the national blood supply).[14]

The depiction of the naive freshman member – Docherty labels him 'the apprentice' – more attuned than the seasoned MP to the concerns of the little man back home is no populist parody. Nor is it intended to be. Because so few scholarly books are published in Canada on Parliament and, even more to the point, on the House of Commons – Docherty's (1997) is the most recent singular study – but largely because it takes the member as its subject, *Mr Smith Goes to Ottawa* can be considered a tract for its times. The analogy between Capra's folk hero and Canada's MPs is false, as other observers have noted: 'In the movies, when a Man of Integrity goes to the capital, you can be sure he'll teach the cynical out-of-touch pols there an important thing or two. Sadly, in reality, it is the capital that dispenses most of the lessons.'[15] Docherty does not disagree. His insight is to see and to demonstrate that voters see that there is a neglected – people's – dimension to the House.

In Great Britain, Norton and Wood maintain that at one time '[c]onstituency parties looked to their Members to make a name at Westminster, not in their constituencies.'[16] They argue that local demand for an MP's services increased as government programs multiplied after the Second World War. In a federation the equation could never be so direct, although members invariably say that constituents show little appreciation for jurisdictional niceties when they seek out an MP to solve a problem. What has happened in Canada at both the federal and provincial levels for the last half-century is the disappearance of small-change patronage that helped hold national parties together and in whose distribution local members had some say. In the age of bureaucracy, 'backbenchers began to feel inferior to the Public Service. They also felt they were losing what had been their *raison de être* for years: patronage.'[17]

Under Macdonald, and then Laurier, power passed from Parliament to the constituencies, where the governing party through judicious use of patronage anchored the political parties. In time this early localism was transformed into ministerialism with a regional or provincial base. Post-war prosperity, North American economic integration, the revolution of mass telecommunication, and the rise of a new politics that disdained patronage devalued, in turn, the more recent certainties of the past.[18] Among these certainties was the fixed link provided by parties, which connected constituencies to the centre in Parliament. One party radically affected by societal change was the Co-operative Commonwealth Federation (CCF). Of parliamentary as well as academic and agrarian lineage, the idealistic and doctrinaire CCF looked to the electorate and Parliament to achieve its economic and social policy objectives. Reconstituted as the New Democratic Party after joining with the Canadian Labour Congress in 1960, it followed the Liberal party's example by concentrating its attention on urban societal issues and on the question of national unity. In so doing, it loosed its programmatic moorings.

The CCF was a parliamentary not a populist party. So too were the Liberals and Progressive Conservatives. For all of them political attention and rhetoric were directed primarily towards the House. The new, participatory politics, mentioned by Ed Broadbent above and indelibly associated with the early years of the first Trudeau government, shifted the focus. In time, enthusiasm and interest in the structures of participatory democracy waned. Nonetheless, belief in the principle grew. The literature on path dependence theory, which concerns itself with the study of the unfolding of social processes over time – 'sometimes an extremely long time' – is extensive, but none of it has been directed to examining the legacy of participatory-democratic attitudes on modern Canadian politics and, especially, conceptions of the people's house.[19] The social revolution of the 1960s and 1970s did not stop: from liberalizing divorce and abortion, and decriminalizing homosexual acts to introducing government-sanctioned gambling, tightening gun-control laws, and, more recently, legislating to permit same-sex marriages. Each of these sets up a tension, deeply felt because the issues touch on moral values, between centre and constituency (for in Canada, as opposed to the United States, all of these matters fall under federal jurisdiction, largely, though not exclusively, as a result of a single criminal code). Parliamentary democracy is about mediating conflict and refining positions. Discipline in Parliament is defended as a way of levelling up, not down. Yet discipline comes under attack for silencing the private members and, thereby, the voice of the people back in the constituency. Service, responsiveness, and sensitivity, all on behalf of the constituency, exert pressure on MPs today that their predecessors never experienced. At the same time, and in part because opinions on moral issues are so disparate, the hand of the whip is felt to be heavier than ever before.

Note that the expanded constituency concerns are not local in content. They raise foundational issues of rights, parliamentary practices, and claims of popular sovereignty. The net is wide because uncertainty is great: the public has difficulty locating itself in politics. Who rules, for whom, and why? The constituency dimension, which once was finite, has transcended its geographic boundaries. Societal transformation in the sense of the arrival of social phenomena that are fluid – mores, attitudes, movements – helps explain the change, but only in part. Another equally broad set of transformative influences might be categorized under the heading 'information.' Here would be included access-to-information laws (Canada's Office of the Information Commissioner was created in 1983). Parliaments and cabinets still work largely in an oral tradition and for that reason depend upon interpreters, such as the late Eugene Forsey. The oral tradition is abetted by discipline and secrecy: it is a measure of the loss of respect for past times that a Liberal private member's bill in 2003 seeking greater access to cabinet records could equate cabinet secrecy to 'a lack of moral confidence.' At the same time, Open Government Canada, 'a nation-wide network formed in spring 2000 to advocate access to government information laws,' predictably called for the information commissioner 'to be given the power to order release of requested documents and to punish those who disobey.' Predictably, because whenever the prerogative arises critics advocate displacing it with statute law.[20] The phrase 'moral confidence' is telling for what it reveals about modern attitudes towards responsible government. At the same time, it is indicative of a revival – if indeed the campaigns early in the last century for prohibition and female franchise qualify as original instances – of 'the great moral political crusades, bringing "new aims, new methods, new spirit" into public life.'[21] The words are G.M. Trevelyan's, the subject John Bright's campaigns in the nineteenth century against the Corn Laws and the Crimean War. They could apply as easily to the Internet and press campaign in opposition to the Martin government's Civil Marriage Bill introduced in 2005: 'Anne McLellan [then minister of justice] should follow in the footsteps of Sheila Copps and the Westminster tradition of Parliament, do the honourable thing and and [sic] resign her seat.'[22]

Compared to television coverage of Parliament – stilted in the image and fragmented in the information it transmits (Question Period dominates) – through which the public sees and hears the proceedings, the Internet allows the public to be heard by parliamentarians. It obliterates boundaries – geographic, political, gender, economic, for example – allowing groups and movements to form and re-form and to move in and out of the traditional political forum. At the same time, satellite communication provides instantaneous and almost total coverage. The audience has changed as a result of the change in technology; reading a biography of a politician of half a century ago underscores the magnitude of the change. Jimmy Gardiner's audience was in the House – Liberals on the backbenches upon whom he depended to propagate the government's message back in the constituencies as often as members of the opposition. Out of the House and off the Hill, the organized farmers arrayed in a few very large (often province-wide) associations were, compared to fifty years later, easy to reach and to proselytize (although never as easy as in 1910, when the farmers laid siege to Ottawa and, at the invitation of Sir Wilfrid Laurier, filled the lower chamber and for four hours read statements and memorials to government ministers). No other interest group (nor farmers since) was ever accorded such a reception.[23]

Specialization in agriculture, as in every other field, fortified by increased technical knowledge and training, presents a problem for government and legislators that goes beyond simple communication. MPs find themselves confronted by multiple and often conflicting claims to expertise possessed by public servants and interest groups. Here is one reason members complain about lack of resources, personally and as members of committees, while drawing invidious comparisons between their inferior state and the support that members of the U.S. Congress receive. Here too the costs of high turnover of MPs (especially striking when compared to the longevity of representatives in Washington) and the lack of experience and knowledge that follow are evident. The House of Commons is not a chamber of specialists in an era where expertise in science and law, economics and health care, for example, would be welcome.[24] There is no consensus on the impact information and communications technology will have on the people's house, although a disruptive impact is one possibility.

Consider, for instance, the vision offered by Reg Alcock, a former parliamentary secretary, a former chair of a standing committee, and, in 2005, president of the Treasury Board: 'The real power ... lies in the potential of ICTs [information and communications technologies] to enable and support a more transparent, accountable and participatory form of government.' He foresaw electronic voting by MPs and citizens, thus allowing 'more frequent use of referenda and [a] shift in the balance of control from Parliament to citizens.' Greater accountability and greater participation could be expected.[25] A less sanguine projection, presented by an academic, Gilles Paquet, speaks of 'the disturbance factor ... ascribable to a de-materialization and de-territorialization of the socio-economy generated by the new technologies.' According to this view, participation can take two forms: designing and implementing policy or, conversely, 'opposing, stalling and sabotaging' it. He argues that information technologies actually embody 'a strategy of deliberate decentralization' and, because they do, pose a serious challenge to 'the foundations of representative democracy.' For instance, 'distributed governance' introduces a 'softer ... 360-degree notion of accountability' than is usually associated with 'Westminster government.'[26] As an illustration, he cites the Canadian armed forces, which – incrementally and without intent – have abandoned a classic, hierarchical structure to embrace a broadened, citizen-oriented perspective. Evidence to support that claim can be found in the recommendation made in 2005 by the first ombudsman of the Canadian Forces (an office created by ministerial directive in 1998 and as a result of the Somalia scandal) to enshrine his office in law. The recommendation appeared in a

'White Paper on Civilian Oversight in the Military,' issued at the time he resigned from office.[27]

It is not necessary to agree with either of these interpretations to appreciate the challenge the new communications technologies pose for parliamentarians. In fact, the contrasting tenor of the two prognoses provides background for the limited use parliamentarians make of the Internet. Differential access to the Internet, the complex demography of many constituencies (for instance, a rural population that is remote and scattered versus an urban one that is concentrated and ethnically diverse), and the uneven quality of technological expertise among members and their staff are practical considerations that qualify any general statement about increased participation.[28] Equally important, but overlooked in the same forecasts, is the grasp of party politics. Politicians in Canada, as elsewhere, 'perceive themselves as part of a team rather than as individual players. They will behave accordingly in their attempt to mobilize electoral support.'[29]

The promise of communications technology contrasts not only with its own reality but also with everyday understanding of the term *information*. The paradox lies in the juxtaposition of electronic plenty and paper scarcity. 'Mismanagement of information,' according to then Information Commissioner John Reid, 'was the root of the $1-billion filing mess in the Human Resources Department.' Nor was it an isolated instance: all around, there is 'a collapse of a culture of record keeping.' The future might be electronic, but in the present there is 'a shortage of file clerks and librarians who are responsible for organizing and maintaining government files.'[30] Three years later, in a report with a title inappropriate for the Canadian system of government, 'Checks and Balances,' the Association of Public Service Financial Administrators reiterated the thesis that 'breakdown in financial controls [lay] at the centre of Liberal scandals.' Poor control of information was not the only culprit – public service practices and philosophy entered the picture, too – but the consequence of impaired management capacity remained the same.[31] Use of the phrase 'checks and balances' is spreading – 'I don't see any checks and balances,' said David Tilson, MP, while questioning expenditures of an officer of Parliament in 2005 – although American author Garry Wills has argued that the phrase has no constitutional provenance in the United States either: 'Nowhere ... does the Constitution mention checks, or balances, or separation of power, or co-equal branches (or even branches) of government.'[32]

Today is a new age for legislators. Demands from constituents for service and a need on the part of members to know about all manner of subjects have transported them from the former hermetic world of partisan loyalties. Nor are they privileged: constituents are better educated than in the past, and many of them have stronger credentials in matters of public affairs than do their MPs. It is now said that elected office does not carry the prestige it once did.[33] While difficult to substantiate in the absence of survey data from half a century ago, still, impressionistically, there is reason to agree. Members of Parliament can no longer dominate the public world because that singular world has disappeared. Rather, there are parallel universes of expert knowledge from which MPs are excluded and which they must strive to enter. Part of the fission arises from the increased use government, and especially the Prime Minister's Office (PMO), makes of task forces, policy forums, and inquiries. In an age of participatory politics, the consultative approach gives 'the impression that it [government] is closer to the people.'[34] While not identical, the task force phenomenon may be viewed as a variation on another theme: 'The delegation of policy-making authority to semi-autonomous, professional bodies has also expanded in other nonjudicial realms.' National authorities (for example, central banks) joined to transnational and supranational bodies, help 'insulat[e] policy-making from the vagaries of democratic politics.'[35]

Thus, to importunities from constituents and impoverishment of information can be added the encroachment of competing organizations on the territory of the Commons. Australian political scientist John Uhr has traced what he calls 'the deliberative deficit of parliamentary systems' to such factors.[36] So too could be attributed the culture of dissatisfaction that infects the Commons and a reorganization imperative that remains forever alluring.

Much could be said about reform of House of Commons rules and procedures. In fact, much has been said about what should be done, what has been done, and what ought to be undone. Take examination of the estimates as an example: did their removal from the whole House acting as Committee of Supply to standing committees strengthen or weaken Parliament, the opposition, and the concept of government accountability? Should they (or at least some of them) be returned to the chamber for plenary examination? In any case, what legislative/democratic theory supports either proposition? These are central questions touching on essential matters of parliamentary government. Nonetheless, they are not fundamental to the analysis of the people's house being presented here, for the following reasons. First, they are complex matters with a long history, a sample of which many be gained from reading John B. Stewart, *The Canadian House of Commons: Procedure*

and Reform.[37] In a political variant of Gresham's law, principles of procedure drive out contemplation of any other kind. Second, and despite
its arcane quality, procedural analysis is a staple of the rather sparse
Canadian parliamentary literature. In his Baedeker of Parliament Hill,
The Parliament of Canada (1987), written a decade after Stewart's book,
C.E.S. Franks offers a sobering explanation for this distortion in parliamentary studies: 'Reform has focused on the obvious and easy things to
change, such as parliamentary committees, procedure and the Senate,
while many of the real problems lie elsewhere ...'[38] Third, and to echo
the thesis of Franks's book, rhetoric does not engage parliamentary
reality in Canada. The ideal of the independent member of Parliament
persists and has even grown in appeal – thus the resonance of a title
(with its populist allusion) such as *Mr Smith Goes to Ottawa*. For this reason, another inquest into committees or another assessment of the
effect of previous inquiries, such as the much-cited McGrath Committee and its broad recommendations, would contribute little to an understanding of the people's house; nor would it answer 'the central
question' posed by Reg Alcock in a round table on 'MPs Views on Committee Organization':

> [S]hould MPs be able to play a larger role? In a sense to me, it is tragic that
> we even have to ask that question. The House of Commons, leaving aside
> parties, exists to give citizens a voice in managing the affairs of their coun-
> try. It exists to give citizens a voice in holding their government to account.
> The very fact that we are worried about the role and we have to ask about
> enlarging the role I think, underscores the concern [found in] a survey of
> public servants who say that of 22 influences on the making of legislation,
> MPs rank at the bottom.[39]

Here is the source for the claim about MPs' insufficiency, inefficacy,
and disempowerment and for the charge that Parliament is illegitimate.
Implicit too is the allegation that, absent a 'responsive' chamber, the
House can accomplish nothing. Yet Parliament is not the passive entity
students of legislatures everywhere in the 1960s once described.

On the contrary, Peter Milliken, now speaker of the House of Commons, maintains that 'the role and importance of committees in the
House of Commons has increased dramatically over the past 20 or 30
years.'[40] Contrary to the claim that legislatures are in decline, there has
been 'a world-wide growth of parliamentary committees.'[41] While this
reversal may be a matter of quantitative record – number of commit-

tees, frequency of their meeting, size of membership – and of qualitative evaluation – disposition of recommendations, public and media response to committee reports – the phenomenon requires explanation because it runs counter to the thesis of an ever-expanding and more powerful executive.

At first glance, Parliament's rehabilitation appears counter-intuitive. The communications revolution, discussed above, has irrevocably altered the relationship between government and Parliament on the one hand and the public (or publics, if the kaleidoscopic diversity of the modern polity is to be acknowledged) on the other. Indeed, it is this transformed condition between leader and led that some observers say explains, first, the 'revolt of the voting classes' – lower turnout, less confidence in government, and a decline in political party loyalty – and second, the power of social movements to set the political agenda. As a result, 'citizens now have an active marketplace of participation in which to shop.'[42]

'Marketplace' is a peculiarly apt description, because social movements enter or leave the political arena at their own choosing; they are movements in both senses of that term. Here, surely, is a recipe for the disintegration of the familiar institutions of politics. And yet the challenge to Parliament that these developments present has elicited a compensatory response. Turning their backs upon their tradition as generalists, members of Parliament seek, through the avenue of standing committees, to become specialists and to speak with authority on the issues that resound through Parliament and that are dominated by expert bureaucrats, academics, interest groups, and scientists. It is this context that frames the familiar plea heard from MPs, of which the following is representative: 'If the committees had more independence from the government, from the executive of cabinet, would it not be more beneficial for legislation and for the feeling that we are here for a purpose and with the ability to do something more than to be a talk shop or to have busy work going on in committees?'[43]

Arthur Kroeger, a former long-time senior civil servant, has said that 'modern communication technologies ... not only increas[e] the public's understanding of political issues but ... whe[t] their appetite for more meaningful involvement.'[44] The first part of that proposition needs testing as well as modification. There is much evidence to suggest, not surprisingly, that public understanding of issues varies according to their complexity. Involvement is another matter. The consequence of the Internet, which is to annihilate distance, will be in Kroeger's words, 'similar to that of the extension of the franchise in the nineteenth century.' Members of Parliament need specialist knowledge not only to hold their own against a proliferation of experts (among whom, for the purpose of this discussion, should be included the occupants of the PMO) but also to respond to an aroused citizenry. The last word is important because specialist MPs speak not on behalf of the voters in the constituency they represent in the House but on behalf of individuals, wherever located, whose particular interests or concerns the MP articulates as a member of the standing committee.

The still calm of a disciplined House of Commons, portrayed by critics, is misleading. It is neither so still nor so calm as it once (even recently) was. Of course, compared to the U.S. Congress, there is no independence of members to be found. Comparison with the British Parliament is less stark but in the same direction: party loyalty is less dependable at Westminster than in Ottawa, with the consequence that governments lose more votes there than here. Reasons unique to British politics, including a lower chamber with twice the number of members as the Canadian, are part of the explanation. In addition, Britain's unitary system of government injects particularistic and local concerns into national politics. By contrast, in Canada, as John Stewart has noted, 'most matters of a local and private nature ... were given to the provinces [and] reduced the room for independent action by the private members at Ottawa.'[45]

For the purpose of the present discussion, the point to note is that, despite this history of political deviance and despite a program of legislative modernization under the Blair government, the reputation of Parliament, and the Commons in particular, has not improved. A former leader of the House diagnosed the problem as follows: 'The Commons remains highly polarized in an era in which the public has become more pluralist and more volatile in their party affiliations.'[46] As a response he urged Parliament to adopt 'a business-like [in contrast to a partisan] approach,' and to show that 'it can be a means of expressing the idealism of the young.' As noted elsewhere in this book, modernization has done nothing to reverse the decline in voter turnout in Britain or the reputation of the Commons.

In a discussion of people's houses, British parallels may be no parallel at all, or at the very least, of minimal application to Canada. The heart of the critique on this side of the Atlantic is not the complexion of the House – a statement made with some care since change to the electoral system to effect mirror representation is a familiar entry on the usual list of reforms – but the orientation of power within it – to be blunt, prime-ministerial dominance, apotheosized in Paul Martin's ironic quip 'Who do you know in the PMO?' when campaigning for leadership of the Liberal party, and in the title of Donald Savoie's much-quoted book, *Governing from the Centre: The Concentration of Power in Canadian Politics.*[47]

The theme of the critique in Canada is less the downward trajectory of the MP as a person of political substance than it is the force propelling the decline – the prime minister and his advisers. The eclipse of Parliament is occasionally described as the presidentialization of Canadian politics. This reference to American politics is inappropriate for both the United States and Canada. Politics is less centralized in the former – Congress can never be taken for granted – and more centralized in the latter – Parliament has no constitutional role in foreign affairs or in appointments of major officials, innovations reformers in Canada demand and Congress in the United States has always possessed. The criticism about concentrated powers is curious in one respect – it has been like this for well over a century. Writing in 1901, C.P. Ilbert observed that 'the Parliament of the present day has largely reverted *in substance* to the practice of the Parliament of the first Edwards, under which the king, by his Ministers, made the law,' a comment with application to Canada, where the executive power 'that enormous part of our constitutional system ... rests upon the common law, and upon that part of it which deals with the King's prerogative.'[48] What may have changed is that cabinet decision making is less collegial than it was in the days of Jimmy Gardiner and C.D. Howe, or, more precisely, that cabinet ministers are no longer semi-sovereign entities. But in either case discipline was as inflexible then as now. The reason why lies in such measures of parliamentarianism as a powerful prime minister, weak bicameralism, the length of the parliamentary term, the single-member electoral system, the role of the speaker, the ease of dissolution, the presence of a leader of the opposition, government control of the agenda, restrictions on private members' bills, control of committee chairs, successive readings for bills with the plenary determining the principles, the government prerogative to introduce money bills, weakly institutionalized committees, low committee influence on parties, effective number of parliamentary parties, and size of the largest party. The list comes from a comparative study by Alan Siaroff, in whose work Canada is but a minor subject of interest.[49] Still, the list has direct application for Canadian politics, where, in the opinion of

another scholar, 'the role and function of the opposition in our vision of
the Westminster model is ... shaped by the essential characteristics of
that model of government.'[50] Comparative parliamentary analysis,
using variables such as those found in the preceding list, helps place
Canadian experience in perspective. Arguably, from that vantage, it
appears that much of what critics oppose in Canada's parliamentary
practices is endemic to this system of politics.

Nonetheless, on all sides there is acquiescence in – or indications of a
willingness to contemplate – change that would lead to 'a greater role
for parliamentarians.' That pledge appeared in the Martin government's 'Action Plan for Democratic Reform,' *Ethics, Responsibility,
Accountability*, released in February 2004, and took concrete form in
provisions for less strict discipline on the government side (a three-line
voting system, extending from one-line or free votes to three-line or confidence votes), an expanded role and greater resources for committees
(with bills subject to one- and two-line votes referred to committee
before second reading so that MPs could have greater influence on legislation), revisions to the estimates process in order to give members
closer scrutiny, a major role for parliamentary secretaries in linking ministers and parliamentarians, and a permanent change to the Standing
Orders providing for election of committee chairs by secret ballot. The
Action Plan also promised prior parliamentary review of appointments
to agencies and crown corporations, and parliamentary participation in
establishing a review process for appointments of judges to the
Supreme Court of Canada.[51] The language ('parliamentary coalitions to
be built across party lines') and the spirit of electoral democracy discussed in chapter 4 pervaded the Action Plan. Cautiously so, however,
since the plan took care to protect, on the one hand, constitutional
democracy, by agreeing only to discuss Parliament's role in judicial
appointments and, on the other hand, parliamentary democracy, by
requiring three-line votes on issues of confidence and 'a limited number
of matters of fundamental importance to the government.'

Labelled 'timid' by critics, and of little practical consequence to the
operation of Parliament, the Action Plan nonetheless represented a crucial modification of traditional government control of House proceedings.[52] More important in a study of the people's house – and contrary
to common complaint – these changes were in line with a long-term
trend towards greater influence by MPs over legislation and the order
of Commons business. Examples are the selection of the speaker by
secret ballot (standing order adopted in 1986), abolition of appeals to

the speaker's rulings (promoted on the proposition that appeals undermine the chair's authority by requiring support from a majority of
members – usually the government – to defeat), committee selection of
chairs (first achieved in 2002 as a result of a defection by fifty-six Liberal
backbenchers in support of an opposition motion), and creation of a
Government Operations and Estimates Committee with extensive
oversight powers.[53]

From outside, if not from within the chamber, the trajectory is clear:
while far from total, members have greater control over their activities
and more opportunity to influence legislation than at any time in the
past century. The work and the effectiveness of committees – indeed the
procedure of the Commons – is a large question separate from the subject at hand, the integration of the House and the people. Clearly, there
is overlap, as in the matter of defining and representing the public
interest. The traditional argument against powerful committees is that
they present themselves as a rival in knowledge and experience to the
plenary body (witness congressional committees in Washington) and,
to the extent that they command authority, depreciate the capacity of
the parent body to speak for the larger interest. It is in the committees of
Congress that gun registry and medicare bills, for instance, have disappeared or been transformed beyond recognition.

Overlap is a peculiarly inaccurate concept when speaking of Parliament, because Parliament is a singular, independent institution. A statutory regime in the form of the Independence of Parliament Act, the
Parliament of Canada Act, and the Canada Elections Act, among other
laws, has sought to protect and guarantee the independence of the
House and its members – thus, the disqualification of certain office
holders as members, the prohibition on pledges (for example, to resign
at some future date), Parliament's power to expel duly elected members (for example, Louis Riel in 1874), protection from civil prosecution,
and more. MPs' independence in the performance of their function
includes independence from political parties. Party discipline is not
absolute. In his ruling on the status in the House of the Progressive
Conservative/Democratic Representative Coalition in 2001, the
speaker noted that 'during the course of a parliament we have seen
members change parties, members suspended from caucus and members expelled from caucus. Each member was elected to the House.
Each member elected to the House may live out the vicissitudes of that
parliament as he or she sees fit. Indeed, each member may self-desig-
nate his or her affiliations or lack thereof.'[54]

Independence has its limits: MPs who desert their party and join another elicit strong, negative feelings among constituents. Demands for their resignation and a by-election are common. Parliamentary democratic theory and practice offer no support for such demands. The speaker's ruling clarifies what is often overlooked in discussion of the House – that is, the continuum between constituency and chamber: 'Once a general election has been held and the writs of election issued, attention turns from external political realities to the internal realities of a new parliament.'

Critics of party discipline say that it vitiates the concept of independence. The arguments for and against party discipline are well rehearsed and need no repeating here, although it is worth noting in this context that Canadians rarely elect independent candidates, and the reasons offered for supporting candidates favour party (leader or platform) over the attraction of individual candidates. A chamber of independent members or even of MPs who consider themselves delegates of their constituents is unimaginable in company with parliamentary government. Still, the criticism and the prescriptions to remedy party discipline continue. Among these, two not yet explored but which their advocates say hold promise for assuring responsive MPs are free votes and private members' bills. Jennifer Smith has asked, 'What does a free vote signify?' 'Who takes responsibility for the outcome?'[55] If several hundred members are free to vote as they wish, how is a majority behind one option to be secured? The answer is through negotiation – coalition building – according to electoral-democracy proponents. Does that not pose a threat familiar to Canadian regions: Ontario with more than one-third of the House members would have to support (or, at least, not oppose) a 'deal,' and 'what will Ontario members demand to buy their votes?'[56] Private members' bills pose an analogous problem. Putting to one side the ease or frequency with which they may be introduced, such bills, once introduced, reflect their provenance. This is to say that the response of MPs to private members' bills 'are not as consistent as [one] may have imagined, since a large degree of vote switching occurs.' Freedom creates uncertainty, which produces inconsistency, which MPs alleviate most directly by looking to party leaders for 'their voting cue.'[57]

The House of Commons is a large, complex institution. Over a long history it has amassed traditions, understandings, conventions, and practices as to its operation and the place of the members. Members each come from a constituency, but they are subject to multiple and often conflicting influences of geography, gender, race, religion, age, occupation, and personal values, as well as career ambitions and concern for individual reputation. One consideration to receive 'limited attention' from academics but periodic and intense scrutiny from the media is remuneration.[58] More than in most professions, MPs serve several masters. Nonetheless, they rise and fall on the esteem of their parties.

Understudied by academics and underestimated by the voter, these cross-pressures contribute to the double-sided personality that frequently appears in discussions of Parliament: the outward versus the inward appearance, the collectivity of the institution in contrast to the singularity of the MP, the adversarial tone of public debate as opposed to the willingness to negotiate and compromise in private. Question Period, the high point of the Commons day for media and the public, is routinely described as a show or theatre, even 'guerrilla theatre.' Although never explored, the implication in these descriptions is the discordant juxtaposition of politics in reality and as illusion.[59] Invariably, the occasion for drawing such contrasts is a discussion of the influence of television on politics and public understanding of politics. (In 2006, there is virtually no one left who remembers what life was like in Parliament before television coverage.) Invariable, also, is the conclusion that television oversimplifies and distorts, both on the part of the speaker and the listener. Edward Blake said the same of *Hansard*: 'It induces a great many men to speak rather for the Hansard than the House. The main object of a deliberative assembly ... to maintain the attention of its audience ... is not accomplished.'[60]

Institutions, legislatures as well as corporations, are living organic entities. In the case of Canada's Parliament, that life embraces, for example, Sir Robert Borden's Naval Aid Bill (1912), which saw the introduction of closure on debate; the Pipeline Debate (1956), which saw closure imposed and an unprecedented and unsuccessful attempt to censure the speaker; the Flag Debate of the 1960s; the Free Trade Agreement, whose negotiation and passage Michael Hart has described as a testament to the Canadian model of parliamentary government; and debates on medicare, abolition of the death penalty, decriminalization of abortion, and much more.[61]

In the history of reform to the House, rule changes are not so much ineffectual as the expectations that accompany them inflated. Here is why hopes are dashed, frustration mounts, and a sense of institutional malaise spreads. More than that, expectations of what is required to make change happen grow more excessive. Early in 2003, the author of a full-page letter to Liberal members of Parliament that appeared in the *National Post*, recommended – along with fixed election dates and free votes in Parliament on all bills except for budgets, non-confidence, and key governmental policy initiatives – the introduction of 'a two-term limit for future Prime Ministers.'[62] To those who seek change – fixed election dates, for example – reference to historical and political context seem smothering. To those who seek a 'level playing field' by removing from the prime minister the prerogative to advise dissolution of Parliament and replacing discretion with a fixed date (as British Columbia legislated in 2002), the unwritten constitution appears impenetrable and nonsensical. In a House debate in 2004 on an opposition motion to institute fixed election dates, reformers cited economy, efficiency, and fairness as their goals. In response, they were told by a government spokesman that 'what at first glance may seem like an innocuous measure which is very easy to implement, in fact could have far-reaching consequences for our Constitution and our system of government without even addressing the question of whether it makes sense.'[63]

The value and utility of fixed election dates are matters for consideration. Living next to the United States, Canadians are familiar with the concept. Except that in that country, there is only one date: all elections, federal, state, and local, are coterminous. What would happen if, including the territories, fourteen different dates were pre-determined? What effect would this have on party organization, electoral financing, and voter mobilization? There is another less practical matter to consider. In the current arrangement, Parliament can be dissolved and a government can go to the people on a matter it deems of sufficient importance and moment. If the value being promoted in electoral reform is responsiveness, how is that reconciled with a fixed election date, which reduces the elasticity of the parliamentary system?

Compared to earlier decades, the expansion of constituency service, the explosion of information and speed of its communication, and the plurality of social, moral, cultural, and economic interests have undermined a sense of common purpose among members of Parliament. If they were seeking guidance, their quest would be confounded by contradictory interpretations. Consider the following three assessments:

'The problem with Parliament is that it has ceased to be a legislative body,' adds [then] Alliance Leader Stephen Harper. 'It provides a public forum for venting reaction or venting ideas, but doesn't have much to do with governing the country. All it really does in the democratic sense is confirm the choices of the prime minister. We make noise. We bring pressure to bear, but we don't have much of a role in legislating.'[64]

The role of MP needs to be better understood (by the public, journalists and the MP's themselves). There is intense pressure on MP's to appear to have a decisive influence in government decisions. In fact, apart from those who are actually in cabinet, the role of MP's is to monitor, critique and hold the government to account.[65]

In the context of British-style cabinet government, the government has no duty – and in fact it has no business – to *share* power with politicians who are not members of the government. Responsible government can only make sense when the government is an identifiable entity within another entity that keeps it responsible. The tasks of the ordinary backbencher are the following: to understand, judge, and occasionally to anticipate and warn about the human consequences of government action and inaction; to get government information and viewpoints critical of it out to the public; and, by sampling the record, to prevent clandestine and corrupt governing by politicians and bureaucrats alike.[66]

While absence of clarity and lack of confidence in what they do might trouble MPs, few are as brutal in their self-assessment as former member Patrick Boyer: 'MPs have basically fulfilled their purpose on election night.'[67] According to this interpretation, docility and futility feed frustration and drive the search for purpose. The explanation has a deeper root still – the lost sense of opposition in parliamentary systems. Helen Suzman, the veteran white anti-apartheid campaigner in South Africa has compared now to then:

In those years when I fought on my own I put up 200 questions a session and innumerable private member's motions. We got an enormous amount of information out of the government and then used the press to get that out to undermine apartheid.

Mind you, it was possible because there was a huge respect for parliament and for the concept of opposition. I often think that Tony Leon today with his 48 Democratic Alliance MPs has a far harder time than I did on my own because the ANC has no respect for parliament and no time at all for an opposition.[68]

The reference to apartheid should not detract from the issue at hand – the role of opposition. The opposition in the people's house has been fragmented to a unrivalled extent since 1993. Still, whether diffused or concentrated, and irrespective of the party in power, respect for opposition from the government side of the House, and from outside the House, has declined. Nor is this attitude limited to Canada, as Suzman's comment about South Africa – and Mrs Thatcher's 'unnervingly decisive' actions in Great Britain – testify.[69] The depreciation of opposition in Canada's Parliament first became evident in the politics of personality that characterized the Diefenbaker-Pearson years but then continued as the official opposition party – PCs in the 1960s, Liberals in the 1980s – entered into bitter contests over leadership succession. Leadership campaigns and conventions, and television coverage of these events and of daily politics, emphasized personalities and circumscribed opposition as a collective entity in Parliament. As a consequence, politics ceased to be played out almost entirely within the parliamentary dimension. One of the larger gaps in scholarly research in Canada is the study of opposition.[70]

The values of electoral democracy, first given coherent expression by the Reform party and carried forward through the Canadian Alliance into the new Conservative party, reinforce the politics of personality. They also pose a challenge to parliamentary democracy and constitutional democracy. An illustration is the debate over the prime minister's monopoly of advice on appointments deriving from exercise of the prerogative. In the words of electoral-democracy proponents, this arrangement leads, in the case of judicial 'appointments,' to 'hand-picked judges,' which by implication taints the impartiality of the bench.[71] The indictment goes beyond judicial appointments.

> Consider just the PM's appointment privileges. The prime minister picks the governor general, the cabinet, all deputy ministers, many ministerial staff, Supreme and superior court judges, senators, the heads of all Crown corporations including the CBC, the chairs of committees, the clerk of the Privy Council, the ethics councillor, the auditor general, the information commissioner, the privacy commissioner and, after diplomatic vetting, Canadian ambassadors. All this without a formal nominations process or public examination. And in many cases, a Liberal membership of exemplary standing is the key consideration for the job.[72]

Nor is concern confined to politicians who espouse the value of electoral democracy. Prominent academics are critical, especially about the prime minister's prominence in the appointment of Supreme Court judges. He is, says Jacob Ziegel, a University of Toronto law professor, in a conflict of interest because the federal government is 'the most frequent litigator before the court.' Others, like Peter Russell, go farther and talk about federal appointees to superior courts and courts of appeal, 'who were "cronies, soulmates, buddies or political friends of political ministers who weighed in and insisted on them getting the nod over someone better."'[73] Patrick Monahan and Peter Hogg speak for more than themselves when they promote review of court nominees by a committee composed of MPs, experts from professional bodies like the Canadian Bar Association, and representatives of provincial attorneys general. Nonetheless, they agree that ultimate selection rests on a recommendation by the prime minister.[74] More radical is the suggestion by Allan Hutchinson, an Osgoode Hall law professor, that 'the power of appointment [be] moved from the executive to an independent commission.' By way of example, he suggests a fifteen-member commission – five MPs, five judges, and five citizens:

> Confident that no particular constituency (i.e., judicial, political or lay) had a lock on the commission's work or decisions, the commission would work to establish appropriate criteria for appointment that seriously considered the need for a diverse and talented judiciary. Candidates could be identified either by application, nomination or search. Candidates would be interviewed, and subjected to intensive vetting. Rules could ensure both geographical representation ... and diversity in terms of women and visible minorities.
>
> The commission might relax threshold rules for eligibility and qualification, so as not to exclude otherwise meritorious candidates ... The commission's recommendations would be final; because the commission itself would be diverse and democratic, there would be no need for approval by the prime minister or for parliamentary confirmation. So structured, the appointments process will be less likely to turn into a media circus, as it has in the United States.[75]

Judges constitute the third branch of government. The adjective that most often accompanies the word *judiciary* is *independent*. In that case, what has the appointment of judges to do with the people's house? A great deal, it would appear, from a reading of the debate on the subject in 2004 and 2005. As part of his pledge to eradicate the democratic deficit, Paul Martin promised to give MPs a role in reviewing Supreme Court nominations. Subsequently, when the Commons Justice Committee recommended an advisory group of eminent (elected and non-elected) persons as part of the selection process, and when this was rejected in favour of a panel of MPs and provincial representatives who would compile a recommended but non-binding shortlist, and when no provision was made for public hearings of nominees, much displeasure was expressed.[76]

The importance of procedural involvement – in the form of eminent persons and pre- or post-nomination committee review, with or without questioning of nominees – lies in what that involvement signifies. The U.S. Senate must give its advice and consent to appointments (Article II, Section II, of the Constitution of the United States) because Congress is the repository of popular sovereignty, and the courts are the people's agents.[77]

What parliamentary participation in the appointment of Canadian judges is intended to signify is less precise. In the interests of consistency and symmetry, one might argue that if the people are part of the charter – the democratic coming of age of Canada, says David Docherty – they should be part of the selection process for judges.[78] Yet nobody does. Critics of the appointment process, who long found fault because it compromised the Supreme Court's role as 'an impartial umpire in the federal system,' have changed tack to focus almost entirely on 'the appropriate balance between the courts and the legislatures in making politically-charged decisions for society.'[79] Individual rights and not federalism are the order of the day. In this atmosphere, critics say the judges and the prime minister 'who chooses them' (an inaccurate description since Section 4 (2) of the Supreme Court Act says 'judges shall be appointed by the Governor General in Council by letters patent under the Great Seal') have too much power.[80] When he was prime minister, Paul Martin agreed: '"I don't think the prime minister should have the unparalleled power that he has now." [T]o adhere to true democracy, there will be checks and balances on everything, including appointments.'[81]

Paul Martin was speaking about more than judicial appointments. Membership on agencies, boards, and commissions totals in the thousands, and each is appointed by governor-in-council. Here, too, he promised parliamentary review of these appointments, but in the event reserved the right to act contrary to a parliamentary recommendation.[82] Parliamentary expectations clashed with prime ministerial pledges and performance. Feeling was aroused in part because of Paul Martin's promises but also because past practices were deprecated. When the

Department of Justice refused to release 'profiles' on candidates for appointments to the Supreme Court, Democracy Watch accused the government of 'excessive secrecy,' while others saw it as 'confirm[ing] ... a political element to the appointments.'[83]

On its surface, scrutiny of appointments is reasonable, and the reputation of some of its proponents gives cause to treat the proposal seriously. Still, it has no theoretical coherence, while appointment on recommendation of the first minister, with or without consultation, is grounded in theory and practice. More than that, central to the evolution of responsible government was the disengagement of government and politics from that which was neither. Church and university dignitaries, office holders, and judges once sat in the colonial legislatures. A key step to clarifying and achieving responsible government was to separate and make independent these positions from the legislature. In his doctoral dissertation (and book), *The Principle of Official Independence*, compiled under the supervision of Graham Wallas at the London School of Economics, R. MacGregor Dawson wrote that the judge 'above all ... is the ideal as it were of other forms of independence.'[84] Among these was the public service, whose slow journey to non-partisanship and, thereafter, remote association with politicians is as cardinal a feature of Canadian government as its much weaker version is to American.

Subjecting judicial nominees to parliamentary scrutiny would, in the words of a former chief justice of the Supreme Court of Canada, 'bring back politics into appointments that we succeeded in getting out.'[85] What kind of politics he did not say, although presumably partisan favouritism is one evil parliamentary vetting is supposed to check. There are other kinds of politics heard in the people's house now that 'the root of the so-called democratic deficit' is said to lie in 'the belief that members are not representing constituents.'[86] The appointments controversy underlines a more general matter – how to reconcile the people with their politicians and, even, their political system. Often implicit in the answer is an inarticulate and mechanical sense of republicanism – thus the crude and unreflective prescription of 'checks and balances' without any thought as to what that term means or how it might be made to work in a parliamentary and constitutional monarchy.

6 Who Are the People?

The answer to the question 'Who are the people?' is more complex than might at first appear. Are the adjectival 'people' of the people's house all, or only some, of Canada's thirty-two million residents? Redistribution – that is, the drawing of constituency or electoral boundaries – uses for its calculation the total population number provided by the decennial census. Under the current formula, that figure is divided by the total number of House seats to determine a quotient, which is then divided into the population of each of the respective provinces. Guarantees under the same formula that no province lose seats at a redistribution distort the purity of the initial calculation, as does the 1915 constitutional amendment that no province shall have fewer MPs than it does senators. Still, the fact remains that total population is the foundation of the exercise. The point requires emphasis since a familiar topic of public debate turns on the proposition that individuals and groups go unrepresented in the House when the candidates they support are defeated. At issue here, and to be examined below, is the operation of the single-member-district, simple-plurality-vote system, which, critics say, leads to 'wasted votes' and failure 'to accurately capture the voice of the people.'[1]

As noted in an earlier chapter, Canada has a history of excluding from the franchise, on racial or religious grounds, those who were otherwise qualified to vote. In so far as the political system claims to be one based on popular will, does voluntary exclusion – that is, not turning out to vote – present any less of a challenge than earlier statutory disqualification? Alarm is regularly expressed at the decline in voter turnout at Canadian general elections, from 70 per cent in 1993, to 67 in 1997, to just over 61 in 2000, and to 60.5 in 2004. More disturbing – the chief electoral officer uses the phrase 'deepening crisis' – is the 25 per cent turnout of eligible voters aged eighteen to twenty-four in the 2000 general election. Indeed, half of the non-voters on that occasion were less than thirty years of age. Ninety-five per cent of the drop in turnout from 1993 could be accounted for by the decline in participation of this age group. Nor is that all the bad news: 'The life-cycle effects, which work to increase the voter turnout rates of initially-lower young cohorts, have not brought the Trudeau and Mulroney cohorts up to the levels of the King, St Laurent, Diefenbaker and Pearson generations.'[2] Age cannot compensate for lower and lower participation to begin with. As a result, the graph of turnout looks like the profile of a staircase.

A general decline, a specific decline, a permanent decline – with these statistics as backdrop it is inevitable, first, that the question will be asked: 'At what stage have we lost legitimacy?' And second, that thresholds – such as 40 or 35 per cent – will be tendentiously proposed.[3] Inevitable, but not helpful in clarifying the issue at hand. First, the decline is not a uniquely Canadian phenomenon: 'A 1999 study by the International Institute for Democracy and Electoral Assistance found youth voter turnout in 15 Western European countries was 10 per cent lower than the overall turnout.'[4] Second, a weakened interest in legislative and electoral politics should not be interpreted as political apathy in general. On the contrary, concentrating on

indicators of conventional political participation ... could ... [lead us to] overlook many of the most important ways that modes of activism have been reinvented in recent decades. In particular, traditional theoretical and conceptual frameworks derived from the literature of the 1960s and 1970s, and even what we mean by 'political participation,' need to be revised and updated to take account of how opportunities for civic engagement have evolved and diversified over the years.[5]

Third, anxiety about the decline in voter turnout feeds agitation for institutional reform: 'Members of Parliament [must] realize they must change the way politics is conducted in this country'; 'Old-fashioned politics is so slow, election campaigns take so long'; 'pressing concerns ... about the levels of electoral participation ...'; '[There is] "a major crisis" because young people no longer care about the political process.'[6]

In this atmosphere and since the year 2000, the chief electoral officer has proposed for consideration lowering the voting age to sixteen (of course, this might lower the turnout percentage even further if the new voters participated at the same level as eighteen- to twenty-four-year-olds do now), introducing online voter registration and, eventually, online voting, and, most controversially, mandatory voting.[7] The new permanent voters' list or National Register of Electors, established in 1997 following criticism by the auditor general of the traditional process of door-to-door enumeration and study by the Royal Commission on Electoral Reform and Party Financing, has been the subject of complaint: 'more attractive in theory than ... in practice ... it's one of the factors now that's helping drive the voter turnout down.'[8] Since it defines the universe of participants for the selection of the people's house, accuracy and completeness are fundamental to the compilation of the voters' list. Labelled as 'dysfunctional' in 2003, described as 'appalling' in its mismanagement in 2005, the national register contributes to the controversy that has arisen to envelope the people's house.[9] Proposals for less party discipline, more free votes and a larger role for MPs on parliamentary committees originate in this atmosphere of uncertainty, although as one extensive study concluded, '[T]here is "no solid evidence" such measures introduced in other countries have boosted voter turnout.'[10]

Although by no means the original proponent, the same study adds its weight – at a time of much unease over political matters – to the cause of electoral reform. It recommends that 'Elections Canada be given the mandate to establish a commission of inquiry into the electoral system and to ask Canadians in a referendum if they want to adopt a system of proportional representation.' Using the language of the title of a well-known book, *Making Votes Count: Reassessing Canada's Electoral System* (1999) – echoed later in a study by the Law Commission of Canada, *Voting Counts: Electoral Reform for Canada* (2004) – the report argues that 'every vote counts (under PR) in a way that it does not under the existing system.'[11] The question to ask is, 'to what effect?'; the report's answer is, 'PR would make elections more interesting and competitive' and 'since the relative standing of the parties in the House of Commons would more clearly reflect their level of popular support the political system would appear more responsive.'[12]

The measured tone of that prediction contrasts sharply with the stronger language of other advocates of PR. Nick Loenen, then a director of Fair Voting B.C., described 'the House of Commons [as] a disgrace to democracy. It is our only institution that supposedly represents all citizens. But the government does not represent the fullness of the nation ... [M]ost votes do not count.'[13] Judy Rebick, holder of the chair in social justice at Ryerson University, and Walter Robinson, federal director of the Canadian Taxpayers' Federation, both of whom sat on the national advisory board of Fair Vote Canada, offered a similar diagnosis of the plurality electoral system: 'So if you vote for the person who comes in second, your vote is wasted ... [T]his routinely results in "faked" majority governments where the party that forms a majority (taking 51 per cent or more of the seats) does so with fewer than 50 per cent of the vote cast.'[14] For Ed Broadbent, former leader of the New Democratic Party, plurality elections are 'disastrous,' leaving the Canadian government 'dysfunctional' and 'millions of Canadians ... effectively disenfranchised.'[15]

The plurality electoral system is triply condemned. First, it is said to weaken national unity and national political parties, because voter support for Party X (say, the Liberals in western Canada) is never enough to translate into seats. As a result, there are few Liberal MPs from the region in caucus and even fewer in cabinet. Liberal governments appear to have no support in the west, when in fact as much as 20 or 25 per cent of voters support them there. In Ontario, in the elections of the 1990s, and in 2000, the shoe was on the other foot: there the Liberals won almost all of the approximately 100 seats, with half or slightly over half of the vote. The political geographic distortion that results from plurality voting was classically set out by Alan Cairns in 1968.[16] Second, the plurality system underrepresents women in the people's house. According to Doris Anderson, president of Fair Vote Canada in 2004, 'when New Zealand, Scotland and Wales changed to P.R., the number of women shot up dramatically.' 'Hoping to look good [parties] include a number of women as well as visible minorities on their lists.'[17] John Courtney, who has written extensively on elections, electoral organization, and representation, agrees, but with this caveat: Scandinavian countries, which use PR, rank highest in the world for the share of women in their parliaments; yet other PR systems, in Brazil, Israel, Greece, Italy, Ireland, and Malta, 'fall well behind the female share of MPs in Canada under plurality voting!' The explanation for the difference lies, he says, in history and culture.

> The representation of any group in an assembly is the result of a complex mix of institutional variables, electoral incentives, political strategies and cultural norms. The six Scandinavian countries at the top of the list of female parliamentarians share a number of distinctive features. They are all developed, territorially small, northern states with a history of women

playing a significant role in public affairs long before most other Western democracies.

Moreover, gender quotas were established in the Scandinavian countries either by these states or their parties to guarantee the election of a predetermined number of women.

Although Canada shares many social values in common with the Nordic countries, it is both structurally and politically different. Ours is a territorially vast, multicultural, officially bilingual and ethnically diverse federation with a unique representational and party history.

How Canadian parties would try to reflect that social diversity in their selection of candidates under a more proportional electoral scheme cannot be foretold with precision. For example, Canadian lawmakers and most of our parties have long resisted electoral quotas on grounds of gender and race. But should governments or parties wish to impose quotas, our current electoral system offers no institutional impediment.[18]

The third indictment is that plurality voting suppresses turnout for the reason given above – winners win, losers lose, and, barring some seismic political upheaval, the electorate knows which is which. PR, on the other hand, rewards a party's share of votes with a comparable share of seats. A vote is a vote is a vote and, as Courtney says, 'parties would have an incentive to encourage their own supporters to participate and voters would have less reason not to vote.'[19] Except that voter turnout appears to be independent of electoral system, and disaffection, especially among the young, knows no national boundaries.

All of these (and more) criticisms of the plurality electoral system are regularly rehearsed in the Canadian press and the academic literature. Organizational imprimatur has followed. In 2004, following the release of a discussion paper and public consultations in major cities across Canada, the 'respected' Law Commission of Canada published *Voting Counts: Electoral Reform for Canada*.[20] The report reviewed electoral systems and electoral options for Canada, discussed democratic values, and evaluated 'the implications of adding an element of proportionality to Canada's electoral system,' that is, using PR to 'top up' the plurality results with additional seats to reduce the discrepancy between a party's share of seats in the people's house and its share of votes. (Looked at from a different direction, after the 2000 election the Liberals would have received 47 per cent of the seats in the Commons compared with the 57 per cent the party won.) The president of the commission spoke of 'the distorted way politicians are elected to the House of Commons,' and of 'the democratic malaise, lack of connectedness in democratic institutions, inability of groups to be well-heard, cynicism towards institutions, lack of confidence ... There is a sense of fatigue about our democratic institutions.' She also said that 'the country's increasingly multicultural and diverse population ... is tuning out from politics in record numbers.'[21] The inference from the last statement is that a change in the electoral system will reverse that trend, although *Voting Counts* is more cautious in its assessment: 'At the very least, proportional representation systems "pose fewer barriers, to achieving demographically representative outcomes than do single member systems."'[22]

At one time women, visible minorities, and First Nations were excluded through disfranchisement. Low participation by these groups now occurs as a result of discouragement on the part of the excluded – why try? – and on the part of the excluders, who, because they consider women, visible minorities, and First Nations candidates less electable under plurality voting than candidates of their own kind – white, male, and middle class – look elsewhere for contenders. Whether a different electoral system than the one in place would produce a different-looking people's house is open to debate. However, that uncertainty lasts only so long as no other objective is being sought through change. According to political scientist Keith Archer, neutrality was not in evidence in the Law Commission's report. On the contrary, increased representation of previously under-represented collectivities – 'social engineering, one which changes the basis of representation from the principle of equality of individuals to a system of representation based on group membership' – was its objective.[23]

Advocates of change argue that statistics do not lie and that there is a smaller percentage of women, visible minorities, or Aboriginals in the House than there are in the general population. For that matter, the percentage of senators from these groups is higher than in the House. A crucial point to note about the 'mirror' argument is that it is all about appearances: X is not represented if X's member does not look like X. Yet, there are other ways of contemplating representation: as an activity – 'My member works for me'; or as a matter of choice – 'X is my member because I voted for him or her. If X had lost, I would have "wasted" my vote.'[24] In *Voting Counts*, these different meanings of representation appear seriatim.[25] Barring a change in attitude towards nominations on the part of the parties, it is not at all clear that any PR system – 'top-up' or total – will achieve the proportionality its proponents desire in six of the ten provinces whose provincial membership in the Commons varies between four and fourteen. In his brief to the U.K. Independent Commission on the Voting System (chaired by Lord Jenkins), British scholar Philip Norton expressed the following note of caution: 'Assessing the weaknesses of the existing system alongside the strengths of the alternative systems would be intellectually dishonest and potentially disastrous.'[26]

Representative government is about government as much as it is representation. This truth makes intelligible if not defensible in an age of electoral democratic values the low participation of Aboriginal voters. There may be 'alienation'; there may be a sense of exclusion from 'white man's politics'; there may be a legitimate scepticism that comes from scarcity of representation – all of this may be true. Still, to say this and no more is to misrepresent the momentum of Aboriginal politics. Similarly, it is a large leap, on the one hand, to talk of 'the failure of the House of Commons to reflect in its make-up the uniqueness and importance of the Aboriginal community of interest' and, on the other, to say that that failure 'calls into question the legitimacy of Parliament itself.'[27] There have been very few Aboriginal members of the people's house, but there has been a long history of bureaucratic as well as, more recently, executive-centred relations. As the National Chief of the Assembly of First Nations observed early in 2005, when the government led by Paul Martin appeared about to be defeated in the House of Commons, 'We have invested thousands of hours in consultations with the federal government, resulting in concrete action plans and proposals that could transform the quality of life for First Nations people. If Parliament were dissolved, this momentum and goodwill would be in danger of being lost.'[28] When the Royal Commission on Aboriginal Peoples reported in 1996, it implicitly dismissed representation in the Commons and opted for an Aboriginal Parliament that would 'supplement rather than substitute for self-government.'[29] While there has been no progress in the direction of creating an Aboriginal Parliament or of designated Aboriginal seats with members elected by Aboriginal voters, 'leaders of five federally recognized aboriginal groups were made permanent members of the Commons aboriginal affairs committee and will be called on to send a representative to committee meetings whenever MPs are studying legislation that relates to their constituents.'[30]

Institutionalized representation within the House of non-elected interests is unprecedented. Then, again, Aboriginal and First Nations collectivities are emerging as unusual communities. In 2004, then Minister of Justice Irwin Cotler put First Nations on a legal par with non-First Nations: '[I]f you look at it ... on the Supreme Court we have three judges

to protect the civil law tradition from Quebec, and we have judges protecting the common law tradition, and we have regional representation
for the purposes of giving expression to the diversity of this country ...
and so the question is ... "What about the tradition of First Nations?" This
is something I think we need to think about.'[31] Unprecedented but of no
precedent, since the Aboriginal Affairs Committee in the new House
after the 2004 election did not make similar appointments.

Explanation for the committee's unusual action was offered by an
NDP member who put forward the motion:

> It was so obvious to me that a bunch of white men in suits were sitting
> around the table passing laws affecting lives (of aboriginal people) and
> they were waiting their turn for a lousy five minutes at the table as
> witnesses.
>
> There's no genuine participation of aboriginal people in the crafting of
> aboriginal legislation and it's offensive. It smacks of colonialism. It's just
> fundamentally wrong.[32]

The logic of this argument is unclear. Is low Aboriginal voter participation the rationale for placing appointed persons on a committee of
elected persons – and if so, why limit the corrective to Aboriginal people? Is colonialism, present and past, the explanation for making
amends in this extraordinary way?

More than reconciliation is at issue here, and more than the political
disadvantage of a minority. Consider, for instance, one argument
advanced for changing the electoral system in order to compensate for
the obstacles encountered by women:

> This emphasis on territorial representation has the effect of muting non-
> territorial claims for representation, effectively rendering them secondary.
> The institutional manifestation of a territorially-defined conception of rep-
> resentation – our single member plurality electoral system – also places
> practical barriers in the way of non-traditional candidates or, more pre-
> cisely, non-traditional candidates who lack a geographically concentrated
> constituency. The most notable group in this regard is women who, unlike
> ethnic groups or gays and lesbians, tend not to live in geographically-con-
> centrated groupings. The most effective means of increasing the diversity
> of Canadian legislatures is to reform the electoral system.[33]

The people's house provides territorially based representation. Acting individually, the people who are qualified to vote select from

among the candidates on offer. The individual elector and the individual member, both territorially defined, are bound in a relationship defined by the length of a parliament. Historically, resignation by a member was not taken lightly, while switching party allegiance in the chamber was a matter of high drama.[34] By contrast, group or collective interests defined by race, or gender, or age, for example, generally lack a territorial dimension. An electoral system that favours the former over the latter will communicate a distinctive representational dimension. Whether one is preferable to the other is not the topic at hand. It is enough to say that representation of interests that transcend territory is traditionally viewed as falling within the category of lobbying activity.

Again, a discussion of interest groups is outside the scope of the people's house, except in the following respect: for a long time, at least since the era of participatory democracy in the late 1960s and 1970s, there has been a strong desire on the part of Liberal governments to enhance 'the participation of as many citizens as possible, [by] encourag[ing] the creation of specific groups to represent those citizens whose voice was not being heard. From ethnocultural and linguistic minorities to women, people with disabilities, consumers and the elderly, efforts were made to level the political playing field by providing assistance to those whose lack of funds and organization had left them mute in the face of strong, well-funded business and industry lobbies.'[35]

The Court Challenges Program, founded in 1978 initially to clarify the scope of language rights then protected under various provisions of Canada's constitution, was one example. According to a history of the program, 'Realizing that the costs of pursuing litigation involving matters of principle and the public interest can constitute a heavy burden on individuals and groups of limited means, the federal government of the time stepped forward and offered financial assistance to a number of litigants.'[36] To name any of these groups is invidious since there are so many of them. Yet, in the context of this discussion, the National Action Committee on the Status of Women is a relevant example. Significantly for a study of the House of Commons, some writers maintain that 'groups should represent the diversity of the society from which they emerge, and should even compensate for some of the representational failures of political parties, legislatures and executives.'[37] The authors of that statement go farther: 'We look to governments to make some effort to even out inequities between various segments of society.' At the same time, since funds from government might compromise a recipient's independence or appearance of independence, they suggest that 'an arms-length government agency with an explicit mandate to provide core, multi-year funding to groups representing marginalized segments of society and diffuse interests would go a long way toward depoliticizing the process of funding these groups.'[38]

Advocacy groups as redressers of defective representative institutions: that is one interpretation of their function, and one reason they cannot be ignored in a discussion of the people's house. Another is the proposition that 'advocacy groups may strengthen citizens' democratic values [because] ... the more citizens are mobilized ... the better democracy is secured.'[39] Since the House of Commons is the only popularly based institution in the Canadian government and since the democratic deficit, as defined by the Martin government and echoed by parliamentarians and the media even after its defeat, is confined to the operation of the legislature (committees and discipline, for example), there is an interest in common between the people's house and those groups that compensate for its representational deficiencies. Notwithstanding the mutuality of interest, broadening the focus of the discussion of the people beyond the electoral base presents logistical and logical difficulties, beginning with that of boundaries.

Whether correctives or not, advocacy groups are not part of the representational system. As discussed in an earlier chapter, critics of modern Canadian politics see advocacy or citizens' interest groups not as supplements to the legislature but as extensions of the executive – what Morton and Knoff call 'the state connection,' visible in government-supported language, ethnic, gender, Aboriginal, and human rights programs.[40] In contrast to this constellation of 'official' interests, there is a parallel alliance of groups opposed to government policy, as for example to firearms legislation.

Illustrative of these opponents is the National Citizens' Coalition (NCC), founded in 1967 and registered as a non-profit corporation 'independent of all political parties.'[41] The NCC claims that it does not 'lobby politicians or bureaucrats' but rather 'speaks directly to our fellow citizens through effective, well-organized, targeted advertising campaigns in mail, electronic and print media.' In 2004 and 2005, that strategy was evident in newspaper advertisements encouraging readers to write to their member of Parliament protesting changes to the definition of marriage that would legalize same-sex unions. Mobilization of public sentiment through the media to influence MPs' behaviour in the people's house endows the NCC with a measure of popular legitimacy that most advocacy groups cannot emulate. In this respect the NCC personifies (for it is a corporation) the values of electoral democracy.

Paradoxically, since advocates of electoral democracy are among the sharpest critics of 'activist' courts in the age of the charter, the NCC boasts in its literature achievements that it 'has won six landmark judicial constitutional court decisions challenging election "gag laws" – laws which would violate citizens' freedom of expression during elections.'[42] (Victory before the Supreme Court of Canada in 2004 in the *Harper* case would have raised the achievement to seven.) The monopoly of the Canadian Wheat Board and 'forced' unionization are other policies the NCC has opposed indirectly through support of court challenges from members of the public.

The boundary question mentioned above is this: where do these non-elected groups fit in the world of representation? That there is a place for interest groups in parliamentary politics there can be no doubt. But the signal characteristic of such groups (whatever their organization's constitution provides) is that they are not popularly elected. State-connected advocacy groups fall even farther into the legislative penumbra. Canada has no shortage of appointed representatives. The need is for a deeper popular electoral base, and for the same reason as that offered by Peter Riddell in Great Britain: 'The various alternatives to a representation system are unconvincing as a means of expressing the will of the people.'[43]

Whatever the conceit of the PMO, hubris of the media, or moral entrepreneurship of public interest groups, the House of Commons is the first, last, and only authoritative voice of the Canadian people. In 1995, two years after its founding, appearing before the Special Joint Committee on a Code of Conduct, Duff Conacher described Democracy Watch as an 'advocacy group ... that represents the citizens' perspective ... We have a small board of three people, ... an advisory committee of three people, and 250 supporters across the country.' He suggested that the committee recommend a check-off provision on tax returns allowing filers to direct ten dollars of additional tax to a national organization. 'It is,' he said (with no sign of irony in light of his audience), 'very difficult for the citizen voice to organize and band together ... We think there should be a group to represent a much greater percentage of Canadians than any organization in Canada currently does.'[44]

The voice of the people but one that speaks in the dialect of party; and it is party more than it is Parliament that is in disrepute. 'Put not your faith in politicians, for they will betray you': extreme perhaps; untrue normally. Still, promise breaking rather than keeping received court sanction in 2005. At issue was a request from the Canadian Taxpayers Federation to quash a health premium, imposed by the new Ontario government led by Dalton McGuinty, 'on the grounds that it broke an election promise,' indeed 'an elaborately signed contract promising not to raise or create new taxes.' In the words of the Ontario Superior Court judge (Paul Rouleau),

> Pledges and promises are made in order to garner support in an election campaign but also to inform voters of a party's plans and intentions. If every individual or organization that expresses support for a politician or party or votes in favour of a politician or party by reason of a pledge or promise made is then free to bring an action in contract against the politician or party to compel the execution of that promise or pledge, our system of government would be rendered dysfunctional. The courts would be called upon to rule on which pledges and promises constitute contracts. The voter or group would then seek to use the court to enforce the promise or pledge. This would hinder if not paralyse the parliamentary system.[45]

Constancy is to be expected from courts not legislatures. Governments have a 'temporally limited mandate,' constitutional democracy and its interpreters a permanent obligation to guarantee fundamental rights to all citizens.[46] The Glorious Revolution (1688-9) earned its name because the power of the crown was broken by Parliament. It would be an exaggeration to say that three hundred years later the power of the Canadian Parliament has been broken by the charter, but only an exaggeration. As the controversy surrounding the Martin government's decision to follow judicial decisions and bring same-sex unions within the legal definition of marriage vividly showed, legislatures today are limited. Do these limits contribute to the low esteem in which legislatures are held? Yet limitations on parliamentary power are what some reformers want, fixed election dates being a modern example. Nor is this response original: proposals to set terms, rotate offices, and look to legislators as individuals and not as members of organized parties are of long descent, in the English-speaking world, back at least to the Levellers. All are aimed at limiting the power of party and promoting the interests of the people. That being the case, why, in the cause of promoting responsiveness (the absence of which is cited as a prime index of the democratic deficit), does no one advocate a shorter life to Parliament – say, three rather than five years – and more frequent recourse to the people?

Who are the people and what do they want? The only answer to these questions is that they cannot be answered. The House makes no distinction among its members except between government and opposition ranks. The members organize according to party, as they have since before Confederation, and while within each party caucus there may be smaller caucuses devoted to the concerns of women or Atlantic members, for example, the House is remarkably free from visible divisions. Language has been the great exception. Otherwise, asymmetrical federalism finds no counterpart in an asymmetrical House. A member is a member is a member, each of whom represents the opinions of his or her constituents, and who together for the life of Parliament personify the people. Their claim, which given their position is hard to deny although largely unstudied, is that they know the feeling on the ground.[47]

And this is the case because of the single-member-district, simple-plurality-vote electoral system, because Commons committees are weak and special interests (to date) pay only modest attention to them and their members, and because of the strength of party sentiment. Despite the dominance of the political parties, parliamentary politics in Canada (as in Great Britain) is highly personalized: voter and candidate, voter and party leader, candidate and party leader. Joan Rydon, an Australian political scientist writing of legislatures, once asked the question 'What sense of life do its forms embody?'[48] In this discussion, the question becomes 'What sense of political life does the Commons embody?' The answer must stress both personality and partisanship.

One of the weaknesses of proportional representation enthusiasts is their susceptibility to numbers: 'They ... are attracted by PR's quantifiable and objective criteria: hard numbers. Democratic representation, however, is a less definite, less precise and more amorphous enterprise.'[49] (A comparable caution might be urged about turnout data, whose precise historic units confer legitimacy on solutions proposed to reverse their downward trend.) The sense of life the parliamentary form embodies is one of action as well as of representation. Adversarial not abstract, personal and partisan not impartial – these adjectives describe politics in the people's house. Yet these are the same adjectives that are used by critics to denigrate the chamber. In language familiar to any recent student of Canadian government and politics, a report commissioned by the clerk of the Privy Council in 2004 spoke of 'public institutions [as] "excessively adversarial."'[50] Traditional defenders of parliamentary government would agree, although they might substitute 'continually' for 'excessively': '[T]hose to whom power is entrusted are made to feel that they must resist in such a manner as to be prepared to meet the criticisms of opponents continually on the watch for any errors they may commit.'[51]

In this atmosphere and in this forum, where politics is so personalized, party discipline is applied to enforce order. In its absence, as Earl Grey observed a century and a half ago,

> discontent, ambition, the love of popularity, and even of notoriety, and various personal feelings, are found in practice to exercise so much influence, and must always be expected to array so many Members of the House of Commons in Opposition, that, unless the Government is enabled by some means or other to throw a considerable weight into the scale, by virtue of its official position, it is impossible it should exercise that authority which, as the very keystone of the whole system of Parliamentary Government, it ought to possess in the decision of questions submitted to the House of Commons.[52]

Grey's sensibility to the motivations of politicians was neither his nor confined to early Victorian England. A minister (and an extraordinary diarist) in the government of Margaret Thatcher confirmed Grey's appraisal: 'It is an awkward thing to say, other than to those one can trust, but policies are neither determined or evolved on a simple assessment of National, or even Party, interest. Personal motives – ambition, mischief making, a view to possible obligations and opportunities in the future, sometimes raw vindictiveness – all come into it.'[53]

Canadians are a federal people, and the conduct of federalism is an original and continuing preoccupation of the country's politics. The first and lasting measure of a prime minister is the conduct of federal (once Dominion)-provincial relations, be it the acquisition of territory (the rounding-out of Confederation) or the preservation of the union through national development and, later, social policies. Political union, economic union, and social union make up the skein of Canadian federalism. Notwithstanding the prominence of these themes in Canada's history, federalism is remarkably invisible in its Parliament. Concern about the poverty of intrastate arrangements in the institutions of the central government is of long standing. Critics who see the Senates of the United States and Australia or the Bundestag of Germany providing the integrative sinews necessary for an effective federation look in vain for a Canadian counterpart. Here is the backdrop for advocates of a Triple-E Senate. Senate reform through election is an issue separate from the people's house, except for the significant fact that its history is both brief and parochial. It is difficult to recall twenty years later, but before the late 1980s there was no proposal for an elected Senate, and when it arose, support was confined largely to the province of Alberta. Again, the explanation for these developments is outside the frame of this discussion.

One last point about the Triple-E cause – this time of direct relevance to the topic at hand – is that it was not a people's movement. Like electoral reform, it is an intellectuals' enthusiasm nurtured in the climate of academic seminars, royal commissions, task forces, legislative committees, and, most particularly in this instance, the Canada West Foundation. One of the great weaknesses of the Triple-E Senate proposal is that it is not a people's movement and that the upper chamber it envisages is a provincial and not a people's house.

By contrast, the House of Commons is a people's and not a provincial house. Structurally, there is no provision to mirror the federation in the chamber, except through the allocation of seats by province. As noted at the opening of this chapter, protective clauses today ensure that provinces do not lose seats at redistribution. The result of these guarantees is that, while the national quotient following the 2001 census was 107,220 persons, the provincial quotients ranged from 33,824 (Prince Edward Island) to 108,548 (British Columbia).[54] At a time when the spectre of wasted votes is summoned to criticize the single-member-district, simple-plurality-vote electoral system, it is surprising that the inequality that results from the redistribution formula does not attract more comment. As the chair of the Royal Commission on Electoral Reform and Party Financing wrote a decade ago, 'The size of these deviations cannot be justified politically or legally if the situation was to be challenged under the guarantees offered by the Canadian Charter of Rights and Freedoms.'[55] As another critic noted, 'Defenders of voting-power disparities between the provinces may justify the status quo by invoking federalism. But the right to vote is an individual right, not a right of the province.'[56]

The recognized instrument of federalism in Ottawa has been the cabinet. The scourge of the Confederation agreement, Christopher Dunkin, was proven right in his criticism of the cabinet (as in so much else). From the outset it proved unnecessarily large and unavoidably diverse in the quality of its members, because every province had to be present in its ranks.[57] Whatever its other weaknesses, in the palmy days of national parties ministers were treated as regional or provincial chieftains and in their persons integrated national and provincial politics. The disengagement of these politics and the amassing of power in the hands of the prime minister and his advisers has depreciated cabinet's claim as the buckle of Canadian federalism. On this point it is worth remembering that Canadian party leaders are selected at conventions by individual delegates voting secretly rather than by provincial delegations voting as a block publicly. Another conduit for injecting provincial concerns into federal politics is through the careers of elected politicians. At one time in Canada (as is still true in the United States), it was common for those with provincial legislative experience to sit in the Commons. (Indeed, until 1873 simultaneous membership in both provincial and federal houses was allowed.) Now, this form of interposition of interests is increasingly uncommon.[58]

A variation on the theme of parliamentarians' careers is the decline in the prominence of MPs with legal training. With a single criminal code and the common law in all but one of the provinces (and where uniformity of the common law has from the outset been the desired goal), law and lawyers played a nationalizing role in Canadian politics. In this context one thesis that deserves to be explored is Parliament's, but actually the House's, command of legal expertise at the very time when legal and constitutional issues demand so much attention because of the charter and the introduction of constitutional democracy in a world once monopolized by parliamentary democratic values. (In Canada's First Parliament, over 31 per cent of the members were lawyers; in the Tenth, more than 37 per cent; the Twentieth, 18; the Thirtieth, 21. In the Thirty-Eighth Parliament, elected in 2004, the percentage was less than 13.)[59]

A caveat to the afederal character and appearance of the people's house lies in the chamber's most prominent feature – the political parties. Until the arrival of the Bloc Québécois in the 1990s, no party seeking to be elected to the Commons confined itself to one province. Social Credit captured fifteen of Alberta's seventeen seats in 1935, but it won two seats in Saskatchewan as well. The Bloc was something new. During the period of the Chrétien government it acted largely like any other party in the House (for instance, it chose not to adopt the obstructionist tactics the Irish Nationalists pioneered a century before at Westminster), but after the election of 2004 and the establishment of a Commission of Inquiry into the Sponsorship Program and Advertising Activities under Mr Justice Gomery, it honed its claim to speak for the people of Quebec and for separation.[60]

A federal people in a house that eschews the regalia of federalism and in a Parliament that makes no alternative provision for their incorporation – reformers see the omission as a flaw and a reason for change. Those of another persuasion think that Canada's double federalism (territorial and linguistic) cannot be accommodated within one set of institutions, and especially in an era which itself finds the hierarchies of parliamentary democracy unattractive. As a federal people, Canadians look to civic associations and political parties and to interest groups and business organizations to realize personal federalism. Public federalism takes the form of intergovernmental agreement and accords, pacts, and ententes.

Canadians are a federal people, but that dimension of their lives is not well expressed in the people's house. Indeed, the Meech Lake and Charlottetown Accords constituted elaborate non-parliamentary responses to the unity issue. In so doing they offered ammunition to institutional critics who perceive a democratic malaise. Whether as a result of events outside of Parliament or because of the fragmentation of parties within, or both, David Docherty has discovered that 'an increasing focus on regional concerns during members' statements mirrors the increasingly regional nature of the House of Commons.' Significantly, in light of the focus of this study, they came not 'at the expense of local concerns but rather of national issues.'[61]

One can overinterpret a causal relationship between voter disenchantment and problems with federalism or the electoral system. Pippa Norris, for instance, has noted that 'similar patterns of declining institutional trust are evident in many post-industrial societies, including those like Sweden with PR electoral systems.' Of equal or greater explanatory value, she says, is '*multilayered governance* [which is] diffusing the process of decision-making to multiple bodies,' such as the European Union or the World Trade Organization.[62] Nonetheless, the massive *Norwegian Study of Power and Democracy* echoes one of Norris's central findings: 'Shape election systems so that government formation follows from the outcome of the vote and governments hold enough power to rule.'[63]

At issue is not the merits of different kinds of electoral systems or the respective advantages of institutional over electoral reform. More fundamental is the widespread and long-running scepticism about the honesty of politicians – at least honesty defined as politicians keeping their electoral promises. Absence of honesty thus defined, however, is not the equivalent of personal dishonesty. On the contrary, the public has a higher regard for the individual legislator than it has for political parties. The member is thwarted in representing constituency opinion (so it is said) to the extent that he or she must follow party discipline. How the MP would represent the multiple and conflicting opinions of tens of thousands of individual constituents is never analysed because the question is never asked. Party discipline remains a perennial subject for complaint because it is the essence of parliamentary democracy.

Canadian political scientist Fred Fletcher has said that 'authority comes from the Crown and from Parliament, not from the people.' Parliament, not the people acting through their representatives, makes decisions about public policies.

> But that set of assumptions is not widely understood or accepted by Canadians; I think that's fairly clear from the data. The deference to authority that marked off Canada from the United States historically is no longer as clear-cut as it once was; it's clearly eroding. The concepts of popular sovereignty and the independence of legislators are moving north, becoming much more widely accepted in Canada. I think it's reasonable to say that those perceptions of how a political system should operate are a little easier to understand than the more arcane arguments about the Crown and accountability through disciplined parties.[64]

To what degree does constitutional abstruseness contribute to the low reputation of politics and politicians? That is an important question, since it may help explain 'a growing body of public opinion that does not believe that politicians can solve the country's problems and, indeed, does not want politicians to solve them. This is the source of support for constituent assemblies and referenda.'[65] Legislators are irrelevant because they are impotent and embedded in a system that grants them no independence. True, or false, or merely exaggerated? The syllogism diverts attention from where it might more profitably be focused – which is not on the flaws of institutions but on the changing nature of the people.

At one time Parliament and 'representative, responsible government' were accepted without question[66] – literally, since knowledge of Parliament's workings was not a basis of the faith. This is no longer true: the decline of deference is the obverse of the rise of knowledge. Understanding the political system goes with knowledge; falling voter turnout manifests its lack. The complexity of the declension is seldom so clearly stated than in the following assessment by Paul Howe:

In 1956, people of all ages tended to vote regardless of their level of knowledge about politics ... In 1984, the relationship between knowledge and
voting started to change. As with political knowledge itself, the source of
the change was those aged 18 to 29. Whereas older Canadians acted much
like voters of the mid-1950s, in that the less knowledgeable among them
were only slightly less likely to vote than the more knowledgeable ...
among those under 30, knowledge started to loom larger in the voting
decision ...

   In 2000, these trends continued and intensified. Those in their thirties
and forties looked a lot as they did as 18- to 29-year-olds in 1984. Knowledge had a considerable effect (... a gap of around 25 per cent between top
and bottom knowledge categories) on whether or not they chose to vote.
Meanwhile, the youngest groups in the 2000 survey, the 18-to-29s,
increased the gap another notch, registering a more than 40 per cent difference in turnout between the most and least knowledgeable respondents.
The pattern of old does still hold, but only among those aged 50 and older,
for whom knowledge continues to have only a small impact on turnout.
Nowadays, then, it is only older Canadians who will vote simply out of
duty. Younger Canadians think differently; without some knowledge to
make the voting decision comprehensible and meaningful, they prefer to
abstain.[67]

Once the House of Commons enfranchised the nation. Now a growing
number of citizens – particularly young Canadians – reject electoral
participation as a necessary condition for political involvement. The
semiotics in an advertisement that appeared in the *Globe and Mail* during the 2006 electoral campaign indicates the transformation that has
taken place: 'Democracy is yours, own it! Your opinions = free music.
Under 25s can complete our 2-minute election survey and claim a free
music download! We want your views on how to improve democracy
in Canada.'[68]

7 The People's House of Commons and Its Study

The three variants of democracy discussed in this book – parliamentary, constitutional, and electoral – are not antagonistic models, although much is said in and out of Parliament that would lend support to that description. As already noted in chapter 3, decisions by the Supreme Court of Canada in *Figueroa* and *Harper* had the effect of broadening, even intensifying, political participation by individuals and, thereby, moderating the dominance of traditional political parties and the influence of large organized interest groups.[1] In that respect, constitutional democracy, which is identified (often negatively) with the charter and the work of the courts, enhances rather than constrains its parliamentary and electoral counterparts. Still, tension remains at the very heart of a system of responsible government.

The two Mr Smiths – Frank Capra's and David Docherty's – have little in common. Unlike his Canadian namesake, Jimmy Stewart's celluloid character never needs to engage in politics because he never sees the need to compromise. Like Preston Manning's Reform party and its successors, he is a severe judge of the existing (in the Canadian case, parliamentary) system, not just in the sense that party discipline is deemed oppressive but in the more important sense that politicians in that system fail to serve the people. Abhorring discipline, they propose coalition building in its place. But this is no answer, since the coalitions reformers propose are of interests, not of parties. Nor is it altogether satisfactory. Freed of party discipline, 'American congressmen and legislators,' says Peter Aucoin, 'are dependent elsewhere. In short, there is no such thing as an independent legislator.'[2]

Electoral systems are rooted in political history and are not some abstract, independent creation. In 2005, the Procedure and House

Affairs Committee of the House of Commons recommended against a national citizens' assembly to consider electoral reform for Canada. The model here was British Columbia's experience with a province-wide, publicly elected body whose single task was to study electoral regimes and propose one to be placed before the people of the province in a referendum. The Commons committee concluded that parliamentarians should have the final word on reforming the election process for the people's house. To this proposition, *Globe and Mail* columnist John Ibbitson countered, 'Why should they?' 'The electoral system ... belongs to the people, not to the politicians.'[3] Here was an unhistorical and constitutionally suspect position: the extension of the franchise – to women and to First Nations, for example – had been Parliament's to make; so, too, the abolition of multi-member seats, the drawing of constituency boundaries, the adoption of an electoral expenses regime, limitations on campaign financing, and more. All had been determined by Parliament. More than a description, however, the citizen as the DNA of democracy has been offered as a prescription, too. In the words of the Canada West Foundation, 'it is us [sic] citizens that must pick up the slack and reinvigorate democracy.'[4]

That language is not confined to exhortation; it is depreciatory as well. There is no end to the invidious parallels drawn between politicians and the archetypically unpopular used-car salesman or big banker.[5] The modern political grammar of dissent draws on familiar characters worthy of Frank Capra, except that now the language has general currency. The dominant mode of talking about the House of Commons today is to denigrate and parody the institution in the media and from both sides of the chamber. Nor have changes to House procedure over the past quarter-century, all intended to strengthen the position of the individual member by loosening to a degree the hand of the party whip, reversed the trend: cynicism about Parliament follows the reform of Parliament like a shadow.

Canada has a better House of Commons than its critics allow, and even, perhaps, better than there are theories to explain it. There is no single, undisputed explanation for this difference between fact and reputation. Nonetheless, an important contributing cause, and one directly related to the theme of this book, can be said to lie in the transformed interpretation of the role of member of Parliament. It is a common complaint on both sides of the chamber, in scholarly literature, and in the media that members are prevented – by parties, the courts, the prime minister, and the Prime Minister's Office – from doing what they should be doing, which is to represent interests – most specifically, those found in their constituency. The frustrated sense of unrealized potential is a thread common to all complaints. Everyone appears to concede that the current system is flawed, and it is constant repetition of that claim that gives it the appearance of truth. The problem with this perspective lies in the distortion it presents: the House of Commons is not a collection of disembodied expressions of interests. On the contrary, it is a concrete entity that does things: for instance, it acts (approves, delays, rejects), publishes, translates, meets, travels, and operates (with the Senate) a library (among other activities). Nor is its power delegated. Along with the other component parts of Parliament, it is a body with the full power to commit. It is the perception of the House as an institution whose primary function is to represent interests that explains the modern preoccupation with electoral reform. Interests go unheard, it is said, because the current single-member, simple-plurality voting system under-represents them or does not represent them at all.

Visually, the House of Commons offers support for the charge that it is uniform and unyielding to difference. Overwhelmingly Caucasian, male, middle class, and middle aged, to the uninitiated the chamber appears as ranks of identical MPs sitting to the left and right of the speaker, who, except for Jeanne Sauvé, has, since Confederation, always been a man, sometimes French speaking sometimes English speaking. Members are grouped by party, although that distinction is not visible to the observer; nor, for that matter, is the most important dichotomy in the Commons – the division between government and opposition. All members fall into one or other of the two categories, but the defining characteristics of 'official' parties and the determination of the Official Opposition (as well as its leader) are matters for the House through the speaker to decide. Bilingualism is recognized, federalism is not. In a material age, the iconography remains surprisingly religious, with oaths and prayers, and sits uneasily with the charter's guarantee of freedom of religion.[6] The superficial wholeness of the nation assembled is reinforced by the formality of rules and procedures that govern debate and perpetuate in the public imagination an image of Parliament at variance with its publicized boisterous partisan practices. All this said, the House of Commons remains, as one scholar has written of Parliament more generally, 'the most intense public image of governance.'[7]

Cabinet and caucus may be closed to scrutiny, but the Commons, even at a time when critics say it has lost its power, commands attention. Part of the current attraction lies in witnessing the hierarchical world of parliamentary democracy subjected to the horizontal pressure exerted by constitutional and electoral democracy. But the tension is not so uniform, or unidirectional; advocates of electoral democracy, for instance, never tire of attacking the presumptions and pretensions of proponents of constitutional democracy.

Yet there is a unifying theme. All three democratic variants – parliamentary, constitutional, and electoral – direct their indictments against the executive rather than the legislature. The issue, it is said, is lack of confidence in leaders who cannot be trusted to serve the public rather than private or partisan interest. In Canada in 2004 and 2005, the hearings and the Fact Finding Report of the Commission of Inquiry into the Sponsorship Program and Advertising Activities (chaired by Mr Justice Gomery), as well as the attacks by the opposition parties on the Liberal government led by Paul Martin, and the previous Liberal government led by Jean Chrétien, helped to condense and intensify the debate about trust that now envelops national politics. The question of trust is not a uniquely Canadian concern. The BBC Reith Lectures for 2002 had this very title; and their author, Onora O'Neill, the principal of Newnham College, Cambridge, maintained that '"loss of trust" has become a cliché of our time.'[8] It arises wherever there is reliance on professional and privileged knowledge – doctors, scientists, politicians, and, in Canada since Walkerton, possibly water-treatment engineers. Legitimacy once arose out of a ballot box; it was conferred not earned. Politicians no longer appear to believe in that morality. The want of confidence that is so favoured a topic of debate lies as much within the legislators as it does in the government, and it explains what Robert Skidelsky has described as 'a trust-denying audit explosion' on all sides of public, and not just political, life.[9]

Accountability is one of the big-topic (the cynic might say, op-ed) issues of the day, much as meritocracy was half a century ago.[10] Party discipline empowers the whips and, in turn, the prime minister and his officials, at the same time as it undermines accountability to the public and a modicum of independence for the individual member. The parallelism continues: government is not deaf to criticism in and out of the House, but instead consults the public (or publics) about its plans. Yet, 'the growing intensity of government consultation prior to tabling legislative proposals plus the increasing involvement of central agencies (for greater policy coherence) are intensifying executive resistance to change during parliamentary consideration.'[11] The response of the members of the people's house to this widening gap between the people and their house takes several forms. First, there is the demand for more resources, as may be found in the report of virtually any parliamentary committee. Often comparisons are drawn, individiously, with the riches U.S. congressional committees command. Uncomparative and constitutionally innovative is the call for 'Parliament [to have] sources and expertise equal to the executive.' Here the traditional understanding that 'executive power is co-extensive with legislative power' is reversed; legislative power now becomes the dependent variable.[12]

The problem with the concept of equivalencies between legislatures and executives is that, in a Westminster-like parliamentary system, it has no meaning. The executive is drawn from the legislature, its members continuing to sit as legislators. The essential feature of parliamentary government in a constitutional monarchy is the symbiosis of the three parts of Parliament and of the judiciary. Checks and balances, a twenty-first century prescription favoured by critics for 'reform' of parliaments, depends for its constitutional logic upon the existence of hermetic branches of government. Such is not the case in a parliamentary system where there is (quite differently) a tripartite division of power.

The theory of parliamentary government is not a subject that excites interest among elected politicians. In this they are representative of the public. Part of the reason in Canada lies in the high turnover of MPs, who have little time to learn the roles they are expected to play, and in the competing practical concerns associated with constituency demands. Debates in the Senate of Canada are more productive of discussion of constitutional theory.[13] The same is true of the U.K.'s House of Lords, although seldom so appositely as in 1996 on 'the relationship between the judiciary, the legislature and the executive, and ... judicial participation in public controversy.' Following a reference to the Queen's coronation oath wherein 'she undertakes "to cause law and justice in mercy to be executed in all judgements,"' that is, the oath which binds the judiciary, Lord Kennet continued,

> The words in the oath which bind the executive are those with which she promised to govern us, 'according to our laws and customs.' And her ministers must regard themselves as her delegates to perform that part of her coronation oath.
>
> The question arises: if that oath is, as it surely must be, binding on the executive, who, in the absence of constitutional and administrative courts, is to judge whether and how well it is being kept? The Government today intensely dislike judicial review because, some Ministers claim, it enables

the judiciary to restrict the sovereign rights of Parliament. In fact it does not do that, as has become clear in this debate. On the contrary, it is a means whereby the judiciary examines whether the executive – the Ministers themselves – have properly respected the will and the Acts of the legislature and whether or not they are breaking, by their executive acts, the laws which Parliament has, usually at the behest of that same executive and often under threat, made.

The judiciary is part and parcel of our customary system of internal sovereignty – 'the Queen in Parliament.' It is one of the three separate but symbiotic powers, and it is a capricious and self-serving contention that it should not have the power to preserve the authority of the legislature over the executive.[14]

Archaic perhaps, but not anachronistic. In a system of parliamentary-cabinet government, the oath of the sovereign to do good becomes the obligation of her ministers, and her judges, to fulfil. The presumption that the executive, or the legislature, or the judiciary should be dominant is false, as is the mechanistic conception of the three working in harmony through an array of checks and balances. By contrast, Bourinot's harmony, elaborated in the nineteenth century (before the Supreme Court of Canada became the final court of appeal, and discussed in chapter 1), arises when the people, the legislature, and the crown agree rather than disagree. No part is subordinate to another, although in 2005 the Supreme Court of Canada elaborated the relationship between the latter two. In *Canada (House of Commons) v. Vaid*, the court defined parliamentary privilege as 'the necessary immunity ... in order for ... legislators to do their legislative work.' That work, the court said, included the legislative and deliberative functions. Then, in unprecedented fashion, the court spoke directly of 'the legislative assembly's work in holding the government to account for the conduct of the country's business.'[15]

In this decision, the court stated that the core function of Parliament is 'to keep the government to account,' and it is due to this particular function (plus the legislative and deliberative ones) that Parliament enjoys rights, powers, and immunities that keep certain aspects of Parliament and its members' activities beyond the reach of the courts. (Upholding lower court decisions, the court found that parliamentary privilege did not extend to the power of the speaker of the House of Commons to hire, manage, or dismiss employees.) This was the first time that the concept of keeping government accountable was recognized by the Supreme Court as a foundational function for privileges of Parliament. The ambit of the decision is broad and, presumably, can be argued to encompass the auditor general, the official languages commissioner, the access to information commissioner, the privacy commissioner, and the chief electoral officer, whose privileges are protected when they exercise functions that are essential for members and senators to hold the government or the administration to account. The court did not go as far as to answer that question, and thus the debate remains open. Still, it is important to mention because the Senate ethics officer and the ethics commissioner of the House of Commons are covered by parliamentary privilege according to the recent constituting act, Bill C-34.

How important this judicial injunction will be for the future operation of Parliament, and the House of Commons in particular, is impossible to say. The probability is that it will be great, in part because it adds to rather than subtracts from the image the House has formed of itself. Thus rather than painting a rival picture, the court has heightened an existing dimension.

The subject of accountability is too broad to explore in detail here. Yet, it is too central to the topic of the people's house to ignore. One might go so far as to say it is the reconceptualization of accountability that is transforming the House of Commons into the people's house. Contrary to what is often said, concern for accountability does not originate in scandal, or the failure of politicians to keep their promises, or the collapse of mega-constitutional schemes. It is not even an obvious component of earlier public debate surrounding the Charter of Rights and Freedoms. Nonetheless, it is in the 1980s that transference occurs or a linkage is made between accountability and rights. Greg Tardi has argued that the first (accountability) is 'the positive duty counterpart' of the defence of the second (rights).[16]

Contrary to the depiction of rights as a distorting influence in legislative politics, in this interpretation they have exerted a subtle but pervasive influence. To cite one example: the Co-operative Commonwealth Federation in Saskatchewan experimented with legislating a Bill of Rights in 1947. That innovation is often seen as a failure, since it led to few prosecutions. By contrast, the human rights tribunal or commission route (used even later in Saskatchewan) became the accustomed method across Canada of dealing with human rights grievances. The significance of that choice of instrument led, in the words of an Ontario report, to 'human rights legislation [being] concerned less with punish-

ment than with attempting to win the offender to the community consensus.'[17] Effecting a settlement rather than settling a score was the
objective. Since so much of politics in the last quarter of the twentieth
century turned on matters of rights and entitlements, the influence of
this mode of resolution cannot be ignored.

In the context of the current discussion, it is relevant that the mecha-
nism for securing accountability personalizes and, as a consequence,
depoliticizes accountability. As illustration, there is a clear trend in
monarchical, Westminster-based parliamentary systems to turn from
ministerial responsibility as a concept that emphasizes tort or culpabil-
ity – the minister speaking for the department and facing down opposition demands in the House to resign – and, instead, to elevate what
some writers in Great Britain and New Zealand, for instance, describe
as amendatory or vindicative action. Accountability not responsibility
is the object sought. In theory, this approach depreciates partisanism;
legislatures demand information (and not heads) in order that mismanagement may not recur. By these means, say proponents of the amendatory or vindicative response, government affirms symbolically that it
cares.[18]

Controversy in 2004 and 2005 over spending under the Sponsorship
Program led the Public Accounts Committee to seek to fix accountability for spending decisions in the future upon senior public servants
(after the British model of appointing permanent secretaries as departmental accounting officers). In its 2005 report, the committee concluded
that such a measure would 'clarify the doctrine of ministerial accountability by making a distinction between a minister's policy role and a
deputy minister's administrative role while preserving the minister's
ultimate responsibility and accountability for the actions of his or her
department.'[19]

For the present discussion, the important point is, first, the broadening of the concept of accountability and, second, its migration from the
front benches of the chamber to committees of the House. And there is
more: in 2005, the Public Accounts Committee was reported to be contemplating laying charges (of contempt, perhaps) against witnesses
who were found to have lied to the committee. How this contemplated
action might proceed and what rules of evidence might apply were
unclear. Such was not true of one likely consequence of the initiative:
'Strong parties and strong committees cannot coexist.' That is the opinion of one of the few academics to study parliamentary committees
closely. The general principle, so to speak, in this matter is that 'the

strength of a legislative committee system varies inversely with the strength of the party system.'[20]

Rules changes in the 1960s, such as referral of estimates to committees, attracted academic study, but not rules changes in the 1980s, such as attempts to free private members from the thrall of party discipline.[21] The contrast is significant and the failure to study the consequence of reform in the latter instance unfortunate. Part of the reason may lie in the competing attractions – especially the charter and the growth of a rights scholarship. If this is true, then there is some irony in the explanation. The McGrath Committee (the Special Committee on the Reform of the House of Commons, 1984-5), whose conception of the work of the House and the rules therefore required remains the measure of the House of Commons twenty years later, argued in its First Report (1984) from what might be interpreted as a rights perspective: 'We do not feel that it is appropriate for only Cabinet Ministers to be responsible for the internal management of the House of Commons. The House of Commons is a community of many interests. They should be reflected in the way Commissioners [of the Board of Internal Economy] are appointed.'[22] The Committee (now Board) of Internal Economy has existed since Confederation. An 1896 order-in-council gave the prime minister the power to appoint (among others) its members. Until 1985 these had consisted solely of members of the Privy Council who were also members of the House. In 1985, following recommendations of the McGrath Committee, the government introduced changes that expanded membership to include members of the opposition. In 1997, another act was introduced to deal with the unprecedented number of opposition parties.

Herein lay the mustard seed of a prescription for participation: 'Private members [should] have an effective voice in the decisions governing the management of the House' – and here the rationale for restraining party discipline and leadership. In the succeeding decade it has germinated and brought forth not only stronger committees than before but also (hitherto rare) subcommittees. Furthermore, it has fed demands for the election of committee chairs and for placing committee chairs on a level with cabinet ministers at least as regards pay.[23] Whatever the issue, the direction of reform in the past quarter-century remains the same – from concentrated to distributed governance. This is one justification for John Ibbitson's comment above on the people's role in electoral reform, and it is the basis for the project of former MP John Bryden 'to make the people the partners in government.'[24] Broaden the base through incorporation of the previously excluded, and lower the barriers to influence by codifying the prerogative power (as in removing prime-ministerial discretion to seek a dissolution of Parliament).

The speed and extent of procedural change are important factors in this discussion. Contrary to repeated claims about the oppressive effects of party discipline, procedural change has been comparatively swift and extensive. More surprising (and also contrary to received opinion that 'pressure to change the status quo normally comes from outsiders. Independent auditors, the media, opposition parties ... are the arbiters of appropriate political conduct in Canada'), the impetus has come as much from within the Commons and from within the governing party caucus as it has from outside.[25] In this respect, the McGrath Committee's call for a reform in members' attitudes towards managing the House has been realized.

But with recursive results. Calls for the reform of Parliament remain forever attractive but of predictable content: well-known favourites include demands for more time for private members' bills, more free votes on bills, less party discipline, and greater autonomy for the individual member in caucus. Bob Rae labels the problems (for example, executive dominance and excessive partisanship) such reforms are meant to address 'political pathologies.' The remedies he recommends are notable for shunning the standard repertoire. Instead, they speak to greater 'citizen consultation,' on the premise that 'powerlessness corrupts, and absolute powerlessness corrupts absolutely'; to public service reform, because in 'an age of transparency ... the inner sanctum of government will have to become less hierarchical and more participatory'; and to a readjustment in public attitudes towards government – more realism and less rhetoric about what government should and can do.[26]

Do these reforms and would these proposals for further reform, which would see the legislature more in charge of the business of the House than has been customary for at least a century, make for better public policy – policy that is more national, or more regional, or more responsive? Or is it an act of faith to say, as one political scientist has said, that 'replicating the British practice of loosening party discipline on some votes would be a step in the right direction,' or 'adopting a different type of electoral system would do a great deal to resolve [the] disjuncture [between the formal electoral arrangements in which voters cast a ballot for an MP, not a party, yet parties form the only meaningful structures in Parliament]'?[27] What empirical evidence substantiates this claim? How is it to be reconciled with research in the United States on

Congress 'as public enemy,' or American democracy as 'stealth democracy,' where citizen distrust and suspicion of government remain high despite less strict party discipline.[28] For that matter, how can the claim be reconciled with British politics, not of today but of more than a century ago?

> Parliament at the end of the nineteenth century displayed many of the features – subordination to the executive, overcrowding of the parliamentary timetable, excessive burden of legislation, control by the party whips, decline of the private member – often attributed by the unhistorically minded to the present day.[29]

Or with Canadian politics of the same period?

> [A] strong bias in favour of the executive, as against the House of Commons ... is the most noticeable single characteristic of the legislature in its formative years, and appears to be part of one of the oldest and most honoured traditions of the Canadian House of Commons.[30]

Still, in the 'cycle of discontent' (the phrase is Rae's) that envelops the reform debate, punches leave their mark even when they are only verbal. Thus, in 2005, when the Martin government refused to participate in the continental missile defence system proposed by the United States, Preston Manning criticized the decision:

> The farsighted approach would have been for leadership on both sides of the House to build a bipartisan consensus on Canada's long-range interests in foreign and defence policy, including continental defence.[31]

Manning's metaphors are wrong, when applied to a parliamentary system. There can be no bipartisan consensus, if by that is meant a strategy of decision making. Except for the wartime Union Government of 1917-19, there has never been a coalition frame of mind in national politics, even though the opportunity, in the form of minority parliaments, has presented itself eight times in the last fifty years. Why this has not happened deserves close study for what it reveals about the act of forming a government, and about the expectations, presumptions, and calculations that lie behind a government's formation – on the part of all parties in Parliament, let it be stressed, and not just the one that forms the government. Where coalition government is the norm, in the Netherlands, for example, negotiations turn on many questions: the distribution of portfolios among participating parties and the allocation of spending priorities are two standard concerns. Significantly, representational considerations, which rank so high for advocates of proportional representation in Canada, do not top (or come close to the top of) the list. In his advocacy of bipartisanism, Preston Manning says nothing about the consequences of that course of conduct for the integrity of the opposition in Parliament. For a former leader of the Official Opposition, this is both curious and revealing, since it demonstrates that Manning and those who share his point of view see Parliament and parliamentarians as aligned in opposition to the executive.

Further evidence to support that dichotomous perspective lies in the antagonism towards and refusal to accept the prerogative. This perspective appears not only in matters of foreign and defence policy, where prerogative power exercised on advice is the sole constitutional authority for incurring international obligations (although it needs also to be said that treaties in a Westminster-based parliamentary system – unlike under the U.S. Constitution – are not self-executing and thus require complementary legislation), but also in the refusal in 2005 by the then leader of the opposition, Stephen Harper, to acknowledge the prime minister's discretion to advise the governor general on the use of the prerogative to dissolve Parliament. Instead, Harper maintained that the decision was not his alone to make.[32] The action of the opposition parties in defeating the Martin government in November 2005 and seeking to set terms to the defeat (for instance, when an election would be held) was without precedent. Still, it would be misleading to suggest that constitutional uncertainties are a monopoly of the opposition. Soon after he became prime minister in December 2003, Paul Martin in an interview observed that 'there ought to be parliamentary review of [Senate] appointments ... which no other prime minister has ever been prepared to do because I really do believe that what we've got to do is make this open and transparent so people have real confidence in the quality of the people who are being named to whatever post.'[33] The following day he retracted the proposal on the grounds that 'the advice I have received is that one house should not review another house of Parliament.'[34]

These examples of constitutional misstatement are cited not to parody politicians but to fix a fundamental point about parliamentary democracy: it is widely misunderstood by the public, the media, academics, and politicians themselves. Here again, politicians imitate the public. 'Political illiteracy bodes ill for reform,' a newspaper story announces, then concludes sombrely that, 'given this low level of awareness, how can Canadians have a reasoned and successful debate about institutional change?'[35] Asserting that much of that debate has been driven by a sense of disenfranchisement, the article cites as its cause 'the domination of elites and corporations,' the alienation of the regions, and the empire of metropolitan concerns. It is not necessary to agree with this diagnosis – one might want to state the problem more expansively: the public has increasing difficulty locating itself in politics, with the result that voter turnout falls while social movements grow – in order to be sympathetic with the article's conclusion: 'It's difficult, if not impossible to create a structural solution for what is, essentially, a political problem.'

It is for this reason that enlightenment about the political system is needed rather than rules changes in the House. Only from this vantage can the latent logic of the constitution encompass the competing claims of parliamentary democracy, constitutional democracy, and electoral democracy. Although the subject of this book is the House of Commons, the pre-eminent legislative chamber of Parliament, legislative power is not the sum total of constitutional law. The constitution embraces among other elements the crown, the judiciary, and the federal arrangement of power (itself a complex creation of compound monarchies, divided jurisdiction, and predominantly unitary courts). To this pluralism must be added the multidimensional personality of the people's house itself. There is its oppositional character and its governmental character; there are its representational duties, its legislative obligations, and its communication functions. The coincidence of activities within and the insinuation of influences from without (the crown and the Senate, for example) undermine a clear sense of institutional boundaries, notwithstanding the hermetic approach reformers often adopt.

Here is one reason institutions are less malleable to reforms than proponents of change assume. In the interests of clarity and to facilitate agreement on the place of the people's house in Canada's constitutional order, several questions need to be posed. Posed, it needs to be stressed, not answered; the distinction is important. The answer cannot be pronounced but only arrived at through discussion among all interested (and not just political) parties. It has been said that in the study of politics the prize goes not to the person who gives the best answer but to the one who asks the best question.[36] Whether the questions that follow meet that test, they are nonetheless fundamental queries. More important, they must be addressed as a prelude to anatomizing the people's house.

1 What are the prerogative powers of the crown as they affect the House of Commons? Dissolution is one; prorogation and the summoning of Parliament are others. These acts, carried out by the governor general solely on advice of the prime minister, affect all parliamentarians. The composition of the minority parliament of 2004–5 led to strong criticism of the prime minister's discretion in this matter and to proposals – phrased, paradoxically, in the language of electoral democracy – to constrain the power to dissolve and go to the people – in other words, to have fixed election dates.

What are the implications of fixed election dates for the operation of the parliamentary system? Could election dates be fixed at one level of jurisdiction in the federation but not the other? Could they be fixed in one province but not all? Legally, of course, they could; but politically, the thrust of change would be towards uniformity. How would this affect the election organization of parties, their campaigning, and their fund-raising? Would it increase or further suppress voter turnout? The answer, presumably, would differ according to whether there was one fixed election date, as in the United States. In Canada there has been a conscious attempt to keep federal and provincial politics (including elections) separate.

Another dimension of prerogative power is appointments. Constitutional monarchy is a governmental system based on appointment, beginning with the prime minister and cabinet ministers. This last is a constant source of confusion for the media, since they widely report governments and politicians as 'elected' and, therefore, have difficulty explaining why there is a government when there is no Parliament. The legal base of the responsibility of ministers lies in the Privy Council oath all cabinet ministers take on becoming members of council. It is the Privy Council that, according to section 11 of the Constitution Act, 1867, 'aid[s] and advise[s] in the Government of Canada.' At any particular time, the current cabinet is the active part of the Privy Council, although it speaks and acts in the name of the entire council. '[T]he Governor General acting by and with the advice of Cabinet [is] the first emanation of executive power.'[37] Ministerial authority for a portfolio established by departmental statute originates in a second oath ministers swear on appointment to cabinet, an Instrument of Advice and Commission under the Great Seal being the necessary formality.

Ministers are chosen by the prime minister, their appointment is recommended to the governor general, and their tenure in a portfolio is at the discretion of the prime minister. Ministerial dismissal or ministerial resignation occurs only on the agreement of the prime minister. Similarly, the life of a government is tied to the decision of the prime minister, since he or she is the sole adviser to the governor general.

Deputy ministers are appointed, and may be dismissed by the prime minister, as one of his or her 'special prerogatives.' That power is regularized in order-in-council going back to Sir Wilfrid Laurier's time. It authorizes the prime minister to recommend to council the appointment and dismissal of deputy ministers and the tabling of the order-in-council that does the same. Reaffirmed by successive prime ministers until Mackenzie King, it is now regarded as conventionally established. As with ministers, the prime minister's control over senior departmental officers underlines, first, the prime minister's importance and, second, the importance of the ministry as a collective entity.[38]

Governments that are responsible, in the Canadian understanding of that term, have an indirect popular foundation for their authority. The same cannot be said of lieutenant-governors, senators, judges, or the governor general, except that these individuals are appointed on the advice of the prime minister, who is indirectly popularly accountable. Lieutenant-governors have attracted little study for half a century, and an elected Senate, the latest iteration of a century-old campaign to reform the upper chamber, enjoys regional but not national popular interest.[39] Attention is concentrated because it draws on the interests and values of parliamentary and electoral and constitutional democracy, and on the courts and the appointment of judges. Actually, most of this attention is focused on appointments to the Supreme Court of Canada, while those to the Federal Court of Canada and the superior courts of the provinces attract little comment. Interpretation by the Supreme Court of the Canadian Charter of Rights and Freedoms constitutes a challenge to parliamentary democracy, reaffirms the higher-law values of constitutional democracy, and depreciates the claims of electoral democracy.

If with the prerogative power of dissolution the answer offered by critics has been to eliminate the power by statutorily fixing election dates, then with the power of appointment the answer has been to share that power with MPs in a manner analogous to the power of the U.S. Senate to advise and consent to presidential nominations. In either instance, the language employed appeals to notions of fairness and 'level playing fields.'

2 What is the scope of parliamentary privilege in the people's house today? Its antique origins and turbulent history mark important stages in the evolution of modern parliamentary government. How to reconcile parliamentary privilege, on the one hand, with constitutional rights and democratic rhetoric, on the other? Can there be prayers in the House at the same time that there is freedom of religion? Can television be denied access to a chamber when at the same time there is freedom of expression? If there are privileges, to what extent should they be codified, remembering that, once they are put into statutory form,

> it would not be Parliament and its machinery that would have the final responsibility of enforcing the obligations, it would be the courts. The constitutional obligation, at present non-justiciable, would have become justiciable. Whether that would be a desirable state of affairs would be open to debate. But it must be recognized that if the obligations of accountability are not accepted by ministers, both in principle and practice, as binding, and are not, where necessary enforced by Parliament, the remedy can only lie in reducing at least that part of our unwritten constitution into statutory form.[40]

How does parliamentary privilege affect (expand, or contract, or entrench) the powers of officers of Parliament?

At a time when Parliament as an institution is widely criticized and its members as a group are said to be distrusted, privilege, which places parliamentarians beyond the law, is neither easily explained nor defended. The logic of the argument that privilege helps members (and senators) in their job of speaking on behalf of the people is not immediately apparent to the people or to the media.

3 How does bicameralism affect the operation of the people's house? Parliament is the only bicameral legislature in Canada today, although at one time five provinces had upper chambers. How does the operation of a unicameral legislature in a large province, such as Ontario, compare to Parliament's operation? That question immediately raises another – what are the respective contributions of the House of Commons and the Senate to public policy? For instance, do the committees of each chamber duplicate or complement the work of the other? In legislative examination of bills, are the same witnesses and interests heard twice, or do the members of each chamber bring different perspectives to their task? If so, to what extent is that difference due to MPs 'representing' constituents? Is the way issues are defined and resolved different in the two chambers? Preston Manning's laudatory comments about coalition building in the U.S. Congress need to be seen in the context of that institution's strong bicameralism. To what extent is coalition building in one chamber a strategy to deal with potential opposition in the other chamber?

4 What is the role of the opposition in the House of Commons? Autocratic governments and impotent legislatures are favourite topics of the media and academics. Almost nothing is written about the Official Opposition or the opposition in general. To the extent that the subject arises, it is portrayed in partisan colours, or as a question of inadequate resources (the invidious comparison with the U.S. Congress being inevitable). How is the opposition today different from what it was half a century ago? To the extent that there is a difference, how much of it is explained by factors such as the nature and volume of work done by the House today as opposed to 1955; the transformation in reporting of parliamentary activities by the media; the replacement of intraparty and, thus, intraparliamentary federalism by intergovernmental negotiation (in other words, the impact of fiscal federalism on national political opposition)?

In this context, a comparative study of the New Democratic Party and the Co-operative Commonwealth Federation in Parliament and their respective relationship to the same party (and usually government) in Saskatchewan would pay dividends. It should be recalled that the NDP in Parliament supported the charter; the NDP in Saskatchewan opposed it for the effect it would have on the operation of Parliament. (The CCF's commitment to parliamentary politics in the 1940s and 1950s was a major factor in explaining its policy successes in these decades.) The charter, concern about Quebec and Canadian unity, and a shift from a regional to a metropolitan voter base have helped transform the party's view of its place in opposition. Is the same true of other parties' views? In all the talk about reforming Parliament, little reference is made to the phenomenon of the unintended consequences of reform. This is curious, since the maligned power of party leaders over their caucuses owes much to the introduction of leadership conventions whose intent was to take the selection of leaders out of the hands of caucus and place it with the party's rank-and-file members.[41]

5 How would altering the electoral system from one based on plurality voting in single-member districts to one of proportional representation alter the House of Commons? There is no conclusive answer to this question, since the answer depends upon the variant of PR chosen. Equally, it depends upon when the estimation is made – that is, before or after the first PR election, or after the fifth, or some other arbitrary length of time. There is a chain of causality to voting choices: what one did last time, or at the election before that, influences (though not necessarily determines) one's choice the next time.

The standard argument for moving to a PR electoral system is that under plurality voting interests go under- or unrepresented. That claim begs several questions: some interest or interests will always be under- or unrepresented; and even among those that are represented, compromise is necessary in order to reach agreement on public policy. In Canada, where population is dispersed unevenly across the country, with some provinces ten or more times larger than other provinces, but where representation in Parliament is nonetheless always distributed among provinces, how is proportionality to be achieved? In Saskatchewan (with fourteen seats), where almost half the population is concentrated in two cities and where the northern half of the province and the enormous non-urban rural south must have some representation, there are at most eight seats where proportionality can be contemplated. Under these circumstances, which Saskatchewan interests have to be heard in Parliament? In this context, it should be recalled, Saskatchewan has the same number of seats as Manitoba, and more MPs than any of the four Atlantic provinces.

The electoral system is about more than the representation of interests. Among other considerations, it is about national unity, effective political parties, and voter participation. These are complicated issues because representation – the product of any voting system – is itself complex. In any study of electoral change in Canada, it is crucially important that balanced research of all options be conducted. Nor need this research be confined to Canadian scholars or to Canadian data. A large authoritative literature exists in the United Kingdom and the United States – countries that have used plurality elections for several centuries.

6 Is party discipline inimical to the functioning of a people's house? The presumption behind the criticism of party discipline is that no one is supposed to like discipline, for the reason that it limits the independence and responsiveness of MPs. Few speak for the other side, although Claude Ryan, a former leader of the Quebec Liberal party, was one who did. He argued that responsible government is government by

a team who depend upon support of the chamber if they are to carry their will forward.[42] Another is Al Johnson, a senior policy adviser to the Saskatchewan CCF government and present at the creation of medicare in 1962. He has written about what a near thing that (now emblematic national) policy was, when the doctors struck, public emotion ran high, and some cabinet ministers began to wobble.[43]

What might have happened to medicare forty years ago is scarcely conclusive proof of the value of party discipline. Second-reading debates on great issues of public policy are not the staple fare of the parliamentary timetable. However, discipline is, on matters great and small. If discipline is valuable, then how and when is it valuable? Indeed, what is the role of the party whip? Scarcely anything has been written in Canada on this central office of party government. British practice, which is considerably looser than Canadian and is invariably cited by critics on this side of the Atlantic, should be studied not only for what is imitable but for what is inimitable. After all, the people's house at Westminster is more than double the size of its counterpart at Ottawa. More than that, Britain is a compact, unitary system and Canada a vast federation, whose regionalism is reinforced, indeed institutionalized, through dual language and legal regimes.

7 What is the relationship between the media and the people's house? The contrast between British and Canadian politics could hardly be greater than it is in regard to the media. London is the epicentre of print and electronic media in the first. Toronto, Montreal, and Ottawa, together, fail to play that role in the second. All Britons live in one time zone; Canadians are spread across six. The tyranny of distance and the invisible walls of regionalism challenge communication. Social theory of the 1960s said that mass communications (particularly television) would homogenize the nation state. That claim now appears extraordinarily unperceptive. Cable and satellite technology today permit narrowcasting, which can be used to make religious, linguistic, ethnic, or other singular appeals. In light of this development, do the media help nationalize or do they fragment politics? The people's house, which is the product of those politics, will look very different depending on the answer to that question.

Do the media privilege one democratic model or rhetoric over another, that is, parliamentary, or constitutional, or electoral? To what extent have the media helped create the tripartite division of democratic ideals? What is the influence of talk radio in Canada? How important is public broadcasting (that is, the Canadian Broadcasting Corporation and Radio-Canada) to citizens' perceptions of the people's house?

Should more be done to make the broadcasting of parliamentary activities – rules and procedures, principal debates, and committee hearings, for example – more accessible (that is to say, more intelligible) to the people? If, as is often said, the public feels unengaged by political debate and issues, part of the problem may lie in a failure to understand legislative processes and terminology. If the language of politics often appears intractable, impenetrable, and interminable, the explanation may lie not in the public's ignorance but in their superior knowledge – superior to previous generations and to that of many parliamentarians today. The issues that increasingly confront Parliament and that concern the public are complex – technically, scientifically, legally, and morally. The media have a central role in bridging the chasm that modern communications technology has helped create between the people and their politicians.

8 Are the people's house and the public interest compatible objectives? Even in the twenty-first century, in a parliamentary system with a constitutional monarchy the first principle of the constitution is the crown. Authority resides in it, and beneficences flow from it. Is the public interest articulated differently in a parliamentary system than in a congressional system such as in the United States? The question is relevant, because the referent in Canadian political debate on issues like reform of the upper chamber or introducing mechanisms of direct democracy is usually drawn from American practice. If, on the other hand, there is a divergence rather than a convergence of values between the two North American democracies, to what extent is this due to the presence in Canada of parliamentary government? How to explain the contrasting legislative responses in the two countries to such matters as gun control, same-sex marriage, abolition of capital punishment, hate propaganda legislation, and national medicare? What accounts for the acceptance here of the equality provisions of the Canadian Charter of Rights and Freedoms and in the same decade the failure to pass the Equal Rights Amendment in the United States? The public interest, as it emerges from Congress, is an accretion of individual interests, the product of negotiation and compromise. How is this different from the public interest that traditional parliamentary procedures produce? How do the different registers of parliamentary, constitutional, and electoral democratic debate affect conceptions and interpretations of the public interest?

The popularity of the Citizens' Assembly in British Columbia and consultative mechanisms elsewhere suggest a compelling reason to listen to pleas such as the following: 'Hear, Hear for Citizen Input: If We Want More Engaged Voters, Let's Have Less Partisan Scoffing at Citizen-Politician Dialogues. They're Key to 21st Century Democracy.'[44] Parliament is often described as dysfunctional. It is not clear what this condemnation comprises, although conflicting interpretations of Parliament's functions seem to be critical components of the indictment. During election campaigns, the media predictably report that some first-time voters will not cast their ballots because they see no policies on offer that speak to them. Does the people's house have a distinctive role to play in articulating these (or other special) interests? If so, how can it incorporate them into the public interest as refined in Canadian politics?

9 What is the place of values in the people's house? Values provide the prism for viewing modern Canadian politics. Studies of political parties and the electoral system for the Lortie Commission a decade and a half ago and electoral reform studies since then radiate values and judge politics, and the legislative system in particular, according to how responsive they are to the people's wishes. In this enterprise much is assumed but little proven. Are values isolable? Whose values are to be studied? More fundamental still, who are the people? The familiar question in legislative studies is, what do voters think of politicians? Equally as informative would be to turn the question around: what do legislators think of voters, which is another way of saying, what is their conception of 'the people'? This question has received little study in Canada, notwithstanding the elevation of legislative responsiveness into a cardinal principle of evaluation.[45]

That values consciousness has become more prominent than in the past is indisputable. Equally compelling as distilling the meaning of that phrase is specifying its origin. Any future study of the people's house must look at social movements or (less formalized still) social awareness, as reflected, for instance, in an exemplary letter to the *National Post* from an undergraduate university student in 2003: 'The use of clothes, demonstrations and marches as tools of intellectual debate must not be underestimated.'[46] How are such sentiments to be understood without the mediating presence of political parties? As political scientist Matthew Mendelsohn has cogently observed, 'Young Canadians support same-sex marriage, but don't vote. Older folk tend to oppose it, and do vote. What's an MP to do?'[47] Indeed – and how does less party discipline, on this question and others, lessen the perplexity? Discipline may not be the central issue. Is it an exaggeration to suggest that, in the matter of the people's house today and in the future, party discipline is a straw man?

Are the values that critics say people want in politics but do not find in political parties to be found in social movements? How then to bring values into partisan politics, which feed (and have since Confederation) the atmosphere of the House of Commons? Is the object in the future to bring social movements into Parliament? Can a social movement also be a successful political party?

Reforms propelled by the argument that the current House is unresponsive to values need to be analysed from the perspective of what values and whose, but equally important, which other values will be affected by the proposed reforms, and how.

10 What is there to learn about the people's house from comparative studies? Canadians are a comparative people. Perhaps because they live next door to a formidable power; perhaps because they lived as a colony, and then autonomous nation, within an empire; perhaps because they were the world's first parliamentary federation; or perhaps because they were mandated in 1867 to have 'a Constitution similar in Principle to that of the United Kingdom' – Canadians have demonstrated acute sensibility to constitutional comparisons. For the Royal Commission on Bilingualism and Biculturalism the interest lay in plural societies, such as Switzerland, Belgium, and the Netherlands. For the Royal Commission on Electoral Reform and Party Financing, the locales of interest when it came to voter registration were Australia, Germany, and the United States. Most recently, when the Gomery Commission came to look at ministerial responsibility, the comparison group was specified as the United Kingdom, Australia, and New Zealand.[48]

Always, too, there have been American parallels, but American exceptionalism in constitutional matters has historically qualified their application to Canada. Indeed, the origin and evolution of republican government in the United States provided a metaphorical backdrop to Canada's parliamentary experiment in the Western hemisphere. The transformation in Canadian attitudes towards American constitutional forms and practices in the last quarter of the twentieth century have generally gone unacknowledged and unstudied. Yet for no subject could this intellectual evolution hold more import than the people's house. Nor is the influence unidimensional: constitutional democracy has looked to American courts (particularly the U.S. Supreme Court) and entrenched rights; electoral democracy to mechanisms of direct democracy; and parliamentary democracy to congressional control of the executive. Where Westminster once held a patent on acceptable political innovation, today there is a free market in choice.

Still, too much can be made of comparison. Canada, the United Kingdom, Australia, and New Zealand share a common constitutional tradition – including a common sovereign – but they are distinctive entities. In the matter of the people's house, the claim to parliamentary privilege in Canada is not the same as in the United Kingdom. Similarly, conceptions of ministerial responsibility differ between each member of the quartet. The roles of committees and their chairs and the extent of party discipline in (and out) of committees vary as well. Again, Canada has a longer and fuller experience with officers of Parliament than the other Westminster systems.

Thus, when studying Canada, it is important to recognize the country's historical and constitutional distinctiveness, especially as it is revealed in and reinforced by its only national elected institution. The nation's economy and popular culture may have escaped its territorial confines. The same cannot be said of its politics. Almost antiquely, the constitution allows the reach of the past to continue into the present. How to deal with this reality is a matter as much (or more) for domestic as for comparative study.

Studies of the prerogative, privilege, bicameralism, opposition, electoral reform, party discipline, the media, the concept of the public interest, values, and the contribution of comparative research illustrate but do not exhaust what must be done before the House of Commons is ready to contemplate fundamental reform in any of these areas. The adjective is appropriate because change in any one of these areas will necessitate compensatory change in others. Even before the studies, however, it is vital that there be investigation of the object of the exercise – what is being sought? Unless there is agreement on the nature of the quest, there will never be consensus on its fulfilment. In a review of one volume in the Canadian Democratic Audit series, an Australian commentator wrote: 'It is arguable that a democratic audit that starts from [a] democratic deficit or democratic malaise undertakes more than an accounting of Canadian citizenship and democracy: it seeks to transform it.'[49] Whether that is a sound assessment of this particular volume is beyond the scope of this discussion. It is immaterial as well, except for the implicit warning it contains – never assume. Too little is known about the House and the conventions and provisions of the constitution that touch upon its work to advocate fundamental change in the absence of close research.

8 Conclusion

Among famous literary first words, few can be more memorable than Steven Shapin's introductory sentence to *The Scientific Revolution*: 'There is no such thing as the Scientific Revolution, and this is a book about it.'[1] A comparable epigrammatic remark could be made of the people's house, in the sense that while the lower chamber has always provided a common place for common people, it has never been that alone. To think of it (or any legislative body in Canada) solely in representational terms, which is the tone proponents for PR communicate – 'STV will lead to a government with a much broader representation of perspectives. It will reflect much more the diversity of the electorate'[2] – is to forget what British constitutional scholar Barry Winetrobe urges should be remembered: 'Parliaments are multi-layered institutions in themselves.' To be specific: '[They] operate on many different, though often inter-related, levels, both in terms of formal proceedings (plenary and committee meetings; PQs [question period] etc) and informal activity (both within and [without] the four walls of the parliament itself), and in terms of activity by individual members, party groups, cross-party groups, and various sub-structures such as committees.'[3]

Parliament is about talking – in three 'democratic' registers now – but it is also about doing. Legislating is a complicated business, and all of it is conveyed at second hand by the media to the public. Winetrobe is not the only commentator to propose that Parliament (in Great Britain, but the same has been said of Parliament in Canada) promote itself. Where he stands apart is in the reason he advances for this strategy.

> It is not simply a PR or public information exercise, but also enables a parliament to fulfil its real role and functions effectively. It also requires a par-

liament to think fundamentally about what it is and what it is for. It can provide a framework for such thinking, which, to be effective, must be relevant and related to the unique political and constitutional environment within which a particular parliament operates.[4]

But is self-study enough? Or is Parliament, and more precisely in the context of this discussion, the people's house, too important to the Canadian people to be left to the design of parliamentarians? Is there a need for a national inquiry, even a royal commission on the constitution? Its terms of reference would include study of the law, conventions, usages, and customary understandings that guide parliamentary government in Canada. More than that, it would look at the participants, issues, and questions raised at the end of chapter 7, according to the multiple reference frames they present for constitutional analysis. Only then will it be known whether the new politics of social movements, of parliamentary-, constitutional-, and electoral-democratic visions, of instantaneous communication, and more, actually decentres Parliament in the Canadian political system.

Donald Savoie, who has written authoritatively on the public service and on central agencies such as the Prime Minister's Office, saw in 2005 'a major debate looming in this country about how we govern ourselves.'[5] The perennial problem of Canadian unity is one inference to be drawn from that comment, but equally credible would be the effect, for instance, of electoral reform on the operation of the people's house. What happens to the concept of the opposition in a system of parliamentary responsible government? What will be the effect of PR on the integrative and absorptive capacity of national political parties?

Unlikely as it may seem at the present time, Savoie's intimation of a gathering constitutional storm could include a campaign to abolish monarchy in favour of a parliamentary republic. While there has been virtually no public debate on the question, and no movement to give the cause institutional expression, the argument that Canada should take the last constitutional (and symbolic) step on the road from 'colony to nation' could prove attractive to a future political leader. This comment should be treated less as a prediction than a caution: constitutional change of this magnitude – altering the first principle of Canadian government – should not take place in an unhistorical and intellectual vacuum. The subject of transforming Canada to a republic goes beyond the present discussion but is not unrelated to it. The crown is one part of a tripartite Parliament. The charter and the language of constitutional and electoral democracy notwithstanding, sovereignty in Canada rests in the crown and not the people. A republic, even a hard-faced, bourgeois arrangement of power devoid of fervour, would signal an alteration in fundamental commitment, one that would presumably have philosophical and philological implications for the concept of the people and their chamber. Constitutional change that is ad hoc, reflexive, or directed by political or electoral calculation will do nothing to counter the critics' charge that the political system lacks real legitimacy and displays only its shell instead.

The Constitution Act, 1867, concerns itself largely with the institutions and jurisdictions of federalism. The workings of responsible government – the hinge of Canadian democracy – must be divined from the preambular statement about 'a Constitution similar in Principle to that of the United Kingdom.' The meaning of this statement for Canada is worthy of a treatise in its own right. But its meaning in the British context warrants attention too. The British constitution could be amended by usage, a practice that blinded British politicians to constitutional matters – politics and the constitution were one.[6] It was this context (perhaps only this context) that made a Whig interpretation of history – the idea of progressive, peaceful change – possible, and that awarded central importance to Parliament. From this perspective, Parliament *is* English (or British) history: Walpole, Pitt, Gladstone, Lloyd-George, Churchill, Atlee, Thatcher, Blair. Thus, the importance of political history and, equally, its study. The continuity between present and past is visible.

The same cannot be said of Canada. Or, paradoxically, it can, in the sense that British prime ministers were for a long time imperial prime ministers and the referent for Canadian observers – at least until after the First World War, and even then disengagement from empire remained a strong political theme. Bourinot and W.P.M. Kennedy, for example, were students of the Empire and Canada's evolving autonomy within it.[7] This is not a history that infuses a parliamentary tradition. Instead of a sense of the majestic unfolding of a story whose last chapter has already been written, the deepest impression (and the one MPs exude) is what Raphael Samuel, the Marxist historian and opponent of the Whig interpretation, labels 'period[s] of trial and tribulation.'[8] In Canada, these take the form of anxiety about national unity, which since the very close referendum result in Quebec endorsing federalism in 1995 has grown, and about various other concerns: regional alienation and regional inequality; First Nations and their place in the

Canadian story (and in the people's house); absorption – at one time territorially, now economically and culturally – by the United States. This is why there is no Thomas Macaulay or George Macaulay Trevelyan in Canada's history to proclaim the importance of its Parliament: what is there to celebrate in the past for its influence on the present? Since the time of R. MacGregor Dawson, James Mallory, and Norman Ward, interest in Parliament among political scientists has declined.

The politician as scapegoat is the substitute for praising famous men. Nor is obloquy conducive to constitutional precision. Governments are not elected, they are appointed. Governments do not have terms (Jean Chrétien was prime minister once – for ten years: Pierre Trudeau twice – for sixteen years). The prime minister does not appoint but recommends appointments to the governor general; ministers do neither. When Parliament is dissolved, there are no members of Parliament. Parliament in all its parts speaks for the Canadian people, but members of the people's house are directly accountable to them as well.

The need for political education is so great that it becomes another reason to look seriously at a comprehensive study of the constitution. T.H.B. Symons, himself personally acquainted with the work of several commissions of inquiry, has cited as one reason for their appointment the 'masterful understatement' of Lord Haldane: '[T]he duty of investigation and thought, as a preliminary to action, might with great advantage be more definitely recognized.'[9] 'Commissions can,' Symons says, 'play a vital role in educating both government and the general public about political and public policy matters.' He usefully notes that inquiries are about much more than their report. As the Gomery Commission demonstrated in 2004 and 2005, they are about their hearings and activities, and public and media commentary on both, which continues until after the appearance of the final report.

Neither the media, nor Parliament, nor Canada's educational system is doing an adequate job of explaining Parliament's functions. The crown and the Senate are subjects separate from this discussion, although education of the public about their work is recognized as deficient.[10] Arguably, negligence with respect to the House of Commons is the most damaging of all. The other parts of Parliament are not elected; the people's house is, and the putative breach between elector and elected, revealed in the unresponsiveness of the latter to the former that is said to exist, stands as a damning if inadequately investigated charge.

The conceptual fragmentation of Parliament, evident in the rivalry between the parliamentary-, constitutional-, and electoral-democratic interpretations of its essential role, is a new phenomenon and, as this book has argued, a spurious one. Reconciliation is possible. Where once the people's house incorporated the nation and enfranchised its inhabitants, it can today accommodate a parliamentary system that has as its fundamental characteristics respect for a higher law, on the one hand, and enhanced popular participation in politics, on the other.

Notes

Preface

1 Kenneth Minogue, 'Democracy as a *Telos*,' in Ellen Frankel Paul, Fred D. Miller, Jr, and Jeffrey Paul, eds, *Democracy* (New York: Cambridge University Press, 2000), 209.

1. The State of the Commons

1 Alpheus Todd, *On Parliamentary Government in England: Its Origins, Development, and Practical Operation*, 2nd ed., 2 vols (London: Longmans, Green and Co., 1889), 2: 112, as cited in General Index, Journals of House of Commons (Westminster), vols 1–17: 425.

2 Janet Ajzenstat, Paul Romney, Ian Gentles, and William D. Gairdner, eds, *Canada's Founding Debates* (Toronto: Stoddart, 1999), 271.
3 George Stead Veitch, *The Genesis of Parliamentary Reform* (London: Constable and Co., 1913), 349 (as cited in *Journal*, 1817–18, Creevey Papers, I: 287, ed. Sir H. Maxwell, 1903).
4 F. Max Muller, ed., *Memoirs of Baron Stockmar* (London: Longmans, Green and Co., 1872), 2: 550.
5 See, for instance, F. Leslie Seidle, 'Expanding the Federal Democratic Reform Agenda,' *Policy Options* 25, no. 9 (October 2004): 48–53.
6 See Todd, *On Parliamentary Government in England*, and J.G. Bourinot, 'Canadian Studies in Comparative Perspective: Parliamentary Compared with Congressional Government,' *TRSC*, Section II (1893), 77–108.
7 Philip Corrigan and Derek Sayer, *The Great Arch: English State Formation as Cultural Revolution* (Oxford: Basil Blackwell, 1985), 29.
8 *Reference re: Secession of Quebec*, [1998] 2 SCR 217.
9 Bourinot, 'Canadian Studies in Comparative Perspective,' 82.
10 R. Kenneth Carty and W. Peter Ward, 'The Making of a Canadian Political Citizenship,' in R. Kenneth Carty and W. Peter Ward, eds, *National Politics and Community in Canada* (Vancouver: University of British Columbia Press, 1986), 73–4; and David E. Smith, 'Indices of Citizenship,' in Pierre Boyer, Linda Cardinal, and David Headon, eds, *From Subjects to Citizens: A Hundred Years of Citizenship in Australia and Canada* (Ottawa: University of Ottawa Press, 2004), 19–30.
11 Norman Ward, *The Canadian House of Commons: Representation*, 2nd ed. (Toronto: University of Toronto Press, 1963), 205.
12 See, for example, Elections Canada On-Line, Elections Canada: Media: Statements and Speeches, 'Symposium on Electoral Participation in Canada,' Speech by Jean-Pierre Kingsley, 21 March 2003, www.elections.ca.
13 J.A.R. Marriott, *Second Chambers: An Inductive Study in Political Science* (Oxford: Clarendon Press, 1910), 270. Hence the 'paradox,' says the author, that 'while the opinions of its leading members ... command respectful attention ... the collective opinion of the House counts for little.'
14 Sir John Willison, *Reminiscences: Political and Personal* (Toronto: McClelland and Stewart, 1919), 122.
15 See John English, *The Decline of Politics: The Conservatives and the Party System, 1901–20* (Toronto: University of Toronto Press, 1977); and *DLAUC*, 10 June 1851 (X.1.1851), 320 (Henry John Boulton).
16 James (Viscount) Bryce, *Canada: An Actual Democracy* (Toronto: Macmillan, 1921), 17.
17 Neil Nevitte, *The Decline of Deference: Canadian Value Change in Cross-National Perspective* (Peterborough: Broadview Press, 1996).

18 Paul Smith, ed., *Bagehot: The English Constitution* (Cambridge: Cambridge University Press, 2001), ix. According to Smith, Todd's Australian counterpart was W.E. Hearne, professor of history and political economy at the University of Melbourne.

19 C.E.S. Franks, 'The Canadian Senate in Modern Times,' in Serge Joyal, ed., *Protecting Canadian Democracy: The Senate You Never Knew* (Montreal and Kingston: McGill-Queen's University Press, 2003), 155f.

20 Lorraine Eisenstat Weinrib, 'Canada's Constitutional Revolution: From Legislative to Constitutional State,' *Israel Law Review* 33, no. 1 (Winter 1999): 38.

21 Pippa Norris, *Democratic Phoenix: Reinventing Political Activism* (Cambridge: Cambridge University Press, 2002), 189–91.

22 Bruce Ackerman, 'The New Separation of Powers,' *Harvard Law Review* 113 (January 2000): 694–5.

23 For more on the officers of Parliament, see chapter 4.

24 C.E.S. Franks, *The Parliament of Canada* (Toronto: University of Toronto Press, 1987). A decade earlier, and with a less catholic perspective, there was John B. Stewart, *The Canadian House of Commons: Procedure and Reform* (Montreal and Kingston: McGill-Queen's University Press, 1977), and a decade later, David C. Docherty, *Mr Smith Goes to Ottawa: Life in the House of Commons* (Vancouver: University of British Columbia Press, 1997). A book of essays with contributions by Franks and Stewart, among others, is John C. Courtney, ed., *The Canadian House of Commons: Essays in Honour of Norman Ward* (Calgary: University of Calgary Press, 1985).

In addition, two books on the Senate appeared in 2003: Joyal, ed., *Protecting Canadian Democracy: The Senate You Never Knew*, and David E. Smith, *The Canadian Senate in Bicameral Perspective* (Toronto: University of Toronto Press). Apart from these individually authored works, the three collections cited in note 25, and two other collections of papers by parliamentary interns – Jean-Pierre Gaboury, ed., *The Canadian House of Commons Observed* (Ottawa: University of Ottawa Press, 1979), and Magnus Gunther and Conrad Winn, eds, *House of Commons Reform* (Ottawa: Parliamentary Internship Program, 1991) – no other scholarly studies of the chambers of Parliament have appeared in the last forty years.

Two exceptions to that generalization should be noted: first, the Reference Section of the Library of Parliament publishes numerous technical studies and reports of the work of Parliament; second, John A. Fraser, a former speaker of the House, wrote *The House of Commons at Work* (Montreal and Fredericton: Editions de la Chenelière, 1993), a work he describes as intended for 'high school students, their teachers ... [and] ordinary Canadians,' x.

A new, synoptic treatment of Canadian legislatures is David C. Docherty, *Legislatures* (Vancouver: University of British Columbia Press, 2005).

25 These publications generally take two forms: collections of conference papers and monographs. Of the first, see Janet Ajzenstat, ed., *Canadian Constitutionalism, 1791–1991* (Ottawa: Canadian Study of Parliament Group, [1992]); F. Leslie Seidle and Louis Massicotte, eds, *Taking Stock of 150 Years of Responsible Government in Canada* (Ottawa: Canadian Study of Parliament Group, 1999); and F. Leslie Seidle and David C. Docherty, eds, *Reforming Parliamentary Democracy* (Montreal and Kingston: McGill-Queen's University Press, 2003). For an example of the second, see Jonathan Malloy, 'The "Responsible Government Approach" and Its Effects on Canadian Legislative Studies' (Ottawa: Canadian Study of Parliament Group, 2002).

26 'Media and Public Appearances,' Democracy Watch on-line, nd, http://www.dwatch.ca/allmedia.htm (28 October 2004).

27 http://www.fairvotecanada.org/fvc.php/ (17 March 2005).

28 Jeffrey Simpson, *The Friendly Dictatorship* (Toronto: McClelland and Stewart, 2001); Michael Bliss, 'Southern Republic and Northern Dictatorship,' *National Post*, 6 September 2002, A18, and 'Canada's House of Ill Repute,' *National Post*, 14 May 2005, A1 and A6; Donald J. Savoie, *Governing from the Centre: The Concentration of Power in Canadian Politics* (Toronto: University of Toronto Press, 1999).

29 R. MacGregor Dawson, *Constitutional Issues in Canada, 1900–1931* (Toronto: Oxford University Press, 1933).

30 G. Calvin Mackenzie, *Scandal Proof: Do Ethics Laws Make Government Ethical?* (Washington: Brookings Institution Press, 2002), 34.

31 Canada West Foundation, *Re-Inventing Parliament ... A Conference on Parliamentary Reform*, 25–6 February 1994 (Calgary: Canada West Foundation, 1994), 2.

32 Seidle, 'Expanding the Federal Democratic Reform Agenda.'

33 See Gordon Stewart, *The Origins of Canadian Politics: A Comparative Approach* (Vancouver: University of British Columbia Press, 1986); David E. Smith, *The Regional Decline of a National Party: Liberals on the Prairies* (Toronto: University of Toronto Press, 1981); David E. Smith, 'Party Government, Representation and National Integration in Canada,' in Peter Aucoin, ed., *Party Government and Regional Representation in Canada* (Toronto: University of Toronto Press in cooperation with the Royal Commission on the Economic Union and Development Prospects for Canada, 1985), 1–68.

34 Peter H. Russell, *Constitutional Odyssey: Can Canadians Become a Sovereign People?* (Toronto: University of Toronto Press, 1992).

35 *Reference re: Secession of Quebec*, para. 72.

36 Hilda Kuper, 'The Language of Sites in the Politics of Space,' *American Anthropologist* 74 (1992): 421.
37 William Kilbourn, *The Firebrand: William Lyon Mackenzie and the Rebellion in Upper Canada* (Toronto: Clarke, Irwin and Co., 1956), xii.
38 Quoted in E.P. Thompson, *The Making of the English Working Class* (London: Penguin Books, 1968), 99.

2. Parliamentary Democracy

1 Phillippe Séguin, 'Reflections on the Future of Parliament and Democracy,' *CPR* 25, no. 4 (Winter 2002–3): 6.
2 Roy Miki, *Redress: Inside the Japanese Canadian Call for Justice* (Vancouver: Raincoast Books, 2004), 24 and 46.
3 Lorraine Eisenstat Weinrib, 'Canada's Constitutional Revolution: From Legislative to Constitutional State,' *Israel Law Review* 33, no. 1 (Winter 1999): 21.
4 See *Sauvé v. Canada (A.G.)*, [1993] 2 SCR 438; *Andrews v. Law Society (British Columbia)*, [1989] 1 SCR 143; and *R. v. Big M Drug Mart Ltd.*, [1985] 1 SCR 295. For a comparative examination of admission and exclusion practices, see Louis Massicotte, André Blais, and Antoine Yoshinaka, *Establishing the Rules of the Game: Election Laws in Democracies* (Toronto: University of Toronto Press, 2004).
5 *New Brunswick Broadcasting Co. v. Nova Scotia (Speaker of the House of Assembly)*, [1993] 1 SCR 319.
6 See Rt Hon. Beverley McLachlin, 'Reflections on the Autonomy of Parliament,' *CPR* 27, no. 1 (Spring 2004): 4–7. *See Canada (House of Commons) v. Vaid*, [2005] 1 SCR 667: 'Legislative bodies created by the Constitution Act, 1867 do not constitute enclaves shielded from the ordinary law of the land ... However, if the existence and scope of a privilege has not been authoritatively established, the court will be required to test the claim against the doctrine of necessity, the foundation of all parliamentary privilege.' Para. 29 (1) and (5).
7 Norman Ward, 'Called to the Bar of the House of Commons,' *CBR* (May 1957): 529–46.
8 A. Beauchesne, *Rules and Forms of the House of Commons of Canada*, 3rd ed. (Toronto: 1943), 81–2, cited in Ward, 'Called to the Bar,' 546.
9 Kathryn May, 'Radwanski to Be Called before House of Commons on Contempt Charge,' *CanWest News*, 4 November 2003, 1.
10 *Kielly v. Carson* (1841), 4 Moore P.C. 63, cited in Ward, 'Called to the Bar,' 530–1 (emphasis added).

11 Murray Goot, 'Public Opinion and the Democratic Deficit; Australia and the War Against Iraq,' *Australian Humanities Review* (May 2003), http://www.lib.latrobe.edu. au/AHR/archive/Issue-May-2003/goot.html (29 August 2005); see too Giandomenico Majone, 'Europe's "Democratic Deficit": The Question of Standards,' *European Law Journal* 4, no. 1 (March 1998): 5–28.

12 For example, Gerhard Loewenberg, ed., *Modern Parliaments: Change or Decline?* (Chicago: Aldine, Atherton, 1971), and Lawrence D. Longley and Roger H. Davidson, 'Parliamentary Committees: Changing Perspectives on Changing Institutions,' in Lawrence D. Longley and Roger H. Davidson, eds, *The New Role of Parliamentary Committees* (London: Frank Cass, 1998), 1.

13 Catherine Bromley, John Curtice, and Ben Seyd, 'Is Britain Facing a Crisis in Democracy?' (Constitution Unit, University College London, July 2004), 22.

14 *The Civics Channel*, 9 December 2004, http://northernblue.ca/cconline/ Iwhycivics.php.

15 Stéphane Dion, 'Rising Cynicism: Who Is to Blame?' *CPR* 16, no. 4 (Winter 1993–4): 33–5; Hugh Segal, 'Failing Legitimacy: The Challenge for Parliamentarians,' *CPR* 27, no. 1 (Spring 2004): 30–2; Chuck Strahl, 'Toward a More Responsive Parliament,' *CPR* 24, no. 1 (Spring 2000): 2–4; J. Patrick Boyer, 'Can Parliamentarians Become Real Players?' *CPR* 27, no. 3 (Autumn 2004): 4–8; Louis Balthazar, 'Is the Decline of Parliament Irreversible?' *CPR* 25, no. 4 (Winter 2002–3): 18–21; Matthias Rioux, 'The Roots of Our Democratic Malaise,' *CPR* 25, no. 4 (Winter 2002–3): 7–9; and J. Patrick Boyer, *'Just Trust Us': The Erosion of Accountability in Canada* (Toronto: Dundurn Press, 2003).

16 Peter Riddell, *Parliament under Blair* (London: Politico's Publishing, 2000), ix.

17 Norman Ward, 'The Formative Years of the House of Commons, 1867–91,' *CJEPS* 15, no. 4 (November 1952): 431–51.

18 The argument, with illustrations, is found in David E. Smith, 'Party Government, Representation and National Integration in Canada,' in Peter Aucoin, ed., *Party Government and Regional Representation in Canada* (Toronto: University of Toronto Press in cooperation with the Royal Commission on the Economic Union and Development Prospects for Canada, 1985), 1–68.

19 John C. Courtney, 'Reflections on Reforming the Canadian Electoral System,' *CPA* 23, no. 3 (1980): 427–57.

20 See David E. Smith, *The Invisible Crown: The First Principle of Canadian Government* (Toronto: University of Toronto Press, 1995), ch. 8.

21 W.L. Morton, *The Progressive Party in Canada* (Toronto: University of Toronto

Press, 1950), and David Laycock, *Populism and Democratic Thought in the Canadian Prairies, 1910 to 1945* (Toronto: University of Toronto Press, 1990).

22 Norman Ward and David E. Smith, *Jimmy Gardiner: Relentless Liberal* (Toronto: University of Toronto Press, 1990), 300.

23 Smith, *Invisible Crown*, 30–7.

24 Michael Bliss, 'A Short Guide to Our "Culture of Corruption."' *National Post*, 13 March 2004, A14.

25 Stanley Bach, *Platypus and Parliament: The Australian Senate in Theory and Practice* (Canberra: Department of the Senate, 2003), 314–16.

26 See *Reference re the Remuneration of Judges of the Provincial Court of Prince Edward Island* [1997] 3 SCR 3 at para. 102.

27 Paco Francoli, 'Parliament's Oversight? Donald Savoie Says Its Role Has Greatly Changed,' *The Hill Times*, 22 April 2002, 1.

28 Roy Jenkins, *Gladstone: A Biography* (New York: Random House Trade Paperbacks, 1997), 206.

29 Michael M. Atkinson and Paul Thomas, 'Studying the Canadian Parliament,' *Legislative Studies Quarterly* 18, no. 3 (August 1993): 436.

30 The nine volumes (the first five appeared in 2004, the next three in 2005, and the last in 2006) are published in Vancouver by the University of British Columbia Press: John Courtney, *Elections*; William Cross, *Political Parties*; Elisabeth Gidengil, André Blais, Neil Nevitte, and Richard Nadeau, *Citizens*; Jennifer Smith, *Federalism*; Lisa Young and Joanna Everitt, *Advocacy Groups*; David Docherty, *Legislatures*; Graham White, *Cabinets and First Ministers*; Darin Barney, *Communication Technology*; Ian Green, *The Courts*.

31 In the 2006 general election, voter turnout increased for the first time in two decades (64.9 per cent versus 60.1 per cent in 2004). Whether this signals a longer-term reversal is unknown. Party membership statistics are difficult to trace. They rise and fall with leadership contests and election defeats, respectively: 'Our best estimate, from an examination of membership patterns over time, is that between one and two per cent of Canadians belong to a political party on a year-to-year basis.' William Cross and Lisa Young, 'Party Membership as Public Service,' paper presented at the conference Responsibilities of Citizenship and Public Service: Crisis or Challenge? organized by the Institute for Research on Public Policy and the Trudeau Foundation, Toronto, 2005.

32 Young and Everitt, *Advocacy Groups*, 82.

33 Rob Merrifield (speaker) in Lincoln, Merrifield, Bergeron, and Nystrom, 'Members Look at Parliamentary Reform,' *CPR* 24, no. 2 (Summer 2001): 12.

34 Anne Dawson, 'Martin Vows to Reform Government,' *Star Phoenix* (Saskatoon), 23 September 2003, A1–2.

35 Segal, 'Failing Legitimacy,' 32.
36 A. Paul Pross, 'Parliamentary Influences and the Diffusion of Power,' *CJPS* 18, no. 2 (June 1985): 256.
37 Rioux, 'The Roots of Our Democratic Malaise,' 7.

3. Constitutional Democracy

1 Royal Commission on the Economic Union and Development Prospects for Canada, *Report*, 3 vols (Ottawa: Minister of Supply and Services Canada, 1985), 3: 519–20.
2 Gordon Gibson, 'Stop: In the Name of Love (for Canada),' *Globe and Mail*, 1 February 2005, A15; 'Top Court "Hijacking" Democracy: Report Says,' *National Post*, 7 August 2003, A1 and A6. The report was published by the Fraser Institute.
3 F.L. Morton and Rainer Knopff, *The Charter Revolution and the Court Party* (Peterborough: Broadview Press, 2000), ch. 3.
4 See Christopher P. Manfredi, *Judicial Power and the Charter: Canada and the Paradox of Liberal Constitutionalism*, 2nd ed. (Don Mills, ON: Oxford University Press, 2001).
5 For further on the law-politics dichotomy, see Byron Sheldrick, *Perils and Possibilities: Social Activism and the Law* (Halifax: Fernwood Publishing, 2004), 26.
6 Garry Wills, *Inventing America: Jefferson's Declaration of Independence* (New York: Doubleday, 1978), xxiv.
7 *Reference re An Act to Amend the Education Act* (Ontario) [1987] 40 DLR (4th) 60, as cited in Manfredi, *Judicial Power and the Charter*, 59.
8 *Mahé v. Alberta* [1990] 1 SCR 350, and *Re Manitoba Public Schools Act Reference* [1993] 1 SCR 839, as cited in Michael Behiels, *Canada's Francophone Minority Communities: Constitutional Renewal and the Winning of School Governance* (Montreal and Kingston: McGill-Queen's University Press, 2004), 174 and 236.
9 Behiels, *Canada's Francophone Minority Communities*, xxvii.
10 John Leonard Taylor, *Canadian Indian Policy during the Inter-War Years, 1918–1939* (Ottawa: Indian and Northern Affairs Canada, 1984), 7. See, too, Hugh Shewell, *'Enough to Keep Them Alive': Indian Welfare in Canada, 1873–1965* (Toronto: University of Toronto Press, 2004), esp. ch. 7, 'The Influence of the Social Sciences: The Secular Understanding of the "Other."'
11 See, for instance, David Smith, 'Saskatchewan Perspectives,' in Federation of Saskatchewan Indian Nations, *Saskatchewan and Aboriginal Peoples in the 21st Century: Social, Economic and Political Changes and Challenges* (Regina: PrintWest Communications Ltd., 1997), 4–36.

12 Sheldrick, *Perils and Possibilities*, 13.

13 Roy Romanow, John Whyte, and Harold Leeson, *Canada ... Notwithstanding: The Making of the Constitution, 1976–1982* (Toronto: Carswell/Methuen, 1984), 247.

14 Barry Strayer, 'Ken Lysyk and the Patriation Reference,' Paper presented at the Symposium Honouring the Late Mr Justice Kenneth Lysyk, University of British Columbia, Vancouver, 5–6 November 2004, 17 (unpublished).

15 *Reference re Motor Vehicle Act (British Columbia) s.94 (2)*, [1985] 2 SCR 486 at 497.

16 Royal Commission on the Economic Union and Development Prospects for Canada, *Report*, 3: 519 and 520.

17 Paul Howe and David Northrup, 'Strengthening Canadian Democracy: The Views of Canadians,' *Policy Matters* 1, no. 5 (July 2000), IRPP, 40 and 42.

18 Rainer Knopff, 'Populism and the Politics of Rights: The Dual Attack on Representative Democracy,' *CJPS* 31, no. 4 (December 1998): 699 and 702–3. See too James B. Kelly, 'The Supreme Court of Canada and the Complexity of Judicial Activism,' in Patrick James, Donald E. Abelson, and Michael Lusztig, eds, *The Myth of the Sacred: The Charter, the Courts, and the Politics of the Constitution in Canada* (Montreal and Kingston: McGill-Queen's University Press, 2002), 97–124.

19 *Figueroa v. Canada (Attorney General)*, [2003] 1 SCR 912; Canada, House of Commons, Standing Committee on Procedure and House Affairs, *Evidence*, 9 March 2004 (32 of 38) (between 1645 and 1650). See too Heather MacIvor, 'The Charter of Rights and Party Politics: The Impact of the Supreme Court Ruling in *Figueroa v. Canada (Attorney General)*,' *Choices* 10, no. 4 (May 2004).

20 Ibid. Summary, paras 39 and 45.

21 The criteria are as follows: 'Have as one of its fundamental purposes participation in public affairs; endorse one or more of its members as candidates and support their election; have at least 250 members and three officers in addition to the leader; and comply with new accountability rules.'

22 Jeffrey Simpson, 'Why Don't We Just Turn Policy over to the Courts?' *Globe and Mail*, 22 July 2003, A15.

23 Lorraine Eisenstat Weinrib, 'Canada's Constitutional Revolution: From Legislative to Constitutional State,' *Israel Law Review* 33, no. 1 (Winter): 42.

24 See, for instance, Standing Committee on Procedure and House Affairs, *Evidence* no. 24 (9 March 2005).

25 MacIvor, 'The Charter of Rights and Party Politics,' 19.

26 Jocelyn Downie, *Dying Justice: A Case for Decriminalizing Euthanasia and Assisted Suicide in Canada* (Toronto: University of Toronto Press, 2004), 55.

27 *Harper v. Canada (Attorney General)*, [2004] 1 SCR 827.

28 'Top Judge Rejects Allegation of Activism,' *Globe and Mail*, 23 November 2004, A10.

29 Peter W. Hogg and Allison A. Bushell, 'The *Charter* Dialogue between Courts and Legislatures (or Perhaps the *Charter of Rights* Isn't Such a Bad Thing After All),' 35 *Osgoode Hall Law Journal* 75 (1997): 105 (internal quotation from: R. Dworkin, 'The Forum of Principle,' *New York University Law Review* 56, 469 (1981). For a strong dissent, see Robert Ivan Martin, *The Most Dangerous Branch: How the Supreme Court of Canada Has Undermined Our Law and Our Democracy* (Montreal and Kingston: McGill-Queen's University Press, 2003).

30 Christopher P. Manfredi, 'Great Policy Books: Donald Horowitz, *The Courts and Social Policy* (1977),' *Policy Options* (January-February 2002): 55.

31 Frances Kahn Zemans, 'Legal Mobilization: The Neglected Role of the Law in the Political System,' *APSR* 77, no. 3 (September 1983): 695.

32 Sheldrick, *Perils and Possibilities*, 90–1 and 98–9.

33 Neil Gerlach, *The Genetic Imaginary: DNA in the Canadian Criminal Justice System* (Toronto: University of Toronto Press, 2004), 27.

34 Elaine Dewar, *The Second Tree: Of Clones, Chimeras and Quests for Immortality* (Toronto: Random House Canada, 2004), 423. The draft legislation – Bill C-13, 'Proposals for Legislation Governing Assisted Human Reproduction'– was the Chrétien government's response to *Proceed with Care*, the final report of the Royal Commission on New Reproductive Technologies, which appeared in 1993.

35 John R. Hibbing and Elizabeth Theiss-Morse, *Stealth Democracy: America's Beliefs about How Government Should Work* (New York: Cambridge University Press, 2002), 140.

36 Gerlach, *The Genetic Imaginary*, 27.

37 Patrick James, Donald E. Abelson, and Micháel Lusztig, 'Introduction: The Myth of the Sacred in the Canadian Constitutional Order,' in James, Abelson, and Lusztig, eds, *The Myth of the Sacred*, 3.

38 Rachel E.L. Whidden, 'Science Controversies and Public Policy: A Case Study of Genetically Engineered Food' (unpublished MA Thesis, University of Saskatchewan, 2004); *Monsanto Canada Inc. v. Schmeiser*, [2004] 1 SCR 902.

39 Royal Commission on Electoral Reform and Party Financing, *Report* (Ottawa: Minister of Supply and Services, 1991), 1: 13. See too Pierre Fortin, 'Ethical Issues in the Debate on Reform of the *Canada Elections Act*: An Ethicological Analysis,' in Janet Hiebert, ed., *Political Ethics: A Canadian Perspective*, Royal Commission on Electoral Reform and Party Financing, Research Studies, vol. 12 (Toronto: Dundurn Press, 1990), 3–72.

40 Royal Commission on the Economic Union and Development Prospects for Canada, *Report*, 3: 306.

41 Canada, Committee on Election Expenses, *Report of the Committee on Election Expenses* (Ottawa: Queen's Printer, 1966), 46.

42 All quotations in this paragraph are from Ian Peach, *The Death of Deference: National Policy-Making in the Aftermath of the Meech Lake and Charlottetown Accords*, Public Policy Paper 26 (Regina: Saskatchewan Institute of Public Policy, September 2004).

43 Keith Spicer, 'Canada: Values in Search of a Vision,' in Robert E. Earle and John D. Wirth, eds, *Identities in North America: The Search for Community* (Stanford: Stanford University Press, 1995), 18–19; and Citizens' Forum on Canada's Future, *Report to the People and Government of Canada* (Ottawa: Minister of Supply and Services Canada, 1991), 141.

44 Darrell Bricker and Edward Greenspon, *Searching for Certainty: Inside the New Canadian Mindset* (Toronto: Doubleday Canada, 2001), 263.

45 Michael Adams, *Fire and Ice: The United States, Canada and the Myth of Converging Values* (Toronto: Penguin Canada, 2003), 52.

46 Commission on the Future of Health Care in Canada, *Building on Values: The Future of Health Care in Canada – Final Report* (Saskatoon: Commission on the Future of Health Care in Canada, November 2002), xx; 'Same-Sex Fight Moves to House,' *Star-Phoenix* (Saskatoon), 1 February 2005, A1, A2; Auditor General, *Report of the Auditor General of Canada to the House of Commons* (November 2003), 2; Department of Foreign Affairs and International Trade, *Canada in the World* (Ottawa: 1995) as cited in Jennifer Welsh, *At Home in the World: Canada's Global Vision for the 21st Century* (Toronto: HarperCollins, 2004), 192–201; and Allan D. English, *Understanding Military Culture: A Canadian Perspective* (Montreal and Kingston: McGill-Queen's University Press, 2004), 148.

47 Bill Cross, 'Members of Parliament, Voters and Democracy in the Canadian House of Commons,' *Parliamentary Perspectives* no. 3 (Ottawa: Canadian Study of Parliament Group, 2003), 5.

48 Ibid., 2. See Norman Ward and David E. Smith, *Jimmy Gardiner: Relentless Liberal* (Toronto: University of Toronto Press, 1990); Robert Bothwell and William Kilbourn, *C.D. Howe: A Biography* (Toronto: McClelland and Stewart, 1979); and Reginald Whitaker, *The Government Party: Organizing and Financing the Liberal Party of Canada, 1930–58* (Toronto: University of Toronto Press, 1977).

49 *Reference re Secession of Quebec*, [1998] 2 SCR 217.

50 *Reference re the Remuneration of Judges of the Provincial Court (P.E.I.)*, [1997] 3 SCR 3.

51 *Singh v. Canada (Attorney General) (C.A.)*, [2000] 3 FC 185 at 189.

52 Ibid., 188. See as well, B.L. Strayer, 'Life under the Canadian Charter: Adjusting the Balance between Legislatures and Courts,' *Public Law* (1988): 347–69.
53 Ibid., 202–3.
54 Carolyn J. Tuohy, *Policy and Politics in Canada: Institutionalized Ambivalence* (Philadelphia: Temple University Press, 1992), 40.
55 This distinction is found in Gerald Leonard, *The Invention of Party Politics: Federalism, Popular Sovereignty, and Constitutional Development in Jacksonian Illinois* (Chapel Hill: University of North Carolina Press, 2002), 15, cited in Larry D. Kramer, *The People Themselves: Popular Constitutionalism and Judicial Review* (New York: Oxford University Press, 2004), 8.
56 Stephen Bindman, 'Off the Bench, Estey Speaks His Mind,' *Star-Phoenix* (Saskatoon), 2 May 1988, A17.
57 Alan C. Cairns, *Citizens Plus: Aboriginal People and the Canadian State* (Vancouver: University of British Columbia Press, 2000), 187; Alan Cairns and Tom Flanagan, 'An Exchange,' *Inroads: A Journal of Opinion* 10 (2001): 1–12.
58 Preston Manning, 'Parliament, Not Judges, Must Make the Laws of the Land,' *Globe and Mail*, 16 June 1998, A23.
59 *Reference re Provincial Electoral Boundaries*, [1991] 2 SCR 160.
60 New Brunswick, Commission on Legislative Democracy, *Final Report* (Fredericton: 2004), 7. For a specific reference to 'equality-minded younger voters,' see Equal Voice, 'Equality-Based Electoral Reform' (2003), online: http://www.equalvoice.ca/index.htm, cited in Law Commission of Canada, *Voting Counts: Electoral Reform in Canada* (Ottawa: 2004), 34.
61 British Columbia Citizens' Assembly on Electoral Reform, 'Making Every Vote Count: The Case for Electoral Reform in British Columbia,' *The Final Report of the British Columbia Citizens' Assembly on Electoral Reform* (October 2004), www.citizensassembly.bc.ca.
62 William E. Scheuerman, 'Liberal Democracy and the Empire of Speed,' *Polity* 34, no. 1 (Fall 2001): 41–67.
63 Commission of Inquiry into the Deployment of Canadian Forces to Somalia, *Dishonoured Legacy: The Lessons of the Somalia Affair. Report of the Commission* (Ottawa: Minister of Public Works and Government Services, 1997), 1: 81–2, cited in A. English, *Understanding Military Culture*, 33–4.
64 New Brunswick, Commission on Legislative Democracy, *Final Report*; Prince Edward Island, Prince Edward Island Commissioner of Electoral Reform, *Prince Edward Island Electoral Reform Report* (Charlottetown: 2003); British Columbia, British Columbia Citizens' Assembly on Electoral Reform, *Final Report*.
65 Canada, Parliament, House of Commons, *Debates*, 16 February 2005, 3575; 16 February 1995, 9707; and 13 June 1995, 13685.

4. Electoral Democracy

1 A.V. Dicey, *An Introduction to the Study of the Law of the Constitution*, 10th ed., intro. E.C.S. Wade (London: Macmillan and Co., 1962); R. MacGregor Dawson, *The Government of Canada*, 5th ed., revised by Norman Ward (Toronto: University of Toronto Press, 1970); Eugene A. Forsey, *The Royal Power of Dissolution of Parliament in the British Commonwealth* (Toronto: Oxford University Press, 1943); Sir Ivor Jennings, *Parliament*, 2nd ed. (Cambridge: Cambridge University Press, 1957); Geoffrey Marshall, *Constitutional Theory* (Oxford: Clarendon Press, 1971).

2 A recent exploration is found in John T. Saywell, *The Lawmakers: Judicial Power and the Shaping of Canadian Federalism*, Osgoode Society for Canadian Legal History (Toronto: University of Toronto Press, 2002).

3 *DLAUC*, 19 October 1852 (xi.11.1852), 1105.

4 On Triple E, see David E. Smith, *The Canadian Senate in Bicameral Perspective* (Toronto: University of Toronto Press, 2003).

5 Peter Mendelson, seminar in Bonn, March 1998, cited in Peter Riddell, *Parliament under Blair* (London: Politico's Publishing, 2000), 182.

6 Preston Manning, 'Democracy in the 21st Century: New Imperatives, Old Restraints,' in Richard M. Bird, ed., *Who Decides? Government in the New Millennium* (Toronto: C.D. Howe Institute, 2004), 33.

7 T.D. Weldon, *The Vocabulary of Politics* (London: Penguin Books, 1953, reprinted Johnson Reprints Co., 1970), 43.

8 John R. Hibbing and Elizabeth Theiss-Morse, *Congress as Public Enemy: Public Attitudes toward American Political Institutions* (New York: Cambridge University Press, 1995), 97.

9 David Laycock, *Populism and Democratic Thought in the Canadian Prairies, 1910 to 1945* (Toronto: University of Toronto Press, 1990), 6.

10 Jim Ness, 'Selling Wheat, Doing Time,' *National Post*, 12 October 2002, A21.

11 David Laycock, *The New Right and Democracy in Canada* (Toronto: Oxford University Press, 2002), 10.

12 Ibid., 61.

13 Riddell, *Parliament under Blair*, 107.

14 Laycock, *The New Right and Democracy,* 10 and 27.

15 Bob Franklin, 'Keeping It "Bright, Light and Trite": Changing Newspaper Reporting in Parliament,' *Parliamentary Affairs* 49 (1996): 303.

16 Richard Hodder-Williams, 'British Politicians: To Rehabilitate or Not,' *Parliamentary Affairs* 49, no. 2 (1996): 292. See too Chris Cobb, *Ego and Ink: The Inside Story of Canada's National Newspaper War* (Toronto: McClelland and Stewart, 2004).

17 Published by the University of Toronto Press, they are W.L. Morton, *The*

Progressive Party in Canada (1950), D.C. Masters, *The Winnipeg General Strike* (1950), Jean Burnet, *Next Year Country* (1951), C.B. Macpherson, *Democracy in Alberta: Social Credit and the Party System* (1953), J.R. Mallory, *Social Credit and the Federal Power in Canada* (1954), W.E. Mann, *Sect, Cult and Church in Alberta* (1955), V.C. Fowke, *The National Policy and the Wheat Economy* (1957), L.G. Thomas, *The Liberal Party in Alberta: A History of Politics in the Province of Alberta* (1959), S.D. Clark, *Movements of Political Protest in Canada* (1959), and John A. Irving, *The Social Credit Movement in Alberta* (1959).

18 Frank H. Underhill in *Canadian Forum*, January 1930, reprinted in R. MacGregor Dawson, ed., *Constitutional Issues in Canada, 1900–1931* (London: Oxford University Press, 1933), 135.

19 David E. Smith, *The Republican Option in Canada: Past and Present* (Toronto: University of Toronto Press, 1999), 139–40.

20 André Blais and Elisabeth Gidengil, *Making Representative Democracy Work: The Views of Canadians*, vol. 17, Research Studies, Royal Commission on Electoral Reform and Party Financing (Toronto: Dundurn Press, 1991), 18.

21 Philip Corrigan and Derek Sayer, *The Great Arch: English State Formation as Cultural Revolution* (Oxford: Basil Blackwell, 1985), 3.

22 *Re Initiative and Referendum Act* (1919), AC 944.

23 Harold A. Innis, ed., *The Diary of Alexander James McPhail* (Toronto: University of Toronto Press, 1940), ch. 2, App. I, 'Last Mountain Federal Constituency: Instructions re Primaries.'

24 See, for instance, British Columbia, 'Recall and Initiative Act,' *RSBC* 1996, c. 398; Saskatchewan, 'An Act Respecting Referendums and Plebiscites,' *Statutes of Saskatchewan*, 1990–1, Chapter R-8.01; and Alberta, Constitutional Referendum Act, *RSA*, 2000, c. C-25.

25 Preston Manning, 'Be Not Afraid,' *Globe and Mail*, 2 November 2004, A15.

26 Norma Greenway, 'Liberal Party Run Like an Oligarchy: Grits,' *National Post*, 2 March 2005, A7.

27 Preston Manning, 'Parliament, Not Judges, Must Make the Laws of the Land,' *Globe and Mail*, 16 June 1998, A23.

28 Preston Manning, 'How to Remake the National Agenda,' *National Post*, 13 February 2003, A18.

29 Preston Manning, *The New Canada* (Toronto: Macmillan Canada, 1992), 325–6.

30 Barry Cooper, 'Parliamentary Government and the Recall,' Unpublished paper, August 1998, 82.

31 *Reform Party Motion to Avoid Judicial Rulings on Legislation*, Speaker of the House of Commons, *Hansard*, 8 June 1998, 7677, reprinted in Gregory Tardi,

The Law of Democratic Governing. Volume 2: Jurisprudence (Toronto: Thomson/ Carswell, 2004), 252–6.

32 *New Brunswick Broadcasting Co. v. Nova Scotia (Speaker of the House of Assembly)* [1993], 1 SCR 319 at 389; b-d. http://www/exum.umontreal.ca/csc-scc/en/pub/1993/vol1/html/1993scr/_0319html.

33 'Manning Set to Have PM Removed,' *Globe and Mail*, 14 December 1995, A4.

34 'Chrétien Names 3 New Senators,' *National Post*, 3 September 1999, A1; Preston Manning, 'Is He [Mr Justice John Gomery] Our Last Best Hope?' *Globe and Mail*, 28 February 2005, A13.

35 See, for instance, Dennis Bueckert, 'Watchdog in Discussion with Greens over Financing,' *Globe and Mail*, 19 December 2005, A4.

36 For a discussion of 'post-Watergate mentality,' see G. Calvin Mackenzie with Michael Hafken, *Scandal Proof: Do Ethics Laws Make Government Ethical?* (Washington: Brookings Institution Press, 2002), 31f. See also, Denis St Martin, 'The "Watergate Effect" and the Diffusion of Ethics Commissions,' 2f, in his 'The Multiple Meanings of "Independence" in Politics: Ethics Watchdogs in Comparative Perspective,' Paper presented at Independence and Responsibility: A Conference on the Officers of Parliament, University of Saskatchewan, 2–3 November 2001; and St Martin, 'Should the Federal Ethics Counsellor Become an Independent Officer of Parliament?' *Canadian Public Policy* 19, no. 1 (2003): 197–212.

37 Norman Ward, *The Public Purse: A Study in Canadian Democracy* (Toronto: University of Toronto Press, 1962). The periodical literature is substantial; it ranges from Herbert R. Balls, 'The Watchdog of Parliament: The Centenary of the Legislative Audit,' *CPA* 21, no. 4 (Winter 1978): 584–617, to S.L. Sutherland, 'The Office of the Auditor General of Canada: Government in Exile,' Paper presented at Independence and Responsibility conference, 2001. Of unpublished literature, see first Megan Furi, 'Officers of Parliament: A Study in Government Adaptation' (MA thesis, University of Saskatchewan, 2002).

38 Carolyn Bennett, 'Canada Needs a Healthcare Commissioner as an Officer of Parliament, Says Bennett: MP and MD Carolyn Bennett Says the Commissioner Would Ensure the Transparency and Accountability of All Health and Health Care Outcomes and Spending,' *The Hill Times*, 28 October 2002, 28.

39 Dyane Adam, 'A Hard Act to Follow: The Commissioner of Official Languages as an Agent of Parliament,' Paper presented at Independence and Responsibility conference, 2001, 8. In his study *Commissioned Ridings: Designing Canada's Electoral Districts* (Montreal and Kingston: McGill-

Queen's University Press, 2001), John Courtney discusses one such incident involving New Brunswick's French-speaking Acadian population, 230–1.

40 Democracy Watch, 'Summary of Democracy Watch's Many Notable Achievements,' http://www.dwatch.ca/aboutdw.html (13 December 2004).

41 Jennifer Smith, 'Responsible Government and the Officers of Parliament,' Paper presented at Independence and Responsibility conference, 2001.

42 Preston Manning, 'How to Remake the National Agenda,' *National Post*, 13 February 2003, A18.

43 'Accountability Pillars Lie in Rubble,' *National Post*, 11 February 2004, A18.

44 'Freeing Party Finance from the Iron Triangle,' *National Post*, 21 January 2003, A16.

45 Maria Barrados and Jean Ste-Marie, 'The Auditor General of Canada: An Independent Servant of Parliament,' Paper presented at Independence and Responsibility conference, 2001, [7] and [8].

46 Jim Bronskill, 'Watchdogs' Bark Commonly Ignored,' *Ottawa Citizen*, 27 September 2002.

47 'It is encouraging to see members of Parliament reassert their role in this process.' Auditor General, *Report of the Auditor General of Canada to the House of Commons, Matters of Special Importance – 2003, Foreword and Main Points* (Ottawa: Office of the Auditor General, November 2003), para 36; 'Straight-Talking Fraser Strikes Fear on the Hill,' *Globe and Mail*, 12 February 2004, 4.

48 'Why the Fuss? AG's Report Deals with a Drop in the Tax Bucket,' *Globe and Mail*, 13 February 2004, A19.

49 'Straight-Talking Fraser Strikes Fear on the Hill,' *Globe and Mail*, 12 February 2004, 4.

50 John R. Hibbing and Elizabeth Theiss-Morse, *Stealth Democracy: Americans' Beliefs about How Government Should Work* (New York: Cambridge University Press, 2002), 140.

51 'The Slippery Slope of Shifting Accountability,' *Globe and Mail*, 21 September 2004, A19. Another columnist, Don Martin, nominated Sheila Fraser as 'My Person of the Year,' *Leader Post* (Regina), 24 December 2002, B7.

52 Michael Foot, *Aneurin Bevan*, 2 vols (London: Granada, 1975), 1: 330.

53 Oonagh Gay and Barry K. Winetrobe, *Officers of Parliament – Transforming the Role* (The Constitution Unit, University College London, April 2003), 9.

54 See Roger Gibbins, Loleen Youngman Berdahl, and Katherine Harmsworth, *Following the Cash: Exploring the Expanding Role of Canada's Auditor General* (Calgary: Canada West Foundation, October 2000), 17–18.

55 Jane Mansbridge, 'Rethinking Representation,' *APSR* 97, no. 4 (November 2003): 520–2.

56 Bruce Ackerman, 'The New Separation of Powers,' *Harvard Law Review* 113 (2000): 633–729.

57 For a discussion of this case, *Raîche v. R.*, Federal Court of Canada – Trial Division; filed 12 September 2003, file T-1730–03, and an earlier case, *Société des Acadiens c. Nouveau-Brunswick (Gouverneur en Conseil)* (1997), 188 N.B.R. (2d) 330, see Tardi, *The Law of Democratic Governing. Volume 2: Jurisprudence*, 484–90.

58 Preston Manning, 'Is He Our Last Best Hope?' *Globe and Mail*, 28 February 2005, A13.

59 Stephen Harper, 'Address to the Joint Empire and Canadian Clubs,' 8 November 2005, http://www.conservative.ca/media/20051108–Harper-EmpireClub.pdf (emphasis added).

60 See Michael Power, *The Audit Society: Rituals of Verification* (Oxford: Oxford University Press, 1997).

61 Susan Sontag, *On Photography* (New York: Anchor Books, 1990), 92.

62 Jeffrey Goldsworthy, *The Sovereignty of Parliament: History and Philosophy* (Oxford: Clarendon Press, 1999), 75.

5. What Is the House?

1 Legislative Assembly of United Canada, *Parliamentary Debates on the Subject of the Confederation of the British North American Provinces* (Quebec: Hunter, Rose and Co. Parliamentary Printers, 1865, reprinted Ottawa: Queen's Printer, 1951), 38.

2 Parliamentary Centre, 'Strengthening the Role of MPs,' *Occasional Papers on Parliamentary Government* no. 7 (November 1998): 3; Parliamentary Centre, 'New MPs,' *Occasional Papers on Parliamentary Government* no. 1 (September 1996): 23–4.

3 Donald J. Savoie, 'All Things Canadian Are Now Regional,' *Journal of Canadian Studies* 35, no. 1 (Spring 2000): 203, and 'Parliament Has Calcified,' *Gazette* (Montreal), editorial, 27 December 2001, B2.

4 Parliamentary Centre, 'New MPs,' 13.

5 Library of Parliament, Political and Social Affairs Division, *The Roles of the Member of Parliament in Canada: Are They Changing?* (Ottawa: Library of Parliament, Research Branch, 2002), 10.

6 See David Docherty, *Mr Smith Goes to Ottawa: Life in the House of Commons* (Vancouver: University of British Columbia Press, 1997), ch. 7, 'Home Style: Members and Their Constituencies'; Boyer is quoted in Kevin Michael Grace, 'Parliament of Ombudsmen; Stripped of Their Powers, MPs Now Serve Their Constituents Not with Advocacy but with Favours,' *Report Newsmagazine* (British Columbia edition), 11 June 2000.

7 Alan Clark, *Diaries* (London: Phoenix Giant, 1993), 120; see also Philip Norton and David Wood, 'Constituency Service by Members of Parliament: Does It Contribute to a Personal Vote?' *Parliamentary Affairs* 40, no. 2 (1990): 196.

8 Library of Parliament, *The Roles of the Member of Parliament in Canada*, 11.

9 See Bea Vongdouangchanh, 'Minister Frulla's Riding Office Is Also ... an Art Gallery,' *The Hill Times*, 15–21 November 2004, 20.

10 Louis Balthazar, 'Is the Decline of Parliament Irreversible?' *CPR* 25, no. 4 (Winter 2002–3): 18.

11 The work of the Canadian Study of Parliament Group is discussed in chapter 1, pp 12–13. For the Parliamentary Centre, see http://www.parlcent.ca/ publications/archive_pub_c.php#Occasional_Papers.

12 David Hoffman and Norman Ward, *Bilingualism and Biculturalism in the Canadian House of Commons*, Documents of the Royal Commission on Bilingualism and Biculturalism (Ottawa: Queen's Printer, 1970), 73.

13 Docherty, *Mr Smith Goes to Ottawa*, ix.

14 David Heyman, 'Democracy Requires More Free Votes: U of C Debate Pits Manning against Nicol,' *Calgary Herald*, 17 March 2004, A5.

15 Vaughn Palmer, 'Ottawa Turns Our Man into a Mouse,' *National Post*, 17 February 2001, A19.

16 Norton and Wood, 'Constituency Service by Members of Parliament,' 197.

17 'Interview, René Blondin: Twenty Years at the National Assembly,' *CPR* 18, no. 2 (Summer 1985): 22.

18 David E. Smith, *The Regional Decline of a National Party: Liberals on the Prairies* (Toronto: University of Toronto Press, 1981).

19 For an introduction to path dependence literature, see Paul Pierson, 'Increasing Returns, Path Dependence, and the Study of Politics,' *APSR* 94, no. 2 (June 2000): 251–67. One application to Canada is David E. Smith, 'Path Dependence and Saskatchewan Politics,' in Gregory P. Marchildon, ed., *The Heavy Hand of History: Interpreting Saskatchewan's Past* (Regina: Canadian Plains Research Center, 2005), 31–50.

20 Joe Paraskevas, 'Private Member's Bill Calls for More Open Government,' *CanWest News*, 27 October 2003, 1. The Open Government Campaign is described on the website of Democracy Watch, a member of Open Government Canada, at http://www.dwatch.ca/camp/accessdir.html.

21 David Cannadine, *G.M. Trevelyan: A Life in History* (London: Penguin Books, 1992), 74.

22 'Anne McLellan Should Resign,' *National Post*, 19 March 2005, A15. Sponsors of the advertisement were defendMarriage.ca. In the 1993 election campaign, Sheila Copps promised to resign her seat if the Liberals did not

repeal the Goods and Services Tax. This she did in 1996, and was re-elected in the by-election.

23 Nathan S. Elliott, '"We Have Asked for Bread and You Gave Us a Stone": Western Farmers and the Siege of Ottawa' (MA thesis, University of Saskatchewan, 2004), 87 f.

24 '[T]he traditional role of MP as gather[ers] of information and decision-makers for constituents could be replaced by one of "coach and guide."' Kathryn May, 'Info Technology Is Turning Democracy Upside Down,' *Can-West News*, 28 March 2001, 1.

25 Reg Alcock, 'Parliament and Democracy in the 21st Century: The Impact of Information and Communication Technologies,' *CPR* 25, no. 1 (Spring 2002): 3.

26 Gilles Paquet, 'Governance in the Face of Sabotage and Bricolage,' *CPR* 24, no. 3 (Autumn 2001): 11–18.

27 'Marin Fires Parting Shot,' *National Post*, 30 March 2005, A4; André Marin, 'Our Military Needs an Independent Ombudsman,' *National Post*, 7 April 2005, A18.

28 Michael K. Barbour, 'Parliament and the Internet: The Present and the Future,' *CPR* 22, no. 3 (Autumn 1999): 24; see too Jonathan Malloy, 'To Better Serve Canadians: How Technology Is Changing the Relationshp between Members of Parliament and Public Servants' (Toronto: Institute of Public Administration of Canada, 2003), and Donald G. Leniham, 'MPs Are Missing the Web Revolution,' *CanWest News*, 18 July 2002. Donald Leni-ham, Director of the Centre for Collaborative Government, Ottawa, initi-ated the 'Changing Government' series of discussion papers, whose titles include 'Collaborative Government in the Post-Industrial Age,' 'Opening the E-Government File,' 'Measuring the Quality of Life: The Use of Societal Outcomes by Parliamentarians,' 'Leveraging Our Diversity,' 'Post-Indus-trial Government,' and 'Realigning Governance: From E-Government to E-Democracy.'

29 Thomas Zittel, 'Political Representation and the Internet: Wither [sic] Responsible Party Government?' American Political Science Association, Legislative Studies Section, *Newsletter* 26, no. 1 (January 2003), http://www.apsanet.org/0/07Elss/Newsletter/jan03/papers.htm.

30 Mike Scandiffio, '"It's a Collapse of Culture of Record Keeping," Reid Says It's an Example of Government's Mismanagement of Information,' *The Hill Times*, 31 January 2000, 9.

31 Association of Public Service Financial Administration, 'Checks and Bal-ances: Rebalancing the Service and Control Features of the Government of Canada (GOC) Financial Control Framework' (December 2003), 14p. The

report can be found on the association's website at www.apsfa-agffp.com. See Kathryn May, 'Federal Accountants Call for Order,' *National Post*, 8 December 2003, A7.

32 David Tilson, Standing Committee on Access to Information, Privacy and Ethics, *Evidence*, 15 February 2005, [26], and 'Balance of Power: Is the PMO so Powerful That Cabinet Is Becoming Irrelevant?' *Star-Phoenix*, 5 October 2002, E1; Garry Wills, *A Necessary Evil: A History of American Distrust of Government* (New York: Simon and Schuster, 1999), 57.

33 Parliamentary Centre, 'Stress and MPs,' *Occasional Papers on Parliamentary Government* no. 9 (November 1999): 4.

34 Matthias Rioux, 'The Roots of Our Democratic Malaise,' *CPR* 25, no. 4 (Winter 2002–3): 8. For similar criticism in Great Britain, see David Beetham, Iain Byrne, Pauline Nagan, and Stuart Weir, *Democracy under Blair: A Democratic Audit of the United Kingdom* (London: Politico's Publishing, 2002), 238.

35 Ran Hirschl, *Toward Juristocracy: The Origin and Consequences of the New Constitutionalism* (Cambridge, MA: Harvard University Press, 2004), 215 and 217.

36 John Uhr, *Deliberative Democracy in Australia: The Changing Place of Parliament* (Cambridge: Cambridge University Press, 1998), 84.

37 John B. Stewart, *The Canadian House of Commons: Procedure and Reform* (Montreal and Kingston: McGill-Queen's University Press, 1977).

38 C.E.S. Franks, *The Parliament of Canada* (Toronto: University of Toronto Press, 1987), 8.

39 Canada, House of Commons, Special Committee on Reform of the House of Commons (the McGrath Committee), *Report*, June 1985; Parliamentary Centre, 'MPs Views on Committee Organization,' *Occasional Papers on Parliamentary Government* no. 11 (May 2002): 5.

40 Peter Milliken, 'The Future of the Committee System,' in Gordon Barnhart, ed., *Parliamentary Committees: Enhancing Democratic Governance* (London: Cavendish Publishing, 1999), at 82–95.

41 Lawrence D. Longley and Roger H. Davidson, 'Parliamentary Committees: Changing Perspectives on Changing Institutions,' in Lawrence D. Longley and Roger H. Davidson, eds, *The New Roles of Parliamentary Committees* (London: Frank Cass, 1998), 1.

42 J. Richardson, *The Market for Political Activism: Interest Groups as a Challenge to Political Parties* (San Domenico: European University Institute, 1994), quoted in Arthur Lipow and Patrick Seyd, 'The Politics of Anti-Partyism,' *Parliamentary Affairs* 49, no. 2 (1996): 276.

43 Parliament, House of Commons, *Debates* (4 October 2002) at 329 (Dick Proctor).

44 Arthur Kroeger, 'How to Keep Parliament Relevant,' in Canadian Study of Parliament Group, 'The Eclipse of Parliament? The Concentration of Power in Canadian Politics' (Ottawa: Canadian Study of Parliament Group, 26–7 November 1999), 1.

45 John Stewart, *The Canadian House of Commons*, 27. 'As a proportion of those who had been on the [Labour] backbenches at any point since 2001, almost two-thirds (65%) had rebelled [by November 2003].' Philip Cowley and Mark Stuart, 'Parliament: More Bleak House than Great Expectations,' *Parliamentary Affairs* 57, no. 2 (2004): 311.

46 Rt Hon. Robin Cook, 'A Modern Parliament in a Modern Democracy,' State of the Union Annual Lecture, Constitution Unit, University College London, December 2001, 5.

47 Donald J. Savoie, *Governing from the Centre: The Concentration of Power in Canadian Politics* (Toronto: University of Toronto Press, 1999).

48 C.P. Ilbert, *Legislative Methods and Forms*, 213, quoted in J.A.G. Griffith, 'The Place of Parliament in the Legislative Process, Part 1,' *Modern Law Review* 14, no. 3 (July 1951): 284 (emphasis in original); C.A. Stuart, 'Our Constitution Outside the British North America Act' (Address to the Saskatchewan Bar Association, 1925), in R. MacGregor Dawson, ed., *Constitutional Issues in Canada, 1900–1931* (London: Oxford University Press, 1933), 7.

49 The list is found in Alan Siaroff, 'Varieties of Parliamentarianism in Advanced Industrial Democracies,' *International Political Science Review* 24, no. 4 (2003): 452.

50 W.T. Stanbury, 'Looking for a Legacy Mr Prime Minister? I Got One for You: Forget the Orgy of Spending and Champion Parliamentary Reform,' *The Hill Times*, 21 October 2002, 18. The office of leader of the opposition is significantly understudied. According to Mackenzie King, speaking as prime minister in 1928, 'it differed in degree rather than in kind' from 'the position of leader of the government.' H. McD. Clokie, 'Formal Recognition of the Leader of the Opposition in Parliaments of the Commonwealth,' *Political Science Quarterly*, 69, no. 3 (1954), 445.

51 Privy Council Office, *Ethics, Responsibility, Accountability: An Action Plan for Democratic Reform* (Ottawa: Privy Council Office, February 2004).

52 For corroboration of this point, see Jonathan Malloy, 'The House of Commons under the Chrétien Government,' in G. Bruce Doern, ed., *How Ottawa Spends, 2003–2004: Regime Change and Policy Shift* (Toronto: Oxford University Press, 2003), 65.

53 See David E. Smith, 'The Affair of the Chairs,' *Constitutional Forum* 13, no. 2 (Fall 2003): 42–9.

54 Parliament, House of Commons, *Debates*, 'Speaker's Ruling on the Application of the Progressive Conservative Democratic Representative Coalition for Recognition in the House of Commons,' 24 September 2001: 5489.

55 Jennifer Smith, 'Democracy and the Canadian House of Commons at the Millennium,' *CPA* 42, no. 4 (Winter 1999): 411.

56 Brenton Harding, 'Free Votes, Term Limits Would Hurt the West,' *Edmonton Journal*, 3 July 2004, A17. For a counter-argument, see David Kilgour and John Kirsner, 'Party Discipline and Canadian Democracy,' *CPR* 11, no. 3 (Autumn 1988): 10–11: 'Coalitions composed of members of all parties could exist for the purpose of working together on issues of common regional or other concerns.'

57 Christopher Garner, 'Confused Signals: Backbench Voting Behaviour on Private Members Bills,' Paper submitted to the British Columbia Political Studies Association, 2000 Conference, Victoria, BC, 5–6 May 2000. On use, see R.R. Walsh, 'By the Numbers: A Statistical Survey of Private Member's [sic] Bills,' *CPR* 25, no. 1 (Spring 2002): 29–33.

58 A rare scholarly study is Christopher Hood, 'Looking After Number One? Politicians' Rewards and the Economics of Politics,' *Political Studies* 40 (1992): 207–26.

59 Parliamentary Centre, 'The Question Period: What Former Members Think,' *Occasional Papers on Parliamentary Government* no. 12 (May 2001): 5 and 7.

60 Parliament, House of Commons, *Debates*, 20 April 1883, 764, cited in Norman Ward, 'The Formative Years of the House of Commons, 1867–91,' *CJEPS* 18, no. 4 (November 1952): 445.

61 See Michael Hart, *A Trading Nation: Canadian Trade Policy from Colonialism to Globalization* (Vancouver: University of British Columbia Press, 2002), ch. 13, 'Full Circle: The New Reciprocity.'

62 T. Caldwell, 'Letter,' *National Post*, 25 January 2003, B12.

63 The speaker, John Harvard, then parliamentary secretary to the minister of international trade, also cited the cautions uttered in the report of the Royal Commission on Electoral Reform and Party Financing, vol. 2, 'Reforming Electoral Democracy,' 77–8, http://www.parl.gc.ca/37/3/parlbus/ chambus/house/debates/042_2004–04–27/han042_1500–E.htm.

64 Don Martin, 'Democracy in Retreat in Canada Today: Power Has Shifted to Single Party with One Leader,' *Edmonton Journal*, 29 September 2002, A1.

65 Public Policy Forum, 'Ministerial Accountability: Suggestions for Reform,' Report of a Series of Roundtables of Experts, June 2004, 3, http:// www.ppforum.com/ow/ministerial_accountability.pdf.

66 Sharon L. Sutherland, 'The Report of the Liaison Committee on the Effectiveness of House of Commons Committees,' *Parliamentary Government* no. 44 (August 1993): 8–9 (emphasis in original).

67 Kevin Michael Grace, 'Parliament of Ombudsmen.'

68 R.W. Johnson, 'The Rainbow Nation Paints Out the Whites,' *The Sunday Times*, 27 July 2003, 4.7.

69 Hugo Young, *The Iron Lady: A Biography of Margaret Thatcher* (New York: Farrar Straus Giroux, 1989), 360.

70 An exception is James Irvine Cairns, 'A New Approach to the Study of a New Party: The Bloc Québécois in Parliament' (MA thesis, University of Saskatchewan, 2003).

71 Fraser Institute, 'Measuring the Growing "Democracy Gap" between the Supreme Court and Parliament,' *Canada NewsWire*, 6 August, 2003. During the Gomery Inquiry, Stephen Harper, then leader of the Official Opposition, warned against any procedural appeal to 'Chrétien-appointed judges' on the Federal Court of Canada.

72 Martin, 'Democracy in Retreat in Canada Today,' A1.

73 Janice Tibbets, 'Legal Experts Agree on Transparent System to Vet Judges,' *CanWest News*, 23 March 2004, 1. Kirk Makin, 'High-Court Reform Proposals Imminent,' *Globe and Mail*, 20 April 2004, A6. See too Jacob S. Ziegel, 'Merit Selection and Democratization of Appointments to the Supreme Court of Canada,' *Choices*, IRPP, 5, no. 2 (June 1999).

74 Patrick J. Monahan and Peter W. Hogg, 'We Need an Open Parliamentary Review of Court Appointments,' *National Post*, 24 April 2004, A19.

75 Allan Hutchinson, 'Let's Try Democracy When Choosing Top Judges,' *Globe and Mail*, 3 March 2004, A15.

76 Janice Tibbetts, "MPs Blast Cotler for Dismissing Judge Report,' *National Post*, 8 November 2004, A5; Campbell Clark, 'Plan for Top Court Judges Attacked by Opposition,' *Globe and Mail*, 9 April 2005, A6. See too, Canada, Parliament, House of Commons, Standing Committee on Justice, Human Rights, Public Safety and Emergency Preparedness, *Improving the Supreme Court of Canada Appointments Process* (May 2004; chair, Derek Lee, MP).

77 Larry D. Kramer, *The People Themselves: Popular Constitutionalism and Judicial Review* (New York: Oxford University Press, 2004).

78 David C. Docherty, *Legislatures* (Vancouver: University of British Columbia Press, 2005), 7.

79 Task Force on Canadian Unity, *A Future Together: Observations and Recommendations* (Ottawa: Minister of Supply and Services Canada, 1979), 101; Ian Peach, *Legitimacy on Trial: A Process for Appointing Justices to the Supreme Court of Canada*, Saskatchewan Institute of Public Policy, Public Policy Paper No. 30 (February 2005), 2–3.

80 C. Gwendolyn Landolt, 'Judging the Judges: Canada's Courts Simply Have Too Much Power,' *Calgary Herald*, 1 June 2003, A11. For example, according to Allan Hutchinson, Supreme Court judgeships are '[c]urrently the gift of

the Prime Minister's Office ...': 'Let's Try Democracy When Choosing Top Judges.'

81 Amy Carmichael, 'PM Promises to Allow MPs Right to Vet Appointments,' *Ottawa Citizen*, 28 February 2004, A3.

82 Mark Kennedy, 'Prime Minister Comes Up Short on Tall Order,' *National Post*, 17 March 2005. For a survey of governor-in-council appointments, see Public Policy Forum, *Governor-in Council Appointments: Best Practices and Recommendations for Reform* (February 2004), 61 pp, http://www.ppforum. com/ow/gov_apt_reform.pdf.

83 Janice Tibbets, 'Supreme Secrets,' *National Post*, 27 April 2004, A6.

84 R. MacGregor Dawson, *The Principle of Official Independence: With Particular Reference to the Political History of Canada* (Toronto: S.B. Gundy, 1922), 28.

85 Cristin Schmitz, 'Martin Idea Would Turn Search for Justices into Circus: Lamer,' *CanWest News*, 18 November 2002, 1.

86 David C. Docherty, *Legislatures*, 157.

6. Who Are the People?

1 Roger Gibbins, 'Re: Free and Honest Elections Are the Lynchpin of Democracy,' Online, retrieved e-mail (19 December 2004).

2 Paco Francoli, '"Deepening Crisis" Grips Canadian Democracy: Kingsley Launches Ambitious Plan to Get Young Canadians to Start Voting,' *The Hill Times*, 31 March 2003, 20, and 'Editorial,' *Windsor Star*, 31 March 2004, A6; see too Jon H. Pammett and Lawrence Le Duc, *Explaining the Turnout Decline in Canadian Federal Elections: A New Survey of Non-Voters* (Ottawa: Elections Canada, March 2003), 21.

3 Bill Graveland, 'Chief Electoral Officer Sounds Alarm over Youth Voters at Calgary Conference,' *Canadian Press NewsWire*, 30 October 2003.

4 Doug Ward, 'Growing Number of Young Voters Can't Be Bothered to Cast Ballot,' *Leader-Post* (Regina), 10 October 2002, B7. For a discussion of comparative turnout, see Pippa Norris, *Democratic Phoenix: Reinventing Political Activism* (New York: Cambridge University Press, 2002), ch. 3, 'Mapping Turnout.'

5 Norris, *Democratic Phoenix*, 188.

6 David Zussman, 'The Danger of Apathy: Good Governance Requires a Belief That Parliament Matters,' *Ottawa Citizen*, 25 May 2004, A19; Graveland, 'Chief Electoral Officer Sounds Alarm'; Gibbins, 'Free and Honest Elections Are the Lynchpin of Democracy'; Francoli, '"Deepening Crisis" Grips Canadian Democracy.'

7 Tim Naumetz, 'Lower Voting Age to 16, Chief Electoral Officer Says,' *Star-*

Phoenix, 27 March 2004, C12; Francoli, '"Deepening Crisis" Grips Canadian Democracy'; 'Parliament May Have to Make Voting Mandatory: Chief Electoral Officer,' *Canadian Press NewsWire*, 19 December 2000; Elections Canada, 'On Line Voter Registration Feasibility Study, Executive Summary,' http://www.elections.ca/content.asp?sections=1oi&dir=fea&document=index&lang.

8 Jerome H. Black, 'The National Register of Electors: Raising Questions about the New Approach to Voter Registration in Canada,' *Policy Matters*, IRPP, 1, no. 10 (December 2000); John C. Courtney and David E. Smith, 'Registering Voters: Canada in a Comparative Context,' in Michael Cassidy, ed., *Democratic Rights and Electoral Reform*, Royal Commission on Electoral Reform and Party Financing, vol. 10, Research Studies (Toronto: Dundurn Press, 1993), 343–461. F. Abbas Rana 'MPs Worried, Permanent Voters' List Drives Down Voter Turnout,' *The Hill Times*, 13 October 2003, 1.

9 Rana, 'MPs Worried, Permanent Voters' List Drives Down Voter Turnout'; Parliament, Senate, Standing Committee on Legal and Constitutional Affairs, *Proceedings* (16 February 2005), 6:18 (Senator Lorna Milne); and Standing Committee on National Finance, *Evidence* (8 February 2005): 'The National Register of Electors is a distinct factor to the low turnout for the voters' list' (Senator Pierrette Ringuette).

10 Centre for Research and Information on Canada, 'Voter Participation in Canada: Is Canadian Democracy in Crisis?' CRIC Papers (Montreal: Centre for Research and Information on Canada, October 2001), 44p; Joan Bryden, 'Reform Needed to Stem Low Voter Turnout: Proportional Representation Advocated to Restore Faith in Government,' *National Post*, 2 January 2002, A2.

11 Henry Milner, ed., *Making Votes Count: Reassessing Canada's Electoral System* (Peterborough: Broadview Press, 1999); Law Commission of Canada, *Voting Counts: Electoral Reform in Canada* (Ottawa: Law Commission of Canada, 2004); Centre for Research and Information on Canada, *Voter Participation in Canada*, 36.

12 Ibid.

13 Nick Loenen, 'Our Parliament Is a Disgrace to Democracy,' *Vancouver Sun*, 30 November 2000, A23.

14 Walter Robinson and Judy Rebick, 'Why We Need to Change Electoral System,' *Toronto Star*, 17 October 2002, A31.

15 Kalvin Reid, 'Electoral System Has Left Canadian Government "Dysfunctional," Says Broadbent,' *Canadian Press NewsWire*, 6 May 2003; 'Canadian Electoral System a "Disaster," Broadbent Says,' *Globe and Mail*, 7 May 2003, A14.

16 Alan Cairns, 'The Electoral System and the Party System in Canada, 1921–1965,' *CJPS* 1, no. 1 (March 1968): 55–80.

17 Doris Anderson, 'Lack of Women Real Deficit,' *Toronto Star*, 25 May 2004, A25.

18 John C. Courtney, 'Can PR Deliver All That It Promises?' *Winnipeg Free Press*, 18 March 2004, http://www.winnipegfreepress.com/westview/v-printerfriendly/story.

19 Ibid.

20 Law Commission of Canada, *Voting Counts*. The adjective 'respected' is John Ibbitson's; see his 'Use Proportional System in Elections, Report Urges,' *Globe and Mail*, 31 March 2004, A1 and A12. Ibbitson also said, 'Although the recommendations are non-binding, the commission's stature and impartiality ... will add considerable impetus to efforts to address the so-called democratic deficit.'

21 Paco Francoli, 'Senior Bureaucrat Urges Changes to Voting System: "There Is a Sense of Fatigue about Our Democratic Institutions,"' *The Hill Times*, 10 March 2003, 16. The president of the commission was Natalie Des Rosiers, a law professor at the University of Ottawa. Following 'preliminary research' but before the 'public consultation process,' the commission's communications director described the plurality system as 'downright undemocratic' and 'dysfunct[ional].' Janice Tibbets, 'Revamp Voting System: Law Panel: Commission Says Poor Turnout Can Be Blamed on "Dysfunction."' *Ottawa Citizen*, 22 October 2002, A3.

22 The quotation comes from B. Schwartz and D. Rettie, *Valuing Canadians: The Options for Voting System Reform in Canada* (Ottawa: Law Commission of Canada, 2002), 51, and Lisa Young, *Electoral Systems and Representative Legislatures: Consideration of Alternative Electoral Systems* (Ottawa: Canadian Advisory Council on the Status of Women, 1994), 6.

23 Keith Archer, 'Reform or Social Engineering,' *Winnipeg Free Press*, 4 April 2004, http://www.winnipegfreepress.com/westview/v-printerfriendly/story.

24 I wish to thank my colleague Duff Spafford for helping clarify these distinctions and for sharing with me his indispensable memorandum 'Representation: What Does It Mean?'

25 Law Commission of Canada, *Voting Counts*, 8–10.

26 Philip Norton, 'The Case for the Existing Electoral System,' Secretary of State for the Home Department, *The Report of the Independent Commission on the Voting System*, 2 vols (London: Stationery Office, October 1998, Cm 4090), 3.

27 Robert A. Milen, 'Aboriginal Constitutional Electoral Reform,' in Robert A. Milen, ed., *Aboriginal Peoples and Electoral Reform in Canada*, vol. 9 of the Research Studies of the Royal Commission on Electoral Reform and Party

Financing (Toronto: Dundurn Press, 1991), 48, cited in Jonathan Malloy and Graham White, 'Aboriginal Participation in Canadian Legislatures,' in R.J. Fleming and J.E. Glenn, eds, *Fleming's Canadian Legislatures 1997* (Toronto: University of Toronto Press, 1997), 62. See as well, Doug Cuthand, 'To Vote or Not to Vote, That Is the Question,' *Leader Post* (Regina), 7 June 2004, B1.

28 John Ibbitson, 'Frazzled in the Forum: A Besieged PM Hangs On,' *Globe and Mail*, 23 April 2005, A8.

29 Malloy and White, 'Aboriginal Participation in Canadian Legislatures,' 65.

30 Chris Lackner and Bill Curry, 'Aboriginal Groups to Sit on House Committee,' *Star-Phoenix* (Saskatoon), 29 March 2004, A6. See too, Bill Curry, 'Native Leaders, PM to Hold First-Ever Budget Talks,' *Star-Phoenix* (Saskatoon), 10 March 2004, A11.

31 Cristin Schmitz, 'Cotler Urges Consideration of Aboriginal Supreme Court Judge,' *CanWest News*, 23 January 2004, 1. One of the 'proposals' passed by the Saskatchewan Conference of the United Church of Canada at its 2005 meeting spoke of 'petition[ing] all government agencies (Provincial, Federal and First Nations Leaders).' 'Important Proposals (formerly "Resolutions") Discussed and Passed at Conference, May 26–28, 2005,' circulated to congregations, 5 June 2005.

32 Chris Lackner and Bill Curry, 'Aboriginal Groups to Sit on House Committee.'

33 Lisa Young, 'Electoral Systems and Representative Legislatures,' *CPR* 21, no. 3 (Autumn 1998): 13.

34 See J.R. Mallory, 'Vacation of Seats in the House of Commons: The Problem of Burnaby-Coquitlam,' *CJEPS*, 30, no. 1 (February 1964): 125–30.

35 Brooke Jeffrey, *Hard Right Turn: The New Face of Neo-Conservatism in Canada* (Toronto: HarperCollins, 1999), 406.

36 Richard Goreham, *Language Rights and the Court Challenges Program: A Review of Its Accomplishments and Impact of Its Abolition*, Report submitted to the Commissioner of Official Languages (Ottawa: Commissioner of Official Languages, 1992), 3. The program was abolished by the Mulroney government in 1992, but reinstated by the Chrétien government in 1994.

37 Lisa Young and Joanna Everitt, *Advocacy Groups* (Vancouver: University of British Columbia Press, 2004), 4.

38 Ibid., 81 and 82.

39 Ibid., 10 and 11.

40 F.L. Morton and Rainer Knopff, *The Charter Revolution and the Court Party* (Peterborough: Broadview Press, 2000), ch. 4.

41 See Murray Dobbin, *The Myth of the Corporate Citizen* (Toronto: Stoddart Publishing, 1998), 182–206; and his *Preston Manning and the Reform Party*

(Toronto: James Lorimer, 1991), 95–8; Brooke Jeffrey, *Hard Right Turn*, 404–13.

42 National Citizens' Coalition, 'Who We Are, What We Do' (Toronto: nd); Mike Scandiffio, 'Wheat War between NCC and Goodale,' *The Hill Times*, 1 June 1998, 2; Frank Luba, ''97 MPs Line Up for Trough Day,' *The Province* (Vancouver), 25 October 1999, A2; NCC website at http://www.morefreedom.org/new_page_42.htm.

43 Peter Riddell, *Parliament under Blair* (London: Politico's Publishing, 2000), 203.

44 Canada, Parliament, Senate of Canada/House of Commons, Special Joint Committee on a Code of Conduct, *Proceedings* (16 October 1995), 5:15 and 5:18.

45 *Canadian Taxpayers Federation v. Ontario (Minister of Finance)*, 2004 CanLll 48177 (ON S.C.), para. 58; Kirk Makin, 'Politician's [sic] Promises Not Set in Stone, Court Says,' *Globe and Mail*, www.GlobeandMail.com (29 January 2005).

46 Lorraine Eisenstat Weinrib, 'Canada's Constitutional Revolution: From Legislative to Constitutional State,' *Israel Law Review*, 33, no. 1 (Winter 1999), 24.

47 Evidence to test this proposition may be forthcoming in The Constituency Project, 'a two-year research programme investigating the state and practice of Canada's federal constituency offices': http://www.the constituencyproject.ca.

48 Joan Rydon, 'Upper Houses – The Australian Experience,' in G.S. Reid, ed., *The Role of Upper Houses Today* (Proceedings of the Fourth Annual Workshop of the Australasian Study of Parliament Group, 1983), 36.

49 Nelson Wiseman, 'Skeptical Reflections on Proportional Representation,' *Policy Options* 18, no. 9 (November 1997): 16.

50 Bill Curry, 'Public Institutions "Excessively Adversarial,"' *National Post*, 13 April 2004, A6.

51 Earl Grey, *Parliamentary Government Considered with Reference to a Reform of Parliament: An Essay* (London: Richard Bentley, 1858), 200–21.

52 Ibid., 99–100.

53 Alan Clark, *Diaries* (London: Phoenix Giant, 1993), 64.

54 John C. Courtney, *Elections* (Vancouver: University of British Columbia Press, 2004), 52.

55 Pierre Lortie, 'A Minimalist Electoral Reform Agenda,' *Policy Options*, IRPP, 18, no. 9 (November 1997): 24.

56 Colin Feasby 'Your Vote Is a Floating Currency: Let's Peg It,' *Globe and Mail*, 16 May 2002, A16.

57 Legislative Assembly of United Canada, *Parliamentary Debates on the Subject of the Confederation of the British North American Provinces* (Quebec: Hunter, Rose and Co., 1865; Ottawa: King's Printer, 1951), 499.

58 Doreen Barrie and Roger Gibbins, 'Parliamentary Careers in the Canadian Federal State,' *CJPS* 22, no. 1 (March 1989): 144.

59 Canada, Library of Parliament, *Members of the House of Commons, Comparative Table of Main Occupations by Category,* http://www.parl.gc.ca/information/about/people/key/occupations/index.asp?sect=sencur&lang=E&hea=6&leg=1&occ=lawyer&param&parl=.

60 See James Irvine Cairns, 'A New Approach to the Study of a New Party: The Bloc Québécois as a Party in Parliament' (MA thesis, University of Saskatchewan, 2003).

61 David C. Docherty, *Legislatures* (Vancouver: University of British Columbia Press, 2005), 109.

62 Pippa Norris, 'The Twilight of Westminster? Electoral Reform and Its Consequences,' *Political Studies* 49 (2001): 885 and 880–1 (emphasis in original).

63 Norwegian Study of Power and Democracy (2005), www.sv.uio.no/mutr/english/index.html. See Stein Ringen, 'Wealth and Decay: Norway Funds a Massive Political Self-Examination – and Finds Trouble for All,' *Times Literary Supplement*, 13 February 2004, 5.

64 Canadian Study of Parliament Group, 'Parliaments and the People: Improving Public Understanding' (Toronto: Canadian Study of Parliament Group, 28 April 1995), 10.

65 Canadian Study of Parliament Group, 'Public Attitudes about Parliament' (Kingston, 2 June 1991), 3. (The speaker was television journalist Don Newman.)

66 The phrase is James G. Gardiner's, forty-some year veteran of Canadian federal and provincial politics and tireless champion of the parliamentary (and party) system. Norman Ward and David E. Smith, *Jimmy Gardiner: Relentless Liberal* (Toronto: University of Toronto Press, 1990).

67 Paul Howe, 'Where Have All the Voters Gone?' *Inroads: The Canadian Journal of Opinion* 12 (Winter/Spring 2003): 80–1.

68 *Globe and Mail*, 10 January 2006, A13. The advertisement appeared as part of 'The Democracy Project, An Initiative of the Dominion Institute.'

7. The People's House of Commons and Its Study

1 See chapter 3, 59–64.

2 Peter Aucoin, 'Accountability: The Key to Restoring Public Confidence in Government' (The Timlin Lecture, University of Saskatchewan, 6 November 1997).

3 John Ibbitson, 'Stonewalling on Electoral Reform,' *Globe and Mail*, 17 June 2005, A4.

4 Robert Roach, 'Putting the *Demos* Back in Democracy' (Canada West Foundation: The West in Canada Project, June 2005), 3.

5 On MPs and used-car salesmen, see Parliamentary Centre, 'Stress and MPs' (Peter Dobell), *Occasional Papers on Parliamentary Government* no. 9 (November 1999), 4; on MPs and bankers, see David Docherty, 'Citizens and Legislators: Different Views on Representation,' in Neil Nevitte, ed., *Value Change and Governance in Canada* (Toronto: University of Toronto Press, 2001), 165.

6 See, for example, *Ontario (Speaker of the Legislative Assembly) v. Ontario (Human Rights Commission)* (2001), DLR (4th) 698 (Ont. C.A.).

7 Greg Tardi, *The Law of Democratic Governing, Volume 1: Principles* (Toronto: Thomson/Carswell, 2004), 107.

8 Onora O'Neill, *A Question of Trust*, BBC Reith Lectures 2002 (Cambridge: Cambridge University Press, 2002), 9; for a general Canadian review, see J. Patrick Boyer, *'Just Trust Us': The Erosion of Accountability in Canada* (Toronto: Dundurn Press, 2003).

9 Robert Skidelsky, 'The Shrinking State,' Review of David Marquand, *Decline of the Public* (London: Polity, 2004), in *Times Literary Supplement*, 24 June 2004.

10 The analogy (but with citizenship) is Ben Pimlott's; see *The Queen: Elizabeth II and the Monarchy* (London: HarperCollins, 1996), 569.

11 *Forum on Parliamentary Reform*, [June 2003], 9, http:www.parlcent.ca/publications/reform_e.pdf. See too Jane Jenson and Susan Philips, 'Regime Shift: New Citizenship Practices in Canada,' *International Journal of Canadian Studies* 14 (Fall 1996): 120.

12 Thomas S. Axworthy, 'Addressing the Accountability Deficit: Why Paul Martin's Minority Government Must Pay More Attention to the Three A's,' www.queensu.ca/csd/AccountabilityDeficit-IRPP.pdf (21 April 2005). See Justice Dickson in *Queen v. Hauser*, [1979] 1 SCR 984 at 1021. Does high turnover of MPs affect the need for resources? There is an allusion to this effect in John Banigan, 'Comptrollership in the Martin Government,' *CMA Management* 38, no. 1, (March 2004): 50.

13 See, for example, Senate of Canada, Standing Committee on Rules, Procedures and the Rights of Parliament, *Evidence*, 15 November 2005. The subject was 'an oath of allegiance to Canada,' the witness, Father Jacques Monet, SJ.

14 Great Britain, House of Lords, *Debates*, 5 June 1996, cols 1254–1313. The quotation is at cols 1275–6.

15 *Canada (House of Commons) v. Vaid*, [2005] 1 SCR 667, para. 41. The first part of the quotation is from J.P. Joseph Maingot, *Parliamentary Privilege in Canada*, 2nd ed. (Montreal and Kingston: McGill-Queen's University Press, 1997).

16 Tardi, *The Law of Democratic Governing, Vol. 1: Principles*, xxxvii.

17 Ontario Human Rights Commission. *Life Together: A Report on Human Rights in Ontario* (Toronto: Queen's Printer for Ontario, 1977), 18. I wish to thank Professor T.H.B. Symons, chair of the Ontario Human Rights Commission at the time of the report's publication, for bringing this report to my attention. The Saskatchewan Bill of Rights has attracted scant scholarly attention. But see Carmela Patrias, 'Socialists, Jews and the 1947 Saskatchewan Bill of Rights,' *Canadian Historical Review* 87, no. 2 (June 2006), 265–92.

18 See Diana Woodhouse, 'The Role of Ministerial Responsibility in Motivating Ministers to Morality,' in Jenny Fleming and Ian Holland, eds, *Motivating Ministers to Morality* (Burlington, VT: Ashgate Dartmouth, 2001), 37–48, and Newcastle Law School Working Papers, 'The Reconstruction of Constitutional Responsibility' (2000/10), www.ncl.ac.uk/nuls/research/wpapers/woodhouse1.html. See too, Robert Gregory, 'Political Responsibility for Bureaucratic Incompetence: Tragedy at Cave Creek,' *Public Administration* 76, no. 3 (Autumn 1998): 519–38. For a fuller discussion of ministerial responsibility, see David E. Smith 'Clarifying the Doctrine of Ministerial Responsibility as It Applies to the Government and Parliament of Canada,' in *Research Studies*, Vol. 1, 'Restoring Accountability,' Commission of Inquiry into the Sponsorship Program and Advertising Activities (February 2006), 101–43.

19 Canada, Parliament, House of Commons, Standing Committee on Public Accounts, *Report: Governance in the Public Service of Canada: Ministerial and Deputy Ministerial Accountability* (Ottawa: May 2005), 21.

20 Paul G. Thomas, 'Parliamentary Reform through Political Parties,' in John C. Courtney, ed., *The Canadian House of Commons: Essays in Honour of Norman Ward* (Calgary: University of Calgary Press, 1985), 43–68 at 51.

21 Michael M. Atkinson and Paul G. Thomas, 'Studying the Canadian Parliament,' *Legislative Studies Quarterly* 18, no. 3 (August 1993): 423–51 at 430–1.

22 Canada, Parliament, House of Commons, Special Committee on Reform of the House of Commons, *First Report*, Minutes of Proceedings and Evidence, 2:10–11, quoted in Library of Parliament, 'Bill C-13: An Act to Amend the Parliament of Canada Act (Composition of the Board of Internal Economy),' prepared by James R. Robertson, Law and Government Division, 31 October 1997, 3.

23 David E. Smith, 'The Affair of the Chairs,' *Constitutional Forum* 13, no. 2

(Fall 2003): 42–9; Thomas S. Axworthy, 'Addressing the Accountability Deficit: Why Paul Martin's Minority Government Must Pay More Attention to the Three A's,' 21 April 2005, www.queensu.ca/csd/AccountabilityDeficit-IRPP.pdf. See also, S.L. Sutherland, 'Federal House Committee Reform: Mindless Adversarialism Well Done,' *Constitutional Forum* 13, no. 2 (Fall 2003): 50–63.

24 John Bryden, 'Reforming the Access to Information Act,' *CPR* 24, no. 2 (Summer 2000): 7.

25 Michael Bliss, 'A Short Guide to Our "Culture of Corruption,"' *National Post*, 13 March 2004, A17.

26 Institute on Governance, 'The Exercise of Power Round Table: Parliament, Politics and Citizens: A Conversation with Bob Rae,' http://www.iog.ca/publications/xrt6.pdf (14 January 1998). Rae attributes the inversion of Lord Acton's dictum to Pierre Trudeau. A sample of the more traditional diagnosis and prescription for Parliament's ills is in Claude Ryan, 'In Defence of Parliament,' *CPR* 25, no. 4 (Winter 2002–03): 13–15.

27 Lisa Young, 'Value Clash: Parliament and Citizens after 150 Years of Responsible Government,' in F. Leslie Seidle and Louis Massicotte, eds, *Taking Stock of 150 Years of Responsible Government in Canada* (Ottawa: Canadian Study of Parliament Group, 1999), 105–36 at 132.

28 John R. Hibbing and Elizabeth Theiss-Morse, *Congress as Public Enemy: Public Attitudes Toward American Political Institutions* (New York: Cambridge University Press, 1995), and John R. Hibbing and Elizabeth Theiss-Morse, *Stealth Democracy: Americans' Beliefs about How Government Should Work* (New York: Cambridge University Press, 2002).

29 Vernon Bogdanor, 'Introduction,' in Vernon Bogdanor, ed., *The British Constitution in the Twentieth Century* (Oxford: Oxford University Press, 2003), 1–28 at 15.

30 Norman Ward, 'The Formative Years of the House of Commons, 1867–1891,' *CJEPS* 18, no. 4 (November 1952): 431–51 at 451.

31 Preston Manning, 'Sleepless in Flanders Fields,' *Globe and Mail*, 19 March 2005, A17.

32 Campbell Clark and Bill Curry, '"Non-Confidence Vote" Plan for Election in February Scorned,' *Globe and Mail*, 15 November 2005, A9. For 'the customary flow of a general election; with annotations,' see Gregory Tardi, 'Political Law Notes in Anticipation of the 39th Federal General Election,' *Perspectives in Political Law*, updated 27 November 2005. The flow includes 'Choice of the timing at the discretion of the Prime Minister and subject to the consent of the Governor General (constitutional convention)'; 'Decision by Cabinet to hold an election, resulting in a recommendation, made

by Order in Council, that the Governor General dissolve the 38th Parliament (constitutional convention)'; 'Prime Minister's visit to the Governor General to request dissolution (constitutional convention)'; 'Governor General consents to dissolve the 38th Parliament (royal prerogative).' tardig@parl.gc.ca.

33 Robert Fife and David Vienneau, 'Senate Reform Awaits Plan from Provinces; Martin Offers Parliamentary Review of Senate Nominations for Now,' *Star-Phoenix* (Saskatoon), 19 December 2003, C11.

34 CanWest News Service, 'PM Backtracks on Senate Remarks,' *Windsor Star* 20 December 2003, C9.

35 Chris Baker, 'Political Illiteracy Bodes Ill for Reform,' *Winnipeg Free Press*, 7 November 2002, A13. Chris Baker was a vice-president at Environics Research Group in November 2002.

36 The social scientist was Richard Rose of the University of Strathclyde, Glasgow, U.K.

37 *Angus v. Canada (1990)*, 72 DLR (4th), 684 (FCA), cited in Gregory Tardi, *The Legal Framework of Government: A Canadian Guide* (Aurora, ON: Canada Law Book, 1992), 83.

38 The list can be found in A.D.P. Heeney, 'Cabinet Government in Canada: Some Recent Developments in the Machinery of the Central Executive,' *CJEPS* 12, no. 3 (August 1946): Appendix A.

39 On lieutenant-governors, the authoritative work remains John T. Saywell, *The Office of Lieutenant-Governor: A Study in Canadian Government and Politics* (Toronto: University of Toronto Press, 1957). On the Senate, see David E. Smith, *The Canadian Senate in Bicameral Perspective* (Toronto: University of Toronto Press, 2003).

40 Vernon Bogdanor, 'Ministerial Accountability,' *Parliamentary Affairs* 50, no. 1 (January 1997): 71–83 at 82.

41 See John C. Courtney, *The Selection of National Party Leaders in Canada* (Toronto: Macmillan of Canada, 1973).

42 Ryan, 'In Defence of Parliament.'

43 A.W. Johnson, *Dream No Little Dreams: A Biography of the Douglas Government of Saskatchewan, 1944–1961* (Toronto: University of Toronto Press, 2004), 281–4.

44 Judith Maxwell, 'Hear, Hear for Citizen Input: If We Want More Engaged Voters, Let's Have Less Partisan Scoffing at Citizen-Politician Dialogues: They're Key to 21st-Century Democracy.' *Globe and Mail*, 30 April 2004, A21; see also, Gloria Galloway, 'Ontario Citizen Juries to Help Plan Budget,' *Globe and Mail*, 8 January 2004, A2.

45 But see Richard F. Fenno, *Home Style: House Members in Their Districts*

(Boston: Little Brown, 1978). For Canada, see David C. Docherty, *Mr Smith Goes to Ottawa: Life in the House of Commons* (Vancouver: University of British Columbia Press, 1997), ch. 7, 'Home Style: Members and Their Constituencies.'

46 'Students Aren't "Blank Slates" under Their Political T-Shirts,' *National Post*, 23 October 2003, A19.

47 Matthew Mendelsohn, 'Same-Sex Statistics,' *Globe and Mail*, 23 August 2003, A17.

48 See John C. Courtney and David E. Smith, 'Registering Voters: Canada in a Comparative Perspective,' in Michael Cassidy, ed., *Democratic Rights and Electoral Reform in Canada* (Toronto: Dundurn Press, 1993), 343–461; and Smith, 'Clarifying the Doctrine of Ministerial Responsibility.'

49 Haig Patapan, review of Elisabeth Gidengil, André Blais, Neil Nevitte, and Richard Nadeau, *Citizens* (Vancouver: University of British Columbia Press, 2004), in H-Net Book Review, H-NetCanada, http://www.h-net.org/~canada/index_en.html (17 March 2005).

8. Conclusion

1 Steven Shapin, *The Scientific Revolution* (Chicago: University of Chicago Press, 1996).

2 'Single Transferable Vote System Encouraged,' *Star-Phoenix* (Saskatoon), 9 May 2005, A7. The speaker was David Suzuki, the occasion the British Columbia referendum campaign on the proposal by the Citizens' Assembly to replace plurality voting with the single transferable vote.

3 Barry K. Winetrobe, 'Working In, With and For Parliaments,' *Newsletter*, Political Marketing Group, Political Studies Association Specialist Group, (April 2003), http://www.psa.ac.uk/spgrp/polmarket/newsletter/pmgn1tapril03.pdf.

4 Ibid.

5 Kathryn May, 'Election May Make [Gomery] Report Futile,' *Leader-Post* (Regina), 12 December 2005, A7.

6 See Larry D. Kramer, *The People Themselves: Popular Constitutionalism and Judicial Review* (New York: Oxford University Press, 2004), 16.

7 J.G. Bourinot, 'Canadian Studies in Comparative Perspective: Parliamentary Compared with Congressional Government,' *TRSC* Section II (1893): 77–108; W.P.M. Kennedy, *The Constitution of Canada, 1534–1937: An Introduction to Its Development, Law and Custom* (London: Oxford University Press, 1938).

8 Raphael Samuel, *Theatres of Memory, Vol. 1: Past and Present in Contemporary Culture* (London: Verso, 1994), 6.

9 Thomas H.B. Symons, 'The Contribution of Investigatory Commissions to Political Education,' in Jon H. Pammett and Jean-Luc Pepin, eds, *Political Education in Canada* (Halifax: Institute for Research on Public Policy, 1988), 127.

10 See David E. Smith, 'The Improvement of the Senate by Non-Constitutional Means,' in Serge Joyal, ed., *Protecting Canadian Democracy: The Senate You Never Knew* (Montreal and Kingston: McGill-Queen's University Press, 2003), 229–70.

Bibliography

Primary Sources

Government Records

CANADA

Citizens' Forum on Canada's Future. *Report to the People and Government of Canada*. Ottawa: Minister of Supply and Services Canada, 1991.

Legislative Assembly of United Canada. *Debates*.

– *Parliamentary Debates on the Subject of the Confederation of the British North American Provinces*. Quebec, 1865. Ottawa: King's Printer, 1951.

Parliament. House of Commons. *Debates*.

– Committee on Election Expenses. *Report of the Committee on Election Expenses*. Ottawa: Queen's Printer, 1966.

– Special Committee on Reform of the House of Commons (the McGrath Committee). *First Report*. December 1984. *Final Report*. June 1985.

– Standing Committee on Access to Information, Privacy and Ethics. *Evidence*. 15 February 2005.

– Standing Committee on Justice, Human Rights, Public Safety and Emergency Preparedness. *Report. Improving the Supreme Court of Canada Appointments Process*. May 2004.

– Standing Committee on Procedure and House Affairs. *Evidence*. 9 March 2004 and 9 March 2005.

– Standing Committee on Public Accounts. *Report. Governance in the Public Service of Canada: Ministerial and Deputy Ministerial Accountability*. Ottawa: May 2005.

Parliament. Senate. Standing Committee on Legal and Constitutional Affairs. *Proceedings*. 16 February 2005.

- Standing Committee on National Finance. *Evidence*. 8 February 2005.
- Standing Committee on Rules, Procedures and the Rights of Parliament. *Evidence*. 15 November 2005.
Parliament. Senate of Canada/House of Commons, Special Joint Committee on a Code of Conduct. *Proceedings*. October 1995.
Privy Council Office. *Ethics, Responsibility, Accountability: An Action Plan for Democratic Reform*. Ottawa: 2004.

ALBERTA
Alberta. 'Constitutional Referendum Act,' *RSA*, 2000, c. C-25.

BRITISH COLUMBIA
British Columbia. 'Recall and Initiative Act,' *RSBC* 1996, c. 398.
- British Columbia Citizens' Assembly on Electoral Reform. *The Final Report of the British Columbia Citizens' Assembly on Electoral Reform*. www.citizens assembly.bc.ca (October 2004).

NEW BRUNSWICK
New Brunswick. Commission on Legislative Democracy. *Final Report and Recommendations*. Fredericton: 2004.

PRINCE EDWARD ISLAND
Prince Edward Island. Prince Edward Island Commissioner of Electoral Reform. *Prince Edward Island Electoral Reform Report*. Charlottetown: 2003.

SASKATCHEWAN
Saskatchewan. 'An Act Respecting Referendums and Plebiscites,' *Statutes of Saskatchewan*, 1990–91, Chapter R-8.01.

GREAT BRITAIN
House of Lords. *Debates*. 5 June 1996, cols 1254–1313.
Secretary of State for the Home Department. *The Report of the Independent Commission on the Voting System*. London: Stationery Office, 1998.

Non-Governmental Records

CANADA
Ajzenstat, Janet, Paul Romney, Ian Gentles, and William D. Gairdner, eds. *Canada's Founding Debates*. Toronto: Stoddart Publishing, 1999.
Auditor General. *Report of the Auditor General of Canada to the House of Commons,*

Matters of Special Importance – 2003, Foreword and Main Points. Ottawa: Office of the Auditor General, November 2003.

Commission on the Future of Health Care in Canada. *Building on Values: The Future of Health Care in Canada – Final Report.* Saskatoon: Commission on the Future of Health Care in Canada, 2002.

Commission of Inquiry into the Deployment of Canadian Forces to Somalia. *Dishonoured Legacy: The Lessons of the Somalia Affair. Report of the Commission, vol. 1.* Ottawa: Minister of Public Works and Government Services, 1997.

Elections Canada. 'On Line Voter Registration Feasibility Study, Executive Summary.' 20 March 2003. http://www.elections.ca/content.asp?section=loi&dir=fea&document=index&lang=e&textonly=false.

Goreham, Richard. *Language Rights and the Court Challenges Program: A Review of Its Accomplishments and Impact of Its Abolition.* Ottawa: Commissioner of Official Languages, 1992.

Hoffman, David, and Norman Ward. *Bilingualism and Biculturalism in the Canadian House of Commons.* Documents of the Royal Commission on Bilingualism and Biculturalism. Ottawa: Queen's Printer, 1970.

Law Commission of Canada. *Voting Counts: Electoral Reform for Canada.* Ottawa: Law Commission of Canada, 2004.

Library of Parliament. 'Bill C-13: An Act to Amend the Parliament of Canada Act (Composition of the Board of Internal Economy).' Ottawa: Law and Government Division, 1997.

– *Members of the House of Commons, Comparative Table of Main Occupations by Category.* http://www.parl.gc.ca/information/about/people/key/occupations/index.asp?sect=sencur&lang=E&hea=6&leg=1&occ=lawyer&param&parl=.

Library of Parliament, Political and Social Affairs Division. *Referendums in Canada: The Effect of Populist Decision-Making on Representative Democracy.* Ottawa: Library of Parliament, 1993.

– *The Roles of the Members of Parliament in Canada: Are They Changing?* Ottawa: Library of Parliament, 2002.

Norton, Philip. 'The Case for the Existing Electoral System.' In Secretary of State for the Home Department, *The Report of the Independent Commission on the Voting System,* 2 vols, Cm 4090. London: Stationery Office, October 1998.

Ontario Human Rights Commission. *Life Together: A Report on Human Rights in Ontario.* Toronto: Queen's Printer for Ontario, 1977.

Pammett, Jon H., and Lawrence Le Duc. *Explaining the Turnout Decline in Canadian Federal Elections: A New Survey of Non-Voters.* Ottawa: Elections Canada, March 2003.

Royal Commission on the Economic Union and Development Prospects for

Canada. *Report*. 3 vols. Ottawa: Minister of Supply and Services Canada, 1985.

Royal Commission on Electoral Reform and Party Financing. *Report*. Ottawa: Minister of Supply and Services, 1991.

Schwartz, B., and D. Rettie. *Valuing Canadians: The Options for Voting System Reform in Canada*. Ottawa: Law Commission of Canada, 2002.

Smith, David E. 'Clarifying the Doctrine of Ministerial Responsibility as It Applies to the Government and Parliament of Canada.' Research Paper for Commission of Inquiry into the Sponsorship Program and Advertising Activities. February 2006.

Task Force on Canadian Unity. *A Future Together: Observations and Recommendations*. Ottawa: Supply and Services, 1979.

Secondary Sources

Books and Monographs

Adams, Michael. *Fire and Ice: The United States, Canada and the Myth of Converging Values*. Toronto: Penguin Canada, 2003.

Ajzenstat, Janet, ed. *Canadian Constitutionalism, 1791–1991*. Ottawa: Canadian Study of Parliament Group, [1992].

Bach, Stanley. *Platypus and Parliament: The Australian Senate in Theory and Practice*. Canberra: Department of the Senate, 2003.

Beauchesne, A. *Rules and Forms of the House of Commons of Canada*. 3rd ed. Toronto: Canada Law Book Co., 1943.

Beetham, David, Iain Byrne, Pauline Nagan, and Stuart Weir. *Democracy under Blair: A Democratic Audit of the United Kingdom*. London: Politico's Publishing, 2002.

Behiels, Michael. *Canada's Francophone Minority Communities: Constitutional Renewal and the Winning of School Governance*. Montreal and Kingston: McGill-Queen's University Press, 2004.

Blais, André, and Elisabeth Gidengil. *Making Representative Democracy Work: The Views of Canadians*. Royal Commission on Electoral Reform and Party Financing, vol. 17, Research Studies. Toronto: Dundurn Press, 1991.

Bothwell, Robert, and William Kilbourn. *C.D. Howe: A Biography*. Toronto: McClelland and Stewart, 1979.

Boyer, J. Patrick. *'Just Trust Us': The Erosion of Accountability in Canada*. Toronto: Dundurn Press, 2003.

Bricker, Darrell, and Edward Greenspon. *Searching for Certainty: Inside the New Canadian Mindset*. Toronto: Doubleday Canada, 2001.

Bryce, James (Viscount). *Canada: An Actual Democracy.* Toronto: Macmillan, 1921.

Cairns, Alan C. *Citizens Plus: Aboriginal People and the Canadian State.* Vancouver: University of British Columbia Press, 2000.

Cannadine, David. *G.M. Trevelyan: A Life in History.* London: Penguin Books, 1992.

Clark, Alan. *Diaries.* London: Phoenix Giant, 1993.

Cobb, Chris. *Ego and Ink: The Inside Story of Canada's National Newspaper War.* Toronto: McClelland and Stewart, 2004.

Corrigan, Philip, and Derek Sayer. *The Great Arch: English State Formation as Cultural Revolution.* Oxford: Basil Blackwell, 1985.

Courtney, John C. *Commissioned Ridings: Designing Canada's Electoral Districts.* Montreal and Kingston: McGill-Queen's University Press, 2001.

– *Elections.* Vancouver: University of British Columbia Press, 2004.

– *The Selection of National Party Leaders in Canada.* Toronto: Macmillan of Canada, 1973.

Courtney, John C., ed. *The Canadian House of Commons: Essays in Honour of Norman Ward.* Calgary: University of Calgary Press, 1985.

Dawson, R. MacGregor. *Constitutional Issues in Canada, 1900–1931.* Toronto: Oxford University Press, 1933.

– *The Government of Canada.* 5th ed. Revised by Norman Ward. Toronto: University of Toronto Press, 1970.

– *The Principle of Official Independence: With Particular Reference to the Political History of Canada.* Toronto: S.B. Gundy, 1922.

Dewar, Elaine. *The Second Tree: Of Clones, Chimeras and Quests for Immortality.* Toronto: Random House Canada, 2004.

Dicey, A.V. *An Introduction to the Study of the Law of the Constitution.* 10th ed. Intro. E.C.S. Wade. London: Macmillan and Co., 1962.

Dobbin, Murray. *The Myth of the Corporate Citizen.* Toronto: Stoddart Publishing, 1998.

– *Preston Manning and the Reform Party.* Toronto: James Lorimer, 1991.

Docherty, David C. *Legislatures.* Vancouver: University of British Columbia Press, 2005.

– *Mr Smith Goes to Ottawa: Life in the House of Commons.* Vancouver: University of British Columbia Press, 1997.

Downie, Jocelyn. *Dying Justice: A Case for Decriminalizing Euthanasia and Assisted Suicide in Canada.* Toronto: University of Toronto Press, 2004.

English, Allan D. *Understanding Military Culture: A Canadian Perspective.* Montreal and Kingston: McGill-Queen's University Press, 2004.

English, John. *The Decline of Politics: The Conservatives and the Party System, 1901–20.* Toronto: University of Toronto Press, 1977.

Fenno, Richard F. *Home Style: House Members in Their Districts*. Boston: Little Brown, 1978.

Foot, Michael. *Aneurin Bevan*. 2 vols. London: Granada, 1975.

Forsey, Eugene A. *The Royal Power of Dissolution of Parliament in the British Commonwealth*. Toronto: Oxford University Press, 1943.

Franks, C.E.S. *The Parliament of Canada*. Toronto: University of Toronto Press, 1987.

Fraser, John A. *The House of Commons at Work*. Montreal and Fredericton: Editions de la Chenelière, 1993.

Gaboury, Jean-Pierre, ed. *The Canadian House of Commons Observed*. Ottawa: University of Ottawa Press, 1979.

Gay, Oonagh, and Barry K. Winetrobe. *Officers of Parliament – Transforming the Role*. The Constitution Unit, University College London, April 2003.

Gerlach, Neil. *The Genetic Imaginary: DNA in the Canadian Criminal Justice System*. Toronto: University of Toronto Press, 2004.

Goldsworthy, Jeffrey. *The Sovereignty of Parliament: History and Philosophy*. Oxford: Clarendon Press, 1999.

Grey, Earl Henry George. *Parliamentary Government Considered with Reference to a Reform of Parliament: An Essay*. London: Richard Bentley, 1858.

Gunther, Magnus, and Conrad Winn, eds. *House of Commons Reform*. Ottawa: Parliamentary Internship Program, 1991.

Hart, Michael. *A Trading Nation: Canadian Trade Policy from Colonialism to Globalization*. Vancouver: University of British Columbia Press, 2002.

Hibbing, John R., and Elizabeth Theiss-Morse. *Congress as Public Enemy: Public Attitudes toward American Political Institutions*. New York: Cambridge University Press, 1995.

– *Stealth Democracy: America's Beliefs about How Government Should Work*. New York: Cambridge University Press, 2002.

Hirschl, Ran. *Toward Juristocracy: The Origin and Consequences of the New Constitutionalism*. Cambridge, MA: Harvard University Press, 2004.

Innis, Harold A., ed. *The Diary of Alexander James McPhail*. Toronto: University of Toronto Press, 1940.

Jeffrey, Brooke. *Hard Right Turn: The New Face of Neo-Conservatism in Canada*. Toronto: HarperCollins, 1999.

Jenkins, Roy. *Gladstone: A Biography*. New York: Random House Trade Paperbacks, 1997.

Jennings, Sir Ivor. *Parliament*. 2nd ed. Cambridge: Cambridge University Press, 1957.

Johnson, A.W. *Dream No Little Dreams: A Biography of the Douglas Government of Saskatchewan, 1944–1961*. Toronto: University of Toronto Press, 2004.

Joyal, Serge, ed. *Protecting Canadian Democracy: The Senate You Never Knew.* Montreal and Kingston: McGill-Queen's University Press, 2003.

Kennedy, W.P.M. *The Constitution of Canada, 1534–1937: An Introduction to Its Development, Law and Custom.* London: Oxford University Press, 1938.

Kilbourn, William. *The Firebrand: William Lyon Mackenzie and the Rebellion in Upper Canada.* Toronto: Clarke, Irwin and Co., 1956.

Kramer, Larry D. *The People Themselves: Popular Constitutionalism and Judicial Review.* New York: Oxford University Press, 2004.

Laycock, David. *The New Right and Democracy in Canada.* Toronto: Oxford University Press, 2002.

– *Populism and Democratic Thought in the Canadian Prairies, 1910 to 1945.* Toronto: University of Toronto Press, 1990.

Leonard, Gerald. *The Invention of Party Politics: Federalism, Popular Sovereignty, and Constitutional Development in Jacksonian Illinois.* Chapel Hill: University of North Carolina Press, 2002.

Loewenberg, Gerhard, ed. *Modern Parliaments: Change or Decline?* Chicago: Aldine, Atherton, 1971.

Mackenzie, G. Calvin. *Scandal Proof: Do Ethics Laws Make Government Ethical?* Washington: Brookings Institution Press, 2002.

Maingot, Joseph P. *Parliamentary Privilege in Canada.* 2nd ed. Montreal and Kingston: McGill-Queen's University Press, 1997.

Manfredi, Christopher P. *Judicial Power and the Charter: Canada and the Paradox of Liberal Constitutionalism.* 2nd ed. Don Mills, ON: Oxford University Press, 2001.

Manning, Preston. *The New Canada.* Toronto: Macmillan Canada, 1992.

Marriott, J.A.R. *Second Chambers: An Inductive Study in Political Science.* Oxford: Clarendon Press, 1910.

Marshall, Geoffrey. *Constitutional Theory.* Oxford: Clarendon Press, 1971.

Martin, Robert Ivan. *The Most Dangerous Branch: How the Supreme Court of Canada Has Undermined Our Law and Our Democracy.* Montreal and Kingston: McGill-Queen's University Press, 2003.

Massicotte, Louis, André Blais, and Antoine Yoshinaka. *Establishing the Rules of the Game: Election Laws in Democracies.* Toronto: University of Toronto Press, 2004.

Miki, Roy. *Redress: Inside the Japanese Canadian Call for Justice.* Vancouver: Raincoast Books, 2004.

Milner, Henry, ed. *Making Votes Count: Reassessing Canada's Electoral System.* Peterborough: Broadview Press, 1999.

Morton, F.L., and Rainer Knopff. *The Charter Revolution and the Court Party.* Peterborough, ON: Broadview Press, 2000.

Morton, W.L. *The Progressive Party in Canada*. Toronto: University of Toronto Press, 1950.

Muller, F. Max, ed. *Memoirs of Baron Stockmar*. London: Longmans, Green and Co., 1872.

Nevitte, Neil. *The Decline of Deference: Canadian Value Change in Cross-National Perspective*. Peterborough, ON: Broadview Press, 1996.

Norris, Pippa. *Democratic Phoenix: Reinventing Political Activism*. New York: Cambridge University Press, 2002.

O'Neill, Onora. *A Question of Trust*. BBC Reith Lectures 2002. Cambridge: Cambridge University Press, 2002.

Pimlott, Ben. *The Queen: Elizabeth II and the Monarchy*. London: HarperCollins, 1996.

Power, Michael. *The Audit Society: Rituals of Verification*. Oxford: Oxford University Press, 1997.

Richardson, J. *The Market for Political Activism: Interest Groups as a Challenge to Political Parties*. San Domenico: European University Institute, 1994.

Riddell, Peter. *Parliament under Blair*. London: Politico's Publishing, 2000.

Romanow, Roy, Harold Leeson, and John Whyte. *Canada ... Notwithstanding: The Making of the Constitution, 1976–1982*. Toronto: Carswell/Methuen, 1984.

Russell, Peter H. *Constitutional Odyssey: Can Canadians Become a Sovereign People?* Toronto: University of Toronto Press, 1992.

Samuel, Raphael. *Theatres of Memory, Vol. 1: Past and Present in Contemporary Culture*. London: Verso, 1994.

Savoie, Donald J. *Governing from the Centre: The Concentration of Power in Canadian Politics*. Toronto: University of Toronto Press, 1999.

Saywell, John T. *The Lawmakers: Judicial Power and the Shaping of Canadian Federalism*. Osgoode Society for Canadian Legal History. Toronto: University of Toronto Press, 2002.

Seidle, F. Leslie, and David Docherty, eds. *Reforming Parliamentary Democracy*. Montreal and Kingston: McGill-Queen's University Press, 2003.

Seidle, F. Leslie, and Louis Massicotte, eds. *Taking Stock of 150 Years of Responsible Government in Canada*. Ottawa: Canadian Study of Parliament Group, 1999.

Shapin, Steven. *The Scientific Revolution*. Chicago: University of Chicago Press, 1996.

Sheldrick, Byron. *Perils and Possibilities: Social Activism and the Law*. Halifax: Fernwood Publishing, 2004.

Shewell, Hugh. *'Enough to Keep Them Alive': Indian Welfare in Canada, 1873–1965*. Toronto: University of Toronto Press, 2004.

Simpson, Jeffrey. *The Friendly Dictatorship*. Toronto: McClelland and Stewart, 2001.

Smith, David E. *The Canadian Senate in Bicameral Perspective*. Toronto: University of Toronto Press, 2003.

– *The Invisible Crown: The First Principle of Canadian Government*. Toronto: University of Toronto Press, 1995.

– *The Regional Decline of a National Party: Liberals on the Prairies*. Toronto: University of Toronto Press, 1981.

– *The Republican Option in Canada: Past and Present*. Toronto: University of Toronto Press, 1999.

Smith, Paul, ed. *Bagehot: The English Constitution*. Cambridge: Cambridge University Press, 2001.

Sontag, Susan. *On Photography*. New York: Anchor Books, 1990.

Stewart, Gordon. *The Origins of Canadian Politics: A Comparative Approach*. Vancouver: University of British Columbia Press, 1986.

Stewart, John B. *The Canadian House of Commons: Procedure and Reform*. Montreal and Kingston: McGill-Queen's University Press, 1977.

Tardi, Gregory. *The Law of Democratic Governing. Volume 1: Principles*. Toronto: Thomson/Carswell, 2004.

– *The Law of Democratic Governing. Volume 2: Jurisprudence*. Toronto: Thomson/Carswell, 2004.

– *The Legal Framework of Government: A Canadian Guide*. Aurora, ON: Canada Law Book, 1992.

Taylor, John Leonard. *Canadian Indian Policy during the Inter-War Years, 1918–1939*. Ottawa: Indian and Northern Affairs Canada, 1984.

Thompson, E.P. *The Making of the English Working Class*. London: Penguin Books, 1968.

Todd, Alpheus. *On Parliamentary Government in England: Its Origins, Development, and Practical Operation*. 2nd ed. 2 vols. London: Longmans, Green and Co., 1887–9.

Tuohy, Carolyn J. *Policy and Politics in Canada: Institutionalized Ambivalence*. Philadelphia: Temple University Press, 1992.

Uhr, John. *Deliberative Democracy in Australia: The Changing Place of Parliament*. Cambridge: Cambridge University Press, 1998.

Veitch, George Stead. *The Genesis of Parliamentary Reform*. London: Constable and Co., 1913.

Ward, Norman. *The Canadian House of Commons: Representation*. Toronto: University of Toronto Press, 1950.

– *The Public Purse: A Study in Canadian Democracy*. Toronto: University of Toronto Press, 1962.

Ward, Norman, and David E. Smith. *Jimmy Gardiner: Relentless Liberal*. Toronto: University of Toronto Press, 1990.

Weldon, T.D. *The Vocabulary of Politics*. London: Penguin Books, 1953; repr. Johnson Reprints Co., 1970.

Whitaker, Reginald. *The Government Party: Organizing and Financing the Liberal Party of Canada, 1930–58*. Toronto: University of Toronto Press, 1977.

Willison, Sir John. *Reminiscences: Political and Personal*. Toronto: McClelland and Stewart, 1919.

Wills, Garry. *Inventing America: Jefferson's Declaration of Independence*. New York: Doubleday, 1978.

– *A Necessary Evil: A History of American Distrust of Government*. New York: Simon and Schuster, 1999.

Young, Hugo. *The Iron Lady: A Biography of Margaret Thatcher*. New York: Farrar Straus Giroux, 1989.

Young, Lisa. *Electoral Systems and Representative Legislatures: Consideration of Alternative Electoral Systems*. Ottawa: Canadian Advisory Council on the Status of Women, 1994.

Young, Lisa, and Joanna Everitt. *Advocacy Groups*. Vancouver: University of British Columbia Press, 2004.

Chapters in Books

Bogdanor, Vernon. 'Introduction.' In Vernon Bogdanor, ed., *The British Constitution in the Twentieth Century*, 1–28. Oxford: Oxford University Press, 2003.

Carty, R. Kenneth, and W. Peter Ward. 'The Making of a Canadian Political Citizenship.' In R. Kenneth Carty and W. Peter Ward, eds, *National Politics and Community in Canada*, 65–79. Vancouver: University of British Columbia Press, 1986.

Courtney, John C., and David E. Smith. 'Registering Voters: Canada in a Comparative Perspective.' In Michael Cassidy, ed., *Democratic Rights and Electoral Reform in Canada*. Royal Commission on Electoral Reform and Party Financing, Vol. 10, Research Studies, 343–461. Toronto: Dundurn Press, 1993.

Docherty, David. 'Citizens and Legislators: Different Views on Representation.' In Neil Nevitte, ed., *Value Change and Governance in Canada*, 165–206. Toronto: University of Toronto Press, 2001.

Fortin, Pierre. 'Ethical Issues in the Debate on Reform of the Canada Elections Act: An Ethicological Analysis.' In Janet Hiebert, ed., *Political Ethics: A Canadian Perspective*. Royal Commission on Electoral Reform and Party Financing, vol. 12, Research Studies, 3–72. Toronto: Dundurn Press, 1990.

Franks, C.E.S. 'The Canadian Senate in Modern Times.' in Serge Joyal, ed., *Pro-*

tecting Canadian Democracy: The Senate You Never Knew, 152–88. Montreal and Kingston: McGill-Queen's University Press, 2003.

James, Patrick, Donald E. Abelson, and Micháel Lusztig. 'Introduction: The Myth of the Sacred in the Canadian Constitutional Order.' In Patrick James, Donald E. Abelson, and Micháel Lusztig, eds, *The Myth of the Sacred: The Charter, the Courts, and the Politics of the Constitution in Canada*, 3–14. Montreal and Kingston: McGill-Queen's University Press, 2002.

Jenson, Jane. 'The Costs of Political Elitism.' In C.E.S. Franks, J.E. Hodgetts, O.P. Dwivedi, Doug Williams, and V. Seymour Wilson, eds, *Canada's Century: Governance in a Maturing Society*, 217–37. Montreal and Kingston: McGill-Queen's University Press, 1995.

Kelly, James B. 'The Supreme Court of Canada and the Complexity of Judicial Activism.' In Patrick James, Donald E. Abelson, and Micháel Lusztig, eds, *The Myth of the Sacred: The Charter, the Courts and the Politics of the Constitution in Canada*, 97–124. Montreal and Kingston: McGill-Queen's University Press, 2002.

Longley, Lawrence D., and Roger H. Davidson. 'Parliamentary Committees: Changing Perspectives on Changing Institutions.' In Lawrence D. Longley and Roger H. Davidson, eds, *The New Roles of Parliamentary Committees*, 1–19. London: Frank Cass, 1998.

Malloy, Jonathan. 'The House of Commons under the Chrétien Government.' In G. Bruce Doern, ed., *How Ottawa Spends, 2003–2004: Regime Change and Policy Shift*, 59–71. Toronto: Oxford University Press, 2003.

Malloy, Jonathan, and Graham White. 'Aboriginal Participation in Canadian Legislatures.' In R.J. Fleming and J.E. Glenn, eds, *Fleming's Canadian Legislatures 1997*, 60–72. Toronto: University of Toronto Press, 1997.

Manning, Preston. 'Democracy in the 21st Century: New Imperatives, Old Restraints.' In Richard M. Bird, ed., *Who Decides? Government in the New Millennium*, 25–35. Toronto: C.D. Howe Institute, 2004.

Milen, Robert A. 'Aboriginal Constitutional Electoral Reform.' In Robert A. Milen, ed., *Aboriginal Peoples and Electoral Reform in Canada*. Royal Commission on Electoral Reform and Party Financing, vol. 9, Research Studies, 3–65. Toronto: Dundurn Press, 1991.

Milliken, Peter. 'The Future of the Committee System.' In Gordon Barnhart, ed., *Parliamentary Committees: Enhancing Democratic Governance*, 135–59. London: Cavendish Publishing, 1999.

Minogue, Kenneth. 'Democracy as a *Telos*,' In Ellen Frankel Paul, Fred D. Miller Jr, and Jeffrey Paul, eds, *Democracy*, 203–24. New York: Cambridge University Press, 2000.

Rydon, Joan. 'Upper Houses – The Australian Experience.' In G.S. Reid, ed.,

The Role of Upper Houses Today, 22–42. Proceedings of the Fourth Annual Workshop of the Australasian Study of Parliament Group, 1983.

Smith David E. 'Clarifying the Doctrine of Ministerial Responsibility as It Applies to the Government and Parliament of Canada.' In Commission of Inquiry into the Sponsorship Program and Advertising Activities, *Research Studies*, Volume I, 'Restoring Accountability,' 101–43. Ottawa: Public Works and Government Services, 2006.

– 'The Improvement of the Senate by Non-Constitutional Means.' In Serge Joyal, ed., *Protecting Canadian Democracy: The Senate You Never Knew*, 229–70. Montreal and Kingston: McGill-Queen's University Press, 2003.

– 'Indices of Citizenship.' In Pierre Boyer, Linda Cardinal, and David Headon, eds, *From Subjects to Citizens: A Hundred Years of Citizenship in Australia and Canada*, 19–30. Ottawa: University of Ottawa Press, 2004.

– 'Party Government, Representation and National Integration in Canada.' In Peter Aucoin, ed., *Party Government and Regional Representation in Canada*, 1–68. Toronto: University of Toronto Press in Cooperation with the Royal Commission on the Economic Union and Development Prospects for Canada, 1985.

– 'Path Dependence and Saskatchewan Politics.' In Gregory P. Marchildon, ed., *The Heavy Hand of History: Interpreting Saskatchewan's Past*, 31–50. Regina: Canadian Plains Research Center, 2005.

– 'Saskatchewan Perspectives.' In Federation of Saskatchewan Indian Nations, *Saskatchewan and Aboriginal Peoples in the 21st Century: Social, Economic and Political Changes and Challenges*, 4–36. Regina: PrintWest Communications Ltd, 1997.

Spicer, Keith. 'Canada: Values in Search of a Vision.' In Robert E. Earle and John D. Wirth, eds, *Identities in North America: The Search for Community*, 13–28. Stanford: Stanford University Press, 1995.

Stuart, C.A. 'Our Constitution outside the British North America Act (An Address to the Saskatchewan Bar Association, 1925).' In R. MacGregor Dawson, ed., *Constitutional Issues in Canada, 1900–1931*, 5–9. Toronto: Oxford University Press, 1933.

Symons, Thomas H.B. 'The Contribution of Investigatory Commissions to Political Education.' In Jon H. Pammett and Jean-Luc Pepin, eds, *Political Education in Canada*, 123–32. Halifax: Institute for Research on Public Policy, 1988.

Thomas, Paul G. 'Parliamentary Reform through Political Parties.' In John C. Courtney, ed., *The Canadian House of Commons: Essays in Honour of Norman Ward*, 43–68. Calgary: University of Calgary Press, 1985.

Woodhouse, Diana. 'The Role of Ministerial Responsibility in Motivating Ministers to Morality.' In Jenny Fleming and Ian Holland, eds, *Motivating Ministers to Morality*, 37–48. Burlington, VT: Ashgate Dartmouth, 2001.

Young, Lisa. 'Value Clash: Parliament and Citizens after 150 Years of Responsible Government.' In F. Leslie Seidle and Louis Massicotte, eds, *Taking Stock of
150 Years of Responsible Government in Canada*, 105–36. Ottawa: Canadian
Study of Parliament Group, 1999.

Articles

Ackerman, Bruce. 'The New Separation of Powers.' *Harvard Law Review* 113
(January 2000): 633–790.
Alcock, Reg. 'Parliament and Democracy in the 21st Century: The Impact of
Information and Communication Technologies.' *CPR* 25, no. 1 (Spring 2002):
2–3.
Atkinson, Michael M., and Paul G. Thomas. 'Studying the Canadian Parlia-
ment.' *Legislative Studies Quarterly* 18, no. 3 (August 1993): 423–51.
Aucoin, Peter, and Lori Turnbull. 'The Democratic Deficit: Paul Martin and
Parliamentary Reform.' *CPA* 46, no. 4 (Winter 2003): 427–49.
Balls, Herbert R. 'The Watchdog of Parliament: The Centenary of the Legisla-
tive Audit.' *CPA* 21, no. 4 (Winter 1978): 584–617.
Balthazar, Louis. 'Is the Decline of Parliament Irreversible?' *CPR* 25, no. 4 (Win-
ter 2002–3): 18–21.
Barbour, Michael K. 'Parliament and the Internet: The Present and the Future.'
CPR 22, no. 3 (Autumn 1999): 23–5.
Barrie, Doreen, and Roger Gibbins. 'Parliamentary Careers in the Canadian
Federal State.' *CJPS* 22, no. 1 (March 1989): 137–46.
Bogdanor, Vernon. 'Ministerial Accountability.' *Parliamentary Affairs* 50, no. 1
(January 1997): 71–83.
Bourinot, J.G. 'Canadian Studies in Comparative Perspective: Parliamentary
Compared with Congressional Government.' *TRSC* Section II (1893): 77–
108.
Boyer, J. Patrick. 'Can Parliamentarians Become Real Players?' *CPR* 27, no. 3
(Autumn 2004): 4–8.
Bryden, John. 'Reforming the Access to Information Act.' *CPR* 24, no. 2 (Sum-
mer 2000): 5–7.
Cairns, Alan.'The Electoral System and the Party System in Canada, 1921–
1965.' *CJPS* 1, no. 1 (March 1968): 55–80.
Cairns, Alan, and Tom Flanagan. 'An Exchange.' *Inroads: A Journal of Opinion*
10 (2001): 1–12.
Clokie, H. McD. 'Formal Recognition of the Leader of the Opposition in Parlia-
ments of the Commonwealth.' *Political Science Quarterly* 69, no. 3 (1954): 438–
52.
Conacher, Duff. 'Power to the People: Initiative, Referendum, Recall and the

Possibility of Popular Sovereignty in Canada.' *University of Toronto Faculty of Law Review* 49, no. 2 (1991): 174–232.

Courtney, John C. 'Reflections on Reforming the Canadian Electoral System.' *CPA* 23, no. 3 (1980): 427–57.

Cowley, Philip, and Mark Stuart. 'Parliament: More Bleak House than Great Expectations.' *Parliamentary Affairs* 57, no. 2, (2004): 301–14.

Dion, Stéphane. 'Rising Cynicism: Who Is to Blame?' *CPR* 16, no. 4 (Winter 1993–4): 33–5.

Dworkin, Robert. 'The Forum of Principle.' *New York University Law Review* 56, (1981): 469–518.

Franklin, Bob. 'Keeping It "Bright, Light and Trite": Changing Newspaper Reporting of Parliament.' *Parliamentary Affairs* 49 no. 2 (April 1996): 298–315.

Giasson, Thierry, and Richard Nadeau. 'Canada's Democratic Malaise, Are the Media to Blame?' *Choices*, IRPP, 9, no.1 (February 2003), www.irpp.org/index.htm (29 August 2005).

Goot, Murray. 'Public Opinion and the Democratic Deficit; Australia and the War against Iraq.' *Australian Humanities Review* (May 2003), http://www.lib.latrobe.edu.au/AHR/archive/Issue-May-2003/goot.html (29 August 2005).

Gregory, Robert. 'Political Responsibility for Bureaucratic Incompetence: Tragedy at Cave Creek.' *Public Administration* 76, no. 3 (Autumn 1998): 519–38.

Griffith, J.A. 'The Place of Parliament in the Legislative Process, Part 1.' *Modern Law Review* 14, no. 3 (July 1951): 279–96.

Heeney, A.D.P. 'Cabinet Government in Canada: Some Recent Developments in the Machinery of the Central Executive.' *CJEPS* 12, no. 3 (August 1946): 282–99.

Hodder-Williams, Richard. 'British Politicians: To Rehabilitate or Not.' *Parliamentary Affairs* 49, no. 2 (April 1996): 285–97.

Hogg, Peter W., and Allison A. Bushell. 'The *Charter* Dialogue between Courts and Legislatures (or Perhaps the *Charter of Rights* Isn't Such a Bad Thing After All).' 35 *Osgoode Hall Law Journal* (1997): 75–124.

Hood, Christopher. 'Looking After Number One? Politicians' Rewards and the Economics of Politics.' *Political Studies* 40 (1992): 207–26.

Howe, Paul. 'Where Have All the Voters Gone?' *Inroads: The Canadian Journal of Opinion* 12 (Winter/Spring 2003): 74–83.

'Interview: René Blondin: Twenty Years at the National Assembly.' *CPR* 18, no. 2 (Summer 1985): 21–3.

Jenson, Jane, and Susan Philips. 'Regime Shift: New Citizenship Practices in Canada.' *International Journal of Canadian Studies* 14 (Fall 1996): 111–36.

Kilgour, David, and John Kirsner. 'Party Discipline and Canadian Democracy.' *CPR* 11, no. 3 (Autumn 1988): 10–11.

Knopff, Rainer. 'Populism and the Politics of Rights: The Dual Attack on Representative Democracy.' *CJPS* 31, no. 4 (December 1998): 683–705.

Kuper, Hilda. 'The Language of Sites in the Politics of Space.' *American Anthropologist* 74 (1972): 411–25.

Lee, Derek. 'Democracy in the 21st Century: The Need for Codification of Parliamentary Privilege.' *CPR* 28, no. 1 (Spring 2005): 2–3.

Lincoln, Clifford, Rob Merrifield, Stephane Bergeron, and Lorne Nystrom. 'Members Look at Parliamentary Reform.' *CPR* 24, no. 2 (Summer 2001): 11–17.

Lipow, Arthur, and Patrick Seyd. 'The Politics of Anti-Partyism.' *Parliamentary Affairs* 49, no. 2 (April 1996): 273–84.

Lortie, Pierre. 'A Minimalist Electoral Reform Agenda.' *Policy Options*, IRPP, 18, no. 9 (November 1997): 22–5.

MacIvor, Heather. 'The Charter of Rights and Party Politics: The Impact of The Supreme Court Ruling in *Figueroa v. Canada (Attorney General)*.' *Choices*, IRPP, 10, no. 4 (May 2004), www.irpp.org/index.htm (29 August 2005).

McLachlin, Rt Hon. Beverley. 'Reflections on the Autonomy of Parliament.' *CPR* 27, no. 1 (Spring 2004): 4–7.

Majone, Giandomenico. 'Europe's "Democratic Deficit": The Question of Standards.' *European Law Journal* 4, no. 1 (March 1998): 5–28.

Mallory, J.R. 'Vacation of Seats in the House of Commons: The Problem of Burnaby-Coquitlam.' *CJEPS* 30, no. 1 (February 1964): 125–30.

Manfredi, Christopher P. 'Great Policy Books: Donald Horowitz, *The Courts and Social Policy* (1977).' *Policy Options* (January-February, 2002): 55.

Mansbridge, Jane. 'Rethinking Representation.' *APSR* 97, no. 4 (November 2003): 515–28.

Norris, Pippa. 'The Twilight of Westminster? Electoral Reform and Its Consequences.' *Political Studies* 49 no. 5 (December 2001): 877–900.

Norton, Philip, and David Wood. 'Constituency Service by Members of Parliament: Does It Contribute to a Personal Vote?' *Parliamentary Affairs* 40, no. 2 (1990): 196–208.

Paquet, Gilles. 'Governance in the Face of Sabotage and Bricolage.' *CPR* 24, no. 3 (Autumn 2001): 11–18.

Patrias, Carmela. 'Socialists, Jews and the 1947 Saskatchewan Bill of Rights.' *Canadian Historical Review* 87, no. 2 (June 2006): 265–92.

Pierson, Paul. 'Increasing Returns, Path Dependence, and the Study of Politics.' *APSR* 94, no. 2 (June 2000): 251–67.

Pross, A. Paul. 'Parliamentary Influences and the Diffusion of Power.' *CJPS* 18, no. 2 (June 1985): 235–66.

Rioux, Matthias. 'The Roots of Our Democratic Malaise.' *CPR* 25, no. 4 (Winter 2002–3): 7–9.

Ryan, Claude. 'In Defence of Parliament.' *CPR* 25, no. 4 (Winter 2002–3): 13–15.

St Martin, Denis. 'Should the Federal Ethics Counsellor Become an Independent Officer of Parliament?' *Canadian Public Policy* 19, no. 1 (2003): 197–212.

Savoie, Donald J. 'All Things Canadian Are Now Regional.' *Journal of Canadian Studies* 35, no. 1 (Spring 2000): 203–17.

Scheuerman, William E. 'Liberal Democracy and the Empire of Speed.' *Polity* 34, no. 1 (Fall 2001): 41–67.

Segal, Hugh. 'Failing Legitimacy: The Challenge for Parliamentarians.' *CPR* 27, no. 1 (Spring 2004): 30–2.

Séguin, Phillippe. 'Reflections on the Future of Parliament and Democracy.' *CPR* 25, no. 4 (Winter 2002–3): 4–6.

Seidle, F. Leslie. 'Expanding the Federal Democratic Reform Agenda.' *Policy Options* 25, no. 9 (October 2004): 48–53.

Siaroff, Alan. 'Varieties of Parliamentarianism in Advanced Industrial Democracies.' *International Political Science Review* 24, no. 4 (2003): 445–64.

Smith, David E. 'The Affair of the Chairs.' *Constitutional Forum* 13, no. 2 (Fall 2003): 42–9.

Smith, Jennifer. 'Democracy and the Canadian House of Commons at the Millennium.' *CPA* 42, no. 4 (Winter 1999): 398–421.

Strahl, Chuck. 'Toward a More Responsive Parliament.' *CPR* 24, no. 1 (Spring 2000): 2–4.

Strayer, B.L. 'Life under the Canadian Charter: Adjusting the Balance between Legislatures and Courts.' *Public Law* (1998): 347–69.

Sutherland, Sharon L. 'The Report of the Liaison Committee on the Effectiveness of House of Commons Committees.' *Parliamentary Government* no. 44 (August 1993): 8–10.

Sutherland, S.L. 'Federal House Committee Reform: Mindless Adversarialism Well Done.' *Constitutional Forum* 13, no. 2 (Fall 2003): 50–63.

Walsh, R.R. 'By the Numbers: A Statistical Survey of Private Member's [sic] Bills.' *CPR* 25, no. 1 (Spring 2002): 29–33.

Ward, Norman. 'Called to the Bar of the House of Commons.' *CBR* (May 1957): 529–46.

– 'The Formative Years of the House of Commons, 1867–91.' *CJEPS* 18, no. 4 (November 1952): 431–51.

Weinrib, Lorraine Eisenstat. 'Canada's Constitutional Revolution: From Legislative to Constitutional State.' *Israel Law Review* 33, no. 1 (Winter 1999): 13–50.

Wiseman, Nelson. 'Skeptical Reflections on Proportional Representation.' *Policy Options*, IRPP, 18, no. 9 (November 1997): 15–18.

Young, Lisa. 'Electoral Systems and Representative Legislatures.' *CPR* 21, no. 3 (Autumn 1998): 12–14.

Zemans, Frances Kahn. 'Legal Mobilization: The Neglected Role of the Law in the Political System.' *APSR* 77, no. 3 (September 1983): 690–703.

Ziegel, Jacob S. 'Merit Selection and Democratization of Appointments to the Supreme Court of Canada.' *Choices*, IRPP, 5, no. 2 (June 1999), www.irpp.org/index.htm (29 August 2005).

Zittel, Thomas. 'Political Representation and the Internet: Wither [sic] Responsible Party Government?' American Political Science Association, Legislative Studies Section, *Newsletter* 26, no. 1 (January 2003), www.apsnet.org/0/07Elss/Newsletter/jan03/papers.htm.

Unpublished Papers

Adam, Dyane. 'A Hard Act to Follow: The Commissioner of Official Languages as an Agent of Parliament.' Paper presented at Independence and Responsibility: A Conference on the Officers of Parliament, University of Saskatchewan, 2–3 November 2001.

Barrados, Maria, and Jean Ste-Marie. 'The Auditor General of Canada: An Independent Servant of Parliament.' Paper presented at Independence and Responsibility: A Conference on the Officers of Parliament, University of Saskatchewan, 2–3 November 2001.

Cooper, Barry. 'Parliamentary Government and the Recall.' Unpublished paper, August 1998.

Cross, William, and Lisa Young. 'Party Membership as Public Service.' Paper presented at the conference Responsibilities of Citizenship and Public Service: Crisis or Challenge? organized by the Institute for Research on Public Policy and the Trudeau Foundation, Toronto, 2005.

Garner, Christopher. 'Confused Signals: Backbench Voting Behaviour on Private Members Bills.' Paper submitted to the British Columbia Political Studies Association, 2000 Conference, Victoria, BC, 5–6 May 2000.

Harper, Stephen. 'Address to the Joint Empire and Canadian Clubs.' 8 November 2005. http://www.conservative.ca/media/20051108-Harper-EmpireClub.pdf (emphasis added).

St Martin, Denis. 'The Multiple Meanings of "Independence" in Politics: Ethics Watchdogs in Comparative Perspective.' Paper presented at Independence and Responsibility: A Conference on the Officers of Parliament, University of Saskatchewan, 2–3 November 2001.

Smith, Jennifer. 'Responsible Government and the Officers of Parliament.' Paper presented at Independence and Responsibility: A Conference on the Officers of Parliament, University of Saskatchewan, 2–3 November 2001.

Strayer, Barry. 'Ken Lysyk and the Patriation Reference.' Paper presented at the

Symposium Honouring the Late Mr Justice Kenneth Lysyk, University of
British Columbia, Vancouver, 5–6 November 2004.
Sutherland, S.L. 'The Office of the Auditor General of Canada: Government in
Exile.' Paper presented at Independence and Responsibility: A Conference
on the Officers of Parliament, University of Saskatchewan, 2–3 November
2001.

Theses

Cairns, James Irvine. 'A New Approach to the Study of a New Party: The Bloc
Québécois as a Party in Parliament.' MA thesis, University of Saskatchewan,
2003.
Elliott, Nathan S. '"We Have Asked for Bread and You Gave Us a Stone": Western Farmers and the Siege of Ottawa.' MA thesis, University of
Saskatchewan, 2004.
Furi, Megan. 'Officers of Parliament: A Study in Government Adaptation.' MA
thesis, University of Saskatchewan, 2002.
Whidden, Rachel E.L. 'Science Controversies and Public Policy: A Case Study
of Genetically Engineered Food.' MA thesis, University of Saskatchewan,
2004.

Occasional Papers, Reports, and Miscellaneous

Association of Public Service Financial Administration. 'Checks and Balances:
Rebalancing the Service and Control Features of the Government of Canada
(GOC) Financial Control Framework.' December 2003, www.apsfa-agffp.
com.
Aucoin, Peter. 'Accountability: The Key to Restoring Public Confidence in
Government.' The Timlin Lecture, University of Saskatchewan, 6 November
1997.
Axworthy, Thomas S. 'Addressing the Accountability Deficit: Why Paul Mar-
tin's Minority Government Must Pay More Attention to the Three A's.'
www.queensu.ca/csd/AccountabilityDeficit-IRPP.pdf (21 April 2005).
Black, Jerome H. 'The National Register of Electors: Raising Questions about
the New Approach to Voter Registration in Canada.' *Policy Matters*, IRPP, 1,
no. 10 (December 2000), www.irpp.org/pm/index.htm (30 August 2005).
Bromley, Catherine, John Curtice, and Ben Seyd. 'Is Britain Facing a Crisis in
Democracy?' Constitution Unit, University College London, July 2004.
Canada West Foundation. *Re-Inventing Parliament ... A Conference on Parliamentary Reform*. 25–6 February 1994. Calgary: Canada West Foundation,
1994.

Canadian Study of Parliament Group. *The Eclipse of Parliament? The Concentra-tion of Power in Canadian Politics.* Ottawa: Canadian Study of Parliament Group, 26–7 November 1999.
– 'Parliaments and the People: Improving Public Understanding.' Toronto: Canadian Study of Parliament Group, 28 April 1995.
– 'Public Attitudes about Parliament.' Kingston: Canadian Study of Parliament Group, 2 June 1991.
Centre for Research and Information on Canada. 'Voter Participation in Canada: Is Canadian Democracy in Crisis?' CRIC Papers. Montreal: Centre for Research and Information on Canada. October 2001.
Cook, Rt Hon. Robin. 'A Modern Parliament in a Modern Democracy.' State of the Union Annual Lecture, Constitution Unit, University College London, December 2001.
Cross, Bill. 'Members of Parliament, Voters and Democracy in the Canadian House of Commons.' *Parliamentary Perspectives* no. 3. Ottawa: Canadian Study of Parliament Group, 2003.
Gibbins, Roger, Loleen Youngman Berdahl, and Katherine Harmsworth. *Fol-lowing the Cash: Exploring the Expanding Role of Canada's Auditor General.* Cal-gary: Canada West Foundation, October 2000.
Howe, Paul, and David Northrup. 'Strengthening Canadian Democracy: The Views of Canadians.' *Policy Matters*, IRPP, 1, no. 5. (July 2000), www.irpp.org/index.htm (29 August 2005).
Institute on Governance. 'The Exercise of Power Round Table: Parliament, Politics and Citizens: A Conversation with Bob Rae.' http://www.iog.ca/publications/xrt6.pdf (14 January 1998).
Málloy, Jonathan. 'The "Responsible Government Approach" and Its Effects on Canadian Legislative Studies.' Ottawa: Canadian Study of Parliament Group, 2002.
Malloy, Jonathan. 'To Better Serve Canadians: How Technology Is Changing the Relationship between Members of Parliament and Public Servants.' Tor-onto: Institute of Public Administration of Canada, 2003.
National Citizens' Coalition. 'Who We Are, What We Do.' Toronto: nd.
Newcastle Law School Working Papers. 'The Reconstruction of Constitutional Responsibility.' (2000/10). www.ncl.ac.uk/nuls/research/wpapers/woodhouse1.html (2000).
Parliamentary Centre. 'MPs' Views on Committee Organization.' *Occasional Papers on Parliamentary Government* no. 11 (March 2001).
– 'New MPs.' *Occasional Papers on Parliamentary Government* no. 1 (September 1996).
– 'The Question Period: What Former Members Think.' *Occasional Papers on Parliamentary Government* no. 12 (May 2001).

– 'Strengthening the Role of MPs.' *Occasional Papers on Parliamentary Government* no. 7 (November 1998).
– 'Stress and MPs.' *Occasional Papers on Parliamentary Government* no. 9 (November 1999).
Patapan, Haig. Review of Elisabeth Gidengil, André Blais, Neil Nevitte, and Richard Nadeau, *Citizens* (Vancouver: University of British Columbia Press, 2004), on H-Net Canada, http://www.h-net.org/~canada/index_en.html (17 March 2005).
Peach, Ian. *The Death of Deference: National Policy-Making in the Aftermath of the Meech Lake and Charlottetown Accords.* Public Policy Paper 26. Regina: Saskatchewan Institute of Public Policy, September 2004.
– *Legitimacy on Trial: A Process for Appointing Justices to the Supreme Court of Canada.* Public Policy Paper No. 30. Regina: Saskatchewan Institute of Public Policy, February 2005.
Public Policy Forum. *Governor-in Council Appointments: Best Practices and Recommendations for Reform.* February 2004. 61 pp. http://www.ppforum.com/ow/gov_apt_reform.pdf.
– 'Ministerial Accountability: Suggestions for Reform.' Report of a Series of Roundtables of Experts, Public Policy Forum, June 2004. http://www.ppforum.com/ow/ministerial_accountability.pdf.
Roach, Robert. 'Putting the *Demos* Back in Democracy.' Canada West Foundation: The West in Canada Project, June 2005.
Skidelsky, Robert. 'The Shrinking State.' Review of David Marquand, *Decline of the Public* (London: Polity, 2004), in *Times Literary Supplement* 24 June 2004.
Winetrobe, Barry K. 'Working In, With and For Parliaments.' *Newsletter.* Political Marketing Group, Political Studies Association Specialist Group. http://www.psa.ac.uk/spgrp/polmarket/newsletter/pmgn1tapril03.pdf (April 2003).

Newspaper and Magazine Articles

'Accountability Pillars Lie in Rubble.' *National Post*, 11 February 2004, A18.
Anderson, Doris. 'Lack of Women Real Deficit.' *Toronto Star*, 25 May 2004, A25.
'Anne McLellan Should Resign.' *National Post*, 19 March 2005, A15.
Archer, Keith. 'Reform or Social Engineering.' *Winnipeg Free Press*, 4 April 2004. www.winnipegfreepress.com/westview/v-printerfriendly/story/.
Baker, Chris. 'Political Illiteracy Bodes Ill for Reform.' *Winnipeg Free Press*, 7 November 2002, A 13.
'Balance of Power: Is the PMO so Powerful That Cabinet Is Becoming Irrelevant?' *Star-Phoenix* (Saskatoon), 5 October 2002, E1.

Banigan, John. 'Comptrollership in the Martin Government.' *CMA Management Magazine* 38, no. 1 (March 2004): 50.

Bennett, Carolyn. 'Canada Needs a Healthcare Commissioner as an Officer of Parliament, Says Bennett: MP and MD Carolyn Bennett Says the Commissioner Would Ensure the Transparency and Accountability of All Health and Health Care Outcomes and Spending.' *The Hill Times*, 28 October 2002, 28.

Bindman, Stephen. 'Off the Bench, Estey Speaks His Mind.' *Star-Phoenix* (Saskatoon), 2 May 1988, A17.

Bliss, Michael. 'Canada's House of Ill Repute.' *National Post*, 14 May 2005, A1, and A6.

– 'A Short Guide to Our "Culture of Corruption."' *National Post*, 13 March 2004, A17.

– 'Southern Republic and Northern Dictatorship.' *National Post*, 6 September 2002, A18.

Bronskill, Jim. 'Watchdogs' Bark Commonly Ignored.' *Ottawa Citizen*, 9 October 2002, A1.

Bryden, Joan. 'Reform Needed to Stem Low Voter Turnout: Proportional Representation Advocated to Restore Faith in Government.' *National Post*, 2 January 2002, A2.

Bueckert, Dennis. 'Watchdog in Discussion with Greens over Financing.' *Globe and Mail*, 19 December 2005, A4.

Caldwell, T. 'Letter.' *National Post*, 25 January 2003, B12.

'Canadian Electoral System a "Disaster," Broadbent Says.' *Globe and Mail*, 7 May 2003, A14.

CanWest News Service. 'PM Backtracks on Senate Remarks.' *Windsor Star*, 20 December 2003, C9.

Carmichael, Amy. 'PM Promises to Allow MPs Right to Vet Appointments.' *Ottawa Citizen*, 28 February 2004, A3.

'Chrétien Names 3 New Senators.' *National Post*, 3 September 1999, A1.

Clark, Campbell. 'Plan for Top Court Judges Attacked by Opposition.' *Globe and Mail*, 9 April 2005, A6.

Clark, Campbell, and Bill Curry, '"Non-Confidence Vote" Plan for Election in February Scorned.' *Globe and Mail*, 15 November 2005, A9.

Courtney, John C. 'Can PR Deliver All That It Promises?' *Winnipeg Free Press*, 18 March 2004. http://www.winnipegfreepress.com/westview/v-printerfriendly/story.

Curry, Bill. 'Native Leaders, PM to Hold First-Ever Budget Talks.' *Star-Phoenix* (Saskatoon), 10 March 2004, A11.

– 'Public Institutions "Excessively Adversarial."' *National Post*, 13 April 2004, A6.

Cuthand, Doug. 'To Vote or Not to Vote, That Is the Question.' *Leader-Post* (Regina), 7 June 2004, B1.

Dawson, Anne. 'Martin Vows to Reform Government.' *Star-Phoenix* (Saskatoon), 23 September 2003, A1, A2.

'Editorial.' *Windsor Star*, 31 March 2004, A6.

Feasby, Colin. 'Your Vote Is a Floating Currency: Let's Peg It.' *Globe and Mail*, 16 May 2002, A16.

Fife, Robert, and David Vienneau. 'Senate Reform Awaits Plan from Provinces; Martin Offers Parliamentary Review of Senate Nominations for Now.' *Star-Phoenix* (Saskatoon), 19 December 2003, C11.

Francoli, Paco. '"Deepening Crisis" Grips Canadian Democracy: Kingsley Launches Ambitious Plan to Get Young Canadians to Start Voting.' *The Hill Times*, 31 March 2003, 20. Online via ProQuest, www.il.pro-quest.com.cyber.usask.ca/proquest/ (30 August 2005).

– 'Parliament's Oversight? Donald Savoie Says Its Role Has Greatly Changed.' *The Hill Times*, 22 April 2002, 1.

– 'Senior Bureaucrat Urges Changes to Voting System: "There is a Sense of Fatigue about Our Democratic Institutions."' *The Hill Times*, 10 March 2003, 16.

Fraser Institute. 'Measuring the Growing "Democracy Gap" between the Supreme Court and Parliament,' *Canada NewsWire*, 6 August 2003.

'Freeing Party Finance from the Iron Triangle.' *National Post*, 21 January 2003, A16.

Galloway, Gloria. 'Ontario Citizen Juries to Help Plan Budget.' *Globe and Mail*, 8 January 2004, A2.

Gibson, Gordon. 'Stop: In the Name of Love (for Canada).' *Globe and Mail*, 1 February 2005, A15.

Grace, Kevin Michael. 'Parliament of Ombudsmen: Stripped of Their Powers, MPs Now Serve Their Constituents Not with Advocacy but with Favours.' *Report Newsmagazine* (British Columbia edition) 28 (11 June 2001): 16.

Graveland, Bill. 'Chief Electoral Officer Sounds Alarm over Youth Voters at Calgary Conference.' *Canadian Press NewsWire*, 30 October 2003.

Greenway, Norma. 'Liberal Party Run Like an Oligarchy: Grits.' *National Post*, 2 March 2005, A7.

Harding, Brenton. 'Free Votes, Term Limits Would Hurt the West.' *Edmonton Journal*, 3 July 2004, A17.

Heyman, David. 'Democracy Requires More Free Votes: U of C Debate Pits Manning against Nicol.' *Calgary Herald*, 17 March 2004, A5.

Hutchinson, Allan. 'Let's Try Democracy When Choosing Top Judges.' *Globe and Mail*, 3 March 2004, A15.

Ibbitson, John. 'Frazzled in the Forum: A Besieged PM Hangs On.' *Globe and Mail*, 23 April 2005, A8.

- 'Stonewalling on Electoral Reform.' *Globe and Mail*, 17 June 2005, A4.
- 'Use Proportional System in Elections, Report Urges.' *Globe and Mail*, 31 March 2004, A1, A12.
Johnson, R.W. 'The Rainbow Nation Paints Out the Whites.' *The Sunday Times*, 27 July 2003, 4–7.
Kennedy, Mark. 'Prime Minister Comes Up Short on Tall Order.' *National Post*, 17 March 2005, A5.
Lackner, Chris, and Bill Curry. 'Aboriginal Groups to Sit on House Committee.' *Star-Phoenix* (Saskatoon), 29 March 2004, A6.
Landolt, C. Gwendolyn. 'Judging the Judges: Canada's Courts Simply Have Too Much Power.' *Calgary Herald*, 1 June 2003, A11.
Leniham, Donald G. 'MPs Are Missing the Web Revolution.' *CanWest News*, 18 July 2002, 1.
Loenen, Nick. 'Our Parliament Is a Disgrace to Democracy.' *Vancouver Sun*, 30 November 2000, A23.
Luba, Frank. '97 MPs Line Up for Trough Day.' *The Province*, 25 October 1999, A2.
Makin, Kirk. 'High-Court Reform Proposals Imminent.' *Globe and Mail*, 20 April 2004, A6.
- 'Politician's [sic] Promises Not Set in Stone, Court Says.' *Globe and Mail*, 29 January 2005. www.GlobeandMail.com.
Manning, Preston. 'Be Not Afraid.' *Globe and Mail*, 2 November 2004, A15.
- 'How to Remake the National Agenda.' *National Post*, 13 February 2003, A18.
- 'Is He [Mr Justice John Gomery] Our Last Best Hope?' *Globe and Mail*, 28 February 2005, A13.
- 'Parliament, Not Judges, Must Make the Laws of the Land.' *Globe and Mail*, 16 June 1998, A23.
- 'Sleepless in Flanders Fields.' *Globe and Mail*, 19 March 2005, A17.
'Manning Set to Have PM Removed.' *Globe and Mail*, 14 December 1995, A4.
Marin, André. 'Our Military Needs an Independent Ombudsman.' *National Post*, 7 April 2005, A18.
'Marin Fires Parting Shot.' *National Post*, 30 March 2005, A4.
Martin, Don. 'Democracy in Retreat in Canada Today: Power Has Shifted to Single Party with One Leader.' *Edmonton Journal*, 29 September 2002, A1.
- 'My Person of the Year.' *Leader-Post* (Regina), 24 December 2002, B7.
Maxwell, Judith. 'Hear, Hear for Citizen Input: If We Want More Engaged Voters, Let's Have Less Partisan Scoffing at Citizen-Politician Dialogues. They're Key to 21st-Century Democracy.' *Globe and Mail*, 30 April 2004, A21.
May, Kathryn. 'Election May Make [Gomery] Report Futile.' *Leader-Post* (Regina), 12 December 2005, A7.
- 'Federal Accountants Call for Order.' *National Post*, 8 December 2003, A7.

– 'Info Technology Is Turning Democracy Upside Down.' *CanWest News*, 28 March 2001, 1.
– 'Radwanski to Be Called Before House of Commons on Contempt Charge.' *CanWest News*, 4 November 2003, 1.
Mendelsohn, Matthew. 'Same-Sex Statistics.' *Globe and Mail*, 23 August 2003, A17.
Monahan, Patrick J., and Peter W. Hogg. 'We Need an Open Parliamentary Review of Court Appointments.' *National Post*, 24 April 2004, A13.
Naumetz, Tim. 'Lower Voting Age to 16, Chief Electoral Officer Says.' *Star-Phoenix* (Saskatoon), 27 March 2004, C12.
Ness, Jim. 'Selling Wheat, Doing Time.' *National Post*, 12 October 2002, A21.
Palmer, Vaughn. 'Ottawa Turns Our Man into a Mouse.' *National Post*, 17 February 2001, A19.
Paraskevas, Joe. 'Private Member's Bill Calls for More Open Government.' *CanWest News*, 27 October 2003, 1.
'Parliament Has Calcified.' *Montreal Gazette*, 27 December 2001, B2.
'Parliament May Have to Make Voting Mandatory: Chief Electoral Officer.' *Canadian Press NewsWire*, 19 December 2000, n/a.
Rana, F. Abbas. '"MPs Worried, Permanent Voters' List Drives Down Voter Turnout.' *The Hill Times*, 13 October 2003, 1.
Reid, Kalvin. 'Electoral System Has Left Canadian Government "Dysfunctional," Says Broadbent.' *Canadian Press NewsWire*, 6 May 2003.
Ringen, Stein. 'Wealth and Decay: Norway Funds a Massive Political Self-Examination – and Finds Trouble for All.' *Times Literary Supplement*, 13 February 2004, 5.
Robinson, Walter, and Judy Rebick. 'Why We Need to Change Electoral System.' *Toronto Star*, 17 October 2002, A31.
'Same-Sex Fight Moves to House.' *Star-Phoenix* (Saskatoon), 1 February 2005, A1, A2.
Scandiffio, Mike. '"It's a Collapse of Culture of Record Keeping," Reid Says It's an Example of Government's Mismanagement of Information.' *The Hill Times*, 31 January 2000, 9.
– 'Wheat War between NCC and Goodale,' *The Hill Times*, 1 June 1998, 2.
Schmitz, Cristin. 'Cotler Urges Consideration of Aboriginal Supreme Court Judge.' *CanWest News*, 23 January 2004, 1.
– 'Martin Idea Would Turn Search for Justices into Circus: Lamer.' *CanWest News*, 8 November 2002, 1.
Simpson, Jeffrey. 'Why Don't We Just Turn Policy over to the Courts?' *Globe and Mail*, 22 July 2003, A15.
'Single Transferable Vote System Encouraged.' *Star-Phoenix* (Saskatoon), 9 May 2005, A7.

'The Slippery Slope of Shifting Accountability.' *Globe and Mail*, 21 September 2004, A19.

Stanbury, W.T. 'Looking for a Legacy Mr Prime Minister? I Got One for You: Forget the Orgy of Spending and Champion Parliamentary Reform.' *The Hill Times*, 21 October 2002, 18.

'Straight-Talking Fraser Strikes Fear on the Hill.' *Globe and Mail*, 12 February 2004, A4.

'Students Aren't "Blank Slates" under Their Political T-Shirts.' *National Post*, 23 October 2003, A19.

Tibbets, Janice. 'Legal Experts Agree on Transparent System to Vet Judges.' *CanWest News*, 23 March 2004, 1.

– 'MPs Blast Cotler for Dismissing Judge Report.' *National Post*, 8 November 2004, A5.

– 'Revamp Voting System: Law Panel: Commission Says Poor Turnout Can be Blamed on "Dysfunction."' *Ottawa Citizen*, 22 October 2002, A3.

– 'Supreme Secrets.' *National Post*, 27 April 2004, A6.

'Top Court "Hijacking" Democracy: Report Says.' *National Post*, 7 August 2003, A1, A6.

'Top Judge Rejects Allegation of Activism.' *Globe and Mail*, 23 November 2004, A10.

Vongdouangchanh, Bea. 'Minister Frulla's Riding Office Is Also ... an Art Gallery.' *The Hill Times*, 15–21 November 2004, 20.

Ward, Doug. 'Growing Number of Young Voters Can't Be Bothered to Cast Ballot.' *Leader-Post* (Regina), 10 October 2002, B7.

'Why the Fuss? AG's Report Deals with a Drop in the Tax Bucket.' *Globe and Mail*, 13 February 2004, A19.

Zussman, David. 'The Danger of Apathy: Good Governance Requires a Belief That Parliament Matters.' *Ottawa Citizen*, 25 May 2004, A19.

Court Cases

Andrews v. Law Society (British Columbia), [1989] 1 SCR 143.

Canada (House of Commons) v. Vaid, [2005] 1 SCR 667.

Canadian Taxpayers Federation v. Ontario (Minister of Finance), [2004] CanL11 48177 (ON S.C.).

Figueroa v. Canada (Attorney General), [2003] 1 SCR 912.

Harper v. Canada (Attorney General), [2004] 1 SCR 827.

Kielly v. Carson (1841), 4 Moore P.C. 63. Cited in Norman Ward, 'Called to the Bar of the House of Commons.' *CBR* (May 1957): 529–46.

Mahé v. Alberta, [1990] 1 SCR 350.

Monsanto Canada Inc. v. Schmeiser, [2004] 1 SCR 902.

New Brunswick Broadcasting Co. v. Nova Scotia (Speaker of the House of Assembly),
    [1993] 1 SCR 319.
*Ontario (Speaker of the Legislative Assembly) v. Ontario (Human Rights Commis-
    sion)* (2001), DLR (4th) 698 (Ont. C.A.).
Queen v. Hauser, [1979] 1 SCR 984.
R. v. Big M Drug Mart Ltd., [1985] 1 SCR 295.
Raîche v. R., Federal Court of Canada – Trial Division; filed 12 September 2003:
    file T-1730–03.
Re Initiative and Referendum Act, [1919] AC 944.
Re Manitoba Public Schools Act Reference, [1993] 1 SCR 839.
Reference re An Act to Amend the Education Act (Ontario), [1987] 40 DLR (4th) 60.
Reference re Motor Vehicle Act (British Columbia) s.94 (2), [1985] 2 SCR 486.
Reference re Provincial Electoral Boundaries, [1991] 2 SCR 158.
*Reference re the Remuneration of Judges of the Provincial Court of Prince Edward
    Island*, [1997] 3 SCR 3.
Reference re Secession of Quebec, [1998] 2 SCR 217.
Sauvé v. Canada (A.G.), [1993] 2 SCR 438.
Singh v. Canada (Attorney General) (C.A.), [2000] 3 FC 185.
Société des Acadiens c. Nouveau-Brunswick (Gouverneur en Conseil) (1997), 188
    N.B.R. (2d) 330 (N.B.Q.B.).

Websites and Electronic Mail

Constituency Project, The. http://www.theconstituencyproject.ca.
Democracy Watch. 'Media and Public Appearances.' www.dwatch.ca/
    allmedia.htm (28 October 2004).
– 'Summary of Democracy Watch's Many Notable Achievements.'
    www.dwatch.ca/aboutdw.html (13 December 2004).
Elections Canada. www.elections.ca.
Equal Voice. 2003. 'Equality-Based Electoral Reform.' www.equalvoice.ca/
    index.htm.
Fair Vote Canada. http://www.fairvotecanada.org/fvc.php/.
Forum on Parliamentary Reform. http:www.parlcent.ca/publications/
    reform_e.pdf (June 2003).
Gibbins, Roger. 'Re: Free and Honest Elections Are the Lynchpin of Democ-
    racy.' Retrieved E-mail. 19 December 2004.
Norwegian Study of Power and Democracy. www.sv.uio.no/mutr/english/
    index. html (30 August 2005).
Tardi, Gregory. 'Political Law Notes in Anticipation of the 39th Federal General
    Election.' *Perspectives in Political Law*. Retrieved E-mail (27 November 2005).

Index

Aboriginal peoples: and franchise, 6, 20, 36, 101, 116; political participation of, 101, 102–3, 141–2; rights of, 6, 25, 35–6, 47, 105. *See also* First Nations

abortion, 57, 77, 89

academic interest and studies, 8, 21, 23, 30–1, 65, 75, 85–6, 104–5, 108, 115–38, 122–3, 126, 140–2; as critical, 13–14, 34, 56, 92–3, 100, 131; declining interest, 10–12, 136; on democratic values, 48–9; interest in the judiciary, 11, 12; interest in MPs, 66, 67, 83, 89, 116; interest in the opposition, 92–3; interest in parties, 58–9; interest in Royal Commissions, 49–50, 110; reflective view of representation, 30–1; and research, 42, 49–50, 58–9, 136–8; on voter turnout, 97–8

accessibility, 11–12, 13, 42, 68, 130, 134

access-to-information: laws, 77–8; commissioner, 121

accountability, 11–14, 24–5, 56, 68, 79, 81, 113, 118–19, 120–2, 129, 130, 132; as a democratic value, 48;

electoral, 63; of the judiciary, 11, 47; of officers of Parliament, 64–5, 66, 69, 70; and Reform party, 56; of the Senate, 4

Ackerman, Bruce, 10, 69

'Action Plan for Democratic Reform, The,' 86

advocacy groups, 30, 68, 105–6

Alberta, 19, 25, 52, 58–9, 110, 111

Alberta government, 16, 35, 60

Alcock, Reg, 79, 82

anti-party/anti-partisan sentiment, 53, 67, 68

appointment(s), 5, 14, 34, 85, 86, 92–3, 106, 142; judicial, 28, 47, 52, 86, 92–5, 128–9; of officers of Parliament, 64–5; patronage, 27–8; prerogative of, 12, 42, 92, 123, 128–9; to the Senate, 14, 22, 27, 29, 52, 126; as subject to scrutiny, 94–5

Aucoin, Peter, 115

auditor general, 63–5, 68, 69, 70, 92, 98, 121; Office of the Auditor General, 10, 68; *Report on Matters of Special Importance*, 44

Australia, 28, 109, 136–7

39–41, 60, 94, 106, 111, 115, 129;
interest in, 11–12, 129; and Parliament, 34–5, 60, 116; and privilege,
22, 34, 130; in the United States,
137. *See also* Supreme Court of
Canada
criminal code, 77, 111
crown, the, 62, 113, 127, 134, 140–1;
and prerogative, 27, 60, 85, 128–9

Dawson, R. MacGregor, 12, 15, 51,
142
debate, 38–9, 49, 52, 89, 93, 134, 135;
on the charter, 36; Confederation,
72; versus electoral democracy, 53–
4, 92, 134; as irrelevant, 8; on the
judiciary, 93; and Parliament, 14,
31, 89, 117, 133; and Reform party,
17, 90; in the Senate, 17, 119
defence policy, 125, 126
deference, 8, 60, 62; decline of, 8, 43–
4, 113
Democracy Watch, 11–12, 66, 68, 95
democratic deficit, 23, 43, 60, 93, 95,
105, 107, 137
democratic values, 34, 39–40, 41, 42–
5, 48–50, 60, 77, 92, 100, 102, 105,
106, 111, 129, 134, 135–6, 137;
defined, 48; as defining Canada,
50, 60; and royal commissions, 49–
50. *See also* fairness
Diefenbaker government, 92, 97; and
Bill of Rights, 29, 50
direct democracy, 11, 13–14, 51, 59–
60, 61, 134
discipline. *See* party discipline.
discretionary powers, 5, 60, 90, 124,
126, 128, 129; as corrupt, 27–8
dissolution of Parliament, 5, 90, 124,
126, 128–9

Docherty, David, 73, 75–6, 82, 94, 112,
115

elections, 20; fixed election dates, 5,
7, 28, 90, 107, 128; interest or participation in, 37, 38–9, 40, 49, 114
(*see also* voter turnout); promises,
107, 112–13. *See also* plurality elections; Canada Elections Act
Elections Canada, 6, 98
electoral boundaries, 70, 96, 105–6,
116; federal, 6, 65–6
electoral democracy, 17–18, 22, 51–5,
57, 59, 86, 106, 128, 134, 137, 141;
and Parliament, 51, 54, 69, 70, 118;
and Reform party, 17, 52, 54–5, 59–
60, 92
electoral systems, 6, 9, 21, 48, 49, 104,
115, 116, 135; changes proposed,
11, 13, 39, 103, 124, 131–2; reform
proposed, 14, 28, 84–5, 90, 98, 110,
112, 116, 117, 123, 135, 137, 140; and
voter turnout, 99–101, 112. *See also*
plurality elections; proportional
representation
elites, 34, 56, 60, 62, 127
English Constitution, The (Bagehot), 5,
8
equality, 35, 42–3, 44, 47, 55, 56, 134;
in the electoral process, 40, 48–9,
101, 110; social, 34, 141
ethics, 44, 66; ethics officers, 63–5, 70,
92, 121; ethics regulation, 28
executive, the, 85, 105, 119, 125; and
cabinet, 5; and Parliament, 29,
58, 62–3; and the legislature, 40,
46, 53–4, 118–20, 125–6; and
officers of Parliament, 64, 66–7;
power of, 3, 83, 93, 119, 124–5,
128